Sharenthood

Why We Should Think before We Talk about Our Kids Online

Leah A. Plunkett

Foreword by John Palfrey

The MIT Press
Cambridge, Massachusetts
London, England

This book was set in Stone Serif and Stone Sans by Jen Jackowitz. Printed and bound in the United States of America.

Library of Congress Cataloging-in-Publication Data

Names: Plunkett, Leah, author.
Title: Sharenthood: Why We Should Think before We Talk about Our Kids Online / Leah A. Plunkett ; foreword by John Palfrey.
Description: Cambridge, MA : MIT Press, [2019] | Series: Strong ideas | Includes bibliographical references and index.
Identifiers: LCCN 2018053938 | ISBN 9780262042697 (hardcover : alk. paper)
Subjects: LCSH: Internet and children. | Parenting. | Caregivers. | Social media.
Classification: LCC HQ784.I58 P58 2019 | DDC 306.874--dc23 LC record available at https://lccn.loc.gov/2018053938

10 9 8 7 6 5 4 3 2 1

For my parents, Jamie and Marcy Plunkett, for always encouraging me to play and playing with me.

For my mentor, Jonathan Zittrain, for first encouraging me to write a book.

For my husband, Mike Lewis, for encouraging me to go to my office and write my book.

For my children, Sam and Alana, and Kermit the Dog, for encouraging me to come home and play with them.

Contents

Foreword

John Palfrey

This book is about some of the crucial questions facing our children in a digital age. Most books on this topic build from research related to young people's changing behavior, sometimes wonderful and oftentimes baffling. We need to understand these changes in youth behavior if we are going be good parents, educators, and lawmakers for an increasingly interconnected, global, and digital world.

This book is different. Leah Plunkett—a law professor and parent—implores us to focus our attention in the first instance on our own behavior as adults. She calls on us to think in new ways about how our daily practices affect the privacy interests of our children, today and long into the future. Her prose is clever and evocative. You're in for a lively and thought-provoking read.

We have reason to worry about the changes to childhood and adolescence that are happening in this ever-more technologically mediated age. Young people in many societies are exhibiting higher levels of stress, anxiety, depression, and suicide. Researchers around the world are trying to figure out whether there is a causal relationship between higher rates of social media usage and these growing problems for youth.

Although these are worthy problems to puzzle over, Plunkett calls our attention to an adjacent set of concerns that are sure to impact young people long into the future. We're missing the mark, she argues, when we try to control too much about the lives of the young people in our care. We are too often "snowplow" parents who try to smooth the path for our children before they encounter the obstacles. We don't give them the chance to fail, skin their knees, and learn to brush themselves off. As parents and teachers, we worry so much about protecting them that we don't adequately support them in their development of the coping skills they will need for living in a complex world. We think we are helping, but too often we compound the problems they will face. And we are potentially causing problems related to data privacy that we can't envision today.

This topic is an urgent one for wealthy societies for a couple of reasons. For one thing, there's no escaping the digital world for most young people. They will grow up in a world in which their every movement is recorded— starting with the sonogram of kicking their mothers inside the womb and continuing through the excitement of birth, first steps, first day of kinder-garten, countless sporting events, parties, and graduations. The digital dos-sier of their entire life establishes a data set that marketers, governments, and potential dates will mine from now until it no longer matters.

For another thing, adolescence itself is getting longer. It is growing in both directions. Young people, especially girls, reach adolescence at a younger age. And adolescence is now believed to stretch well into the twen-ties for most young people. The consequences of this extended period are meaningful for many young people. It also means that our influence as parents, teachers, coaches, and mentors extends longer than ever before. Our own actions cast a longer and longer shadow as time passes.

In situating our attention where it should first belong—on what we can directly control—Plunkett is careful not to let the rest of society off the hook. A law professor, she appreciates the enduring importance of institu-tional constraints and enablers. The law is one of these mechanisms. Cor-porate practice is another. Adults are sharenting because the structure of the online world makes it very easy to do and even encourages it.

As Plunkett points out, most of this bad parenting is encouraged by every major technology company and is entirely lawful today. When we give away data about the young people in our care, it is perfectly fine to do so from the perspective of the state. In fact, the current legal regime fur-ther endorses these practices in permitting the kinds of business practices that yield huge profits for data-hungry social media services and market-ing companies. The default setting today prompts parents to share, rather than protect, data about their children. A very profitable business model depends on this practice.

There is much to be gained from a different type of focus on this prob-lem of data about young people. The generation that is coming of age today can benefit from many good things as a result of new technological developments. They can mean rewarding avenues for learning, exciting new types of jobs (ironically perhaps, most especially in data science), promising ways to solve global problems, and avenues for deepening civic engagement. At the moment, young people are getting too few of these benefits while bearing too many of the costs of the new digital environment.

Plunkett offers a way forward for better parenting in an increasingly data-rich world. As companies and governments trip over themselves to invest more and more in the development of machine learning and other forms of artificial intelligence, the need for data on which to run these systems will grow sharply as this generation comes of age. We owe today's young people a better structure in which to grow up in a digital era. And along the way, we should clean up our own habits and practices as parents and guardians before it proves too costly to those we care the most about.

Now, buckle up! Professor Plunkett offers a bumpy, exciting ride that she promises points us toward True North.

Acknowledgments

Thank you to these people and places for invaluable conversations about and contributions to this project over the years: the Youth and Media team (past and present) at the Berkman Klein Center for Internet & Society at Harvard University, especially Urs Gasser, Sandra Cortesi, Alicia Solow-Niederman, Paulina Haduong, Dalia Topelson Ritvo, Andres Lombana-Bermudez, and Rey Junco; Berkman Klein fellows hour participants; University of New Hampshire (UNH) School of Law faculty workshop participants; Cyber Alliance Speaker Series at Boston University School of Law & Hariri Institute for Computing participants; UNH Law Library; Albany Law School Faculty Workshop participants; Monica Bulger; Megan Carpenter; Mike McCann; John Greabe; Alex Roberts; Roger Ford; Tonya Evans; Kathy Fletcher; Deb Paige; Mary O'Malley; Adam Plunkett; Sarah Haskins; the Rettew family; Sarah Tiano; Justina Johnson; Sarah and Asa Dustin; Julia Sabot; Tal Astrachan; the Lewis family; David Plunkett; Brianna Deschenes; and Janet Eggert. Special thanks to David Weinberger for stewarding the project; Caitlin Poole for research assistance; Lauren Cawse for original artwork; and Gita Devi Manaktala, Kyle Gipson, Nhora Lucia Serrano, and the MIT Press team for bringing these conversations together into book form and inviting others to participate.

Introduction

If Tom Sawyer were a real boy, alive today, he'd be arrested for what he does in the first chapter of Mark Twain's famous novel.[1] Tom skips school. He beats up the new kid in town, then sneaks into his guardian's house in the middle of the night. In the 1840s, towns along the Mississippi River lacked professional police forces,[2] so Tom escaped the fate he would face today.

Let's call today's Tom Sawyer "Tommy S." to avoid confusion with the classic. Today Tommy S. would be known to the local police. Officers, teachers, and court officials would be monitoring and logging his activities using digital technologies. And in the legal case of *In re* Tommy S., Tommy would inadvertently give the government all the evidence it needed to find him delinquent. By chronicling his activities on Instagram, Snapchat, and other digital platforms, Tommy himself would create exhibits A through Z in the court case against him.[3]

This book is not about Tommy's self-incriminating conduct, however. It's about his Aunt Polly, Tommy's guardian. It's about how she might well write her own Facebook post about the affair: "Blue lights flashing outside my bedroom window. Cops woke me up again tonite. Tommy!!! How do you deal with #teentroubles? #bailmoney #xtralargecoffee."

This book is about what Aunt Polly says and does. It's about her role in shaping Tommy's narrative by sharing information about him through many new digital means without knowing all of the ways in which her choices affect her young charge. Aunt Polly is a *sharent*. This new term is still in limited circulation but already has a variety of meanings.[4] Here, it refers to a parent, teacher, or other adult caregiver who publishes, transmits, stores, or engages in other activities involving private information about a child in her or his care via digital channels.[5]

Today, we are all in Aunt Polly's position. This book examines how parents, teachers, and other adult caregivers in the United States make decisions to disclose digital data about children that invade traditional zones of privacy and threaten kids' and teens' current and future opportunities, as well as their ability to develop their own sense of self.

Privacy means different things to all of us. This book proceeds from a broad understanding that privacy is about self-creation, "establishing a locus which we can call our own without undue intervention or interruption—a place where we can vest our identities."[6] And it invites individual reflection on whether that definition, a similar one, or an entirely different one resonates in your own life.

Sharenting decisions impact individual kids and teens. Collectively, they also disrupt any common understanding we may have of childhood and adolescence as protected spaces for play. How can our kids and teens discover who they are when we adults are tracking them, analyzing them, and attempting to decide for them—based on the data we gather—who they are and should become? We owe them greater freedom, in many ways, than we give ourselves to engage in self-discovery.

This book offers a legal analysis of the sharenting problem, both to identify the ways that our laws enable it and also to offer some initial direction on how we could fix it. This direction takes as its North Star the following vision of youth: kids and teenagers should have room to play, to mess up, and to grow up better for having done so.

Like privacy, the concepts of childhood and adolescence can be defined in countless ways. This book advances a play-centered theory: childhood and adolescence should be valued as unique life stages that are anchored in play so that agency and autonomy can be developed through bounded experimentation.[7] Exploration is essential. Making and learning from mistakes is inevitable, even beneficial. Especially in the early years, boundaries between the imagined and the real are minimal.

This play paradigm breaks from the dominant view that today's legal system has of youth, which is grounded in parental and state control of kids and teens.[8] However, it may resonate with us on an intuitive, experiential, cultural, or other level, suggesting that we should think about reconceptualizing the law's understanding of youth.[9] This book also invites you to explore your personal paradigm of how youth should be understood, whether you are using legal or other lenses as your starting point.

You may be wondering why this book is necessary. Aunt Polly meant well. So what's the problem? The problem is that meaning well still leaves our children at risk. We adults are not consciously trying to mess up our children's lives. Sharenting decisions tend to be made with the best of intentions. At worst, they tend to be negligent, even though under the current legal regime, they are lawful. They also occur as part of an often unacknowledged and misunderstood economic bargain between adults and the providers of the tech products and services they use. Adults give up valuable information about children to get free or low-cost devices and services. Tech providers then use that information in myriad profit-oriented ways. Kids and teens are not full participants in this bargain and so may be marginalized in the deal.

The underlying technology itself isn't to blame. Nothing about the connections between computers that brought us the internet, the machine learning that is now giving us artificial intelligence (AI), and many other innovations needs to be inherently threatening to youth. Tech could be an adventure for youth. Twain's Tom had his band of pirates and buried treasure. Today's Toms can make their own robot pirates and try to teach them to trade cryptocurrency. Unfortunately, we're a long way off from unearthing the full wealth of opportunities that digital tech could bring to youth. Instead, different sets of stakeholders are making choices about how to structure, use, and monetize existing and emerging digital technologies in ways that threaten kids and teens both today and tomorrow.

In its focus on parents, teachers, and other caregivers, this book zooms in on certain grown-ups. Others are not off the hook. Tech providers, lawmakers, regulators, and many others also contribute to the threatening turn that digital tech is taking.

And the tech community has been taking the lead. Providers generally want a digital "wild west." This term is thrown around a lot with respect to digital life and can mean different things at different times. Here, it means a landscape where the sheriff spends his days drinking at the local salon and waving his gun around from time to time and where prospectors mine for and use the gold of personal digital data however they think best, with little respect for the sheriff and the law he represents. They are supposed to hang up signs in their camps that explain what they're up to, but the signs are darn hard to read. People pay them about as much attention as the tumbleweed. In this town, lawlessness isn't on the menu. But a nice cold can of law lite sure is. Crack one open, and give a toast as your answers to surveys on a Facebook app are mined to microtarget you for digital ads in a presidential election.[10]

Much has been said already about the impact that tech providers, lawmakers, and other familiar players in the digital tech ecosystem have on privacy. This book will not attempt to say it all again. What this book does have to say is that privacy and related tech choices made by parents and other trusted adults need to be looked at more closely. These everyday decisions play an underappreciated yet outsized role in determining youths' digital dossier, as well as their life prospects in childhood, adolescence, and adulthood.[11] Youth "currently enjoy almost no privacy rights vis-à-vis their parents," and because parents are typically gatekeepers for their children's privacy rights in educational and other settings outside the home, the lack of youth privacy rights may be even more acute with respect to nonparental adults, like teachers.[12] The privacy and related tech choices that adults make so fundamentally shape our children's current lives and future prospects that we are almost unaware of their magnitude.

Parents, teachers, and other caregivers also make many tech choices that have positive impacts on young people's lives.[13] But there is a significant trend that runs in the opposite direction. This trend has implications both for adult choices about individual children and for the types of laws, regulations, policies, companies, nonprofits, and other structures that adults put in place more broadly. This default setting of poorly understood and problematic adult behavior is the concern of this book.

How can we as parents, teachers, and other caregivers make privacy and related choices about children's digital lives that protect and empower the children and teenagers we care for and the life stage of childhood itself?[14] These choices are about what we do in our individual lives. They are also about what we can do as individuals to drive change in our institutions, including legislative bodies, regulatory agencies, and tech companies.

To answer this question, this book sets up a dialogue, inspired by the traditional "case method" approach of law school classrooms.[15] Professors take students through decisions that judges have written to resolve past disputes. Through dissecting a specific situation, students come to understand the broader type of legal problem it contains. They start to think about other manifestations of that problem and similar ones, both those that exist and those that could exist. They unpack the rules that apply to solve that problem, the bedrock legal principles that shape those rules, and the places where there may be gaps or room to improve those rules. They argue about whether and how the law could be used to improve individual and institutional behavior and to avoid that problem or similar ones—by establishing norms that inspire people and institutions to uphold the values embodied in the law beyond what the law requires. And they learn where the law may not be the best or the only way to solve the problem.

The study of law is for everyone, not just law students and their professors. We study law all the time, although we may not realize it. Our daily lives are one long "Law & Ordinary" episode. When we look at the speed limit sign on the highway and figure we can go five miles over without much risk because everyone else is doing it, we're making a snap judgment about how to interpret the letter of the law. When we comfort a friend who feels wronged in a divorce settlement by explaining all the reasons she's right to be upset, we're doing legal analysis. When we look at the health insurance options available to us and develop opinions about how they could be better, we're identifying avenues for law reform.

All of us are students of law out of fear. We live under a "government of laws" rather than of people or robots (yet).[16] If we want to avoid being arrested and incarcerated, we need to understand how to follow the law. We are also students of law because we hope. Whatever we aspire to for ourselves, our families, and our society, we implicitly or explicitly look to the law to help actualize that hope. We all need to study law, especially for a part of society as complex and rapidly changing as the digital tech realm and especially as it affects a group of people as vitally important to us as our children. We need to understand better what the existing laws cover; what they don't cover; and where, why, and how we might want to think about changing them. We also need to talk about the tools that we have that go beyond the law. We want our kids to grow up finding treasure within themselves rather than being mined as part of the adult world's digital gold rush. How can we get them there?

Let's discuss. The study of law in this book proceeds in four parts:

First, the book tells a short story. The story is pretend, but it's not fantasy. It is Tommy S.'s story, a representative real-world scenario of adult decision making about youth digital data. This story reveals just how much private information adults share about youth on a regular basis. Think of this story as the "case" part of our law study. It's not a case in the technical sense of the term—a legal dispute resolved by a court. Think of it more as a "case study"—information tailored for exploring a set of challenges. This book discusses many existing digital technologies, often in hypothetical circumstances. It also discusses hypothetical but realistic near-future digital technologies (some closer than others) as well as the situations likely to accompany them.

Second, the book builds on Tommy's tale to bring in other examples and outline current and future problems that data disclosures from sharenting can pose for children and teenagers, as well as key areas of positive opportunities these disclosures can facilitate. It also shines a spotlight on a subgenre of sharenting—"commercial sharenting," in which parents use their families' private experiences, with a focus on their children, to try to make money.

Third, the book unpacks the faulty assumptions that our legal system makes about children, parents, families, privacy, and related areas that enable and even encourage the sharenting problem.

Fourth, it proposes a "thought compass" to reorient adults to how best to navigate digital terrain such that childhood and adolescence are protected as unique and valuable life stages that empower youths' current and future selves. All life stories begin here. Just as a real compass is grounded in cardinal directions, this compass is oriented toward the everyday ethical principles of play, forget, connect, and respect. All of the principles are laid out at a high level. This design is intentional. It invites debate and different ways to think about "walking the walk" of these principles. Some of these principles are accompanied by mapping of concrete legal or related reforms. Others are not. But the singular ability of the law to set societal norms that go beyond specific statutory, regulatory, or policy requirements means that the law almost always could play some role in charting any new collective course, even if it's not the only or best way.

What would it look like to stop sharenting and reclaim parenting, teaching, and other caregiving? Would digital tech still have a role as we reboot? Or is it a search for fool's gold to speculate on how we might reprogram our relationship to our kids and digital life? As a feature, not a bug, this book has more questions than it does answers. Questions anchor every chapter. Some of these questions are focused; others are more foundational, such as the meaning of privacy or childhood and adolescence. This book is a conversation starter, not a "how to fix all the things" book. It is for everyone who wants to think and talk about how adults' choices around children's digital lives impact youth privacy, opportunity, and sense of self, as well as our collective treatment of childhood and adolescence.

Because this book is for students of "Law & Ordinary," it is not intended as a strictly scholarly analysis. Its heart is in the author's past work as a legal aid lawyer who represented youth clients in school discipline, special education, and similar cases, thereby gaining "expertise . . . in the gritty fisticuffs of legal culture's trenches,"[17] in the words of another public-interest lawyer turned legal academic. It draws on media and other popular accounts of the tech transformation of daily life, with the goal of connecting with people's real-life experiences and participating in the wide-ranging public dialogue on digital life.

The book is filled with ideas and findings from academic literature, primarily from the legal academy. There are many other valuable modes of academic inquiry into the sharenting problem, including media studies, sociology, anthropology, ethics, and more.[18] And the conversation here draws on some of these insights, arguments, and questions to focus the legal analysis.

It also draws on literary, pop culture, and similar references. These tidbits are not proffered as literary, media, or related academic analysis. They are meant to keep the conversation going and to help find some shared points of reference, especially around stories about childhood.

Has the book gotten off on the right foot? Let's tackle a question that may come to many minds: should there still be a spot for Tom Sawyer in the twenty-first century? He is a white, cisgender, able-bodied, Christian boy. He was born in this country to American parents. He isn't rich, but thanks to Aunt Polly, his basic needs are met.

The identities and experiences of a growing number of kids and teens in the United States today are nothing like Tom's. This disconnect is not just because he's a fictional character. It is because he embodies prejudices, privileges, and power dynamics that could make his representation of American childhood one of exclusion and domination of those who are not like him.

As an archetype, Tom Sawyer is imbued with the "original sin" of this country—enslavement and extermination of native peoples, Africans, and other minorities. He uses the n-word, which has earned him the distinction of being banned in schools. (His best buddy, Huckleberry Finn, does help a former slave escape along a river, but one rafting trip does not make Huck an abolitionist.)

Twain's Tom was a product of his time, which tolerated many beliefs, practices, and institutions that today we find reprehensible. The Tom that's conjured up here isn't meant to be limited to Twain's creation. The Tom Sawyer archetype evoked here aims to be timeless. This book uses Tom and other make-believe figures as touchstones to evoke a spirit of childhood as a protected space for exploration and development that every child should have. This book incorporates these stories because they are familiar to many of us as part of a childhood literary canon, not because they are immune from criticism. This book leaves those powerful analyses to others. Here, Tom Sawyer, Peter Pan, and other creatures of childhood fantasy are presented as being for everyone.

In addition to old characters from old stories, this book uses a new word for our new lived experiences. In this book, the word *sharenting* is understood as the publication, transmission, storage, or other uses of private information about children through digital channels by parents, teachers, or other adult caregivers. In other contexts, this term may have different connotations. It may refer to parents' actions or be focused on social media. This specificity is appealing. If a term is grounded in the word *parent*, why should it include people other than parents? And it's accepted to say that we share information on social media. It's less accepted to talk about sharing information with our smart refrigerators or other nonsocial media digital services and products.

What this more limited definition gains in precision, it loses in power to facilitate a big-picture discussion. Today, kids and teens grow up within a circle of trusted adults who routinely share details of their lives through an ever-expanding range of digital affordances with an ever-growing number of other people and institutions for a never-ending set of reasons. Parents play a uniquely important role and are likely to account for the majority of the sharing, either directly or indirectly. However, they are not the only grown-ups with their fingers on the Post, Submit, and Accept buttons. Also, they are doing more than what we conventionally think of as sharing. The term technically should be "shar-using-enting-eaching-other-ing." Unfortunately, the portmanteau police won't issue a permit for terms with more syllables than *Brangelina*.[19] Thus, *sharenting* it is!

As students of the law, we can push back on this word from more than one angle. One of the many fun things about studying law is strength-testing an idea by trying to destroy it. Let's move away from the accuracy argument and launch a more substantive attack: is it fair to speak of sharenting when parents, teachers, and other adults inhabit a confusing, ever-evolving digital tech landscape? Implicit in the concept of sharenting is some degree of individual choice: an adult is choosing to act in certain ways with respect to information about her children.

Today, tech providers tend to lack transparency about what data they are collecting, why they are collecting it, what they will do with it, and whether users can set meaningful boundaries. There is a lack of comprehensive data privacy protection from the legal system, for youth and adults alike. There is almost a necessity to be digital in one's work and social doings. So are we making choices to sharent? Or are we "sharent-trapped"[20] and stuck in our routine by forces outside ourselves?

The short answer to both questions is yes. The relationship between choice and structural context is not "either/or." It's "yes and." In general, people have capacity for individual decision making. Our legal system relies on these first principles of agency and autonomy. We justify sending people convicted of crimes to jail because they *chose* to violate the law. We garnish the wages of absentee fathers who don't pay child support because they *chose* to have sex, thereby *choosing* to become parents. We require people to perform their end of a contract or pay damages because they *chose* to make the bargain. But if they can prove that they entered into the contract under duress, they are off the hook because it is not fair to hold them to a bargain they did not *choose* to make.

Even when people may not be subject to coercive power, the full exercise of their decision-making capacity will be impacted and sometimes limited by external variables. These variables include difficult or dangerous circumstances they are experiencing through such adversity as poverty, discrimination, or violence. They also include less toxic factors, such as lack of full information on which to make decisions or pressure from social norms. These factors significantly shape sharenting for all of us. And for those of us experiencing more toxic factors as well, decision making becomes far more difficult. We're doing our best, but it's hard to know what that should look like.

Sharenthood can feel as clunky as the word itself sounds. We're riding on a bumpy, makeshift, Tom and Huck–style raft down the rapids of the digital world. The gadgets are sleek, the goals are lofty, but our process is age-old. We're passing down folk wisdom to one another while having quick chats in supermarket lanes or watching our kids on a play date.

But is our wisdom really ours, or is it just shared content from social media? We're deciding on the fly: Do we post that picture or not? Do we give our kids the Fitbit they want for Christmas? Do we send a YouTube holiday message or an old-fashioned card? If we're using a card, do we use a website to upload a picture and send a personal one? Do we have time to read the privacy policies and other terms of use for any of these options that are more complex than a pen and paper? We don't even have time to find our reading glasses. Or a pen. But in a few years, our pen and our glasses will have nowhere to hide, courtesy of our in-home robot and its sensor-based tracking system. We mostly think this is awesome, although we also find it a little weird.

The currents are swift. They're also swirly. We're dragged this way and that. But we haven't gone under yet. We have some open water now. Our society is paying more attention to digital privacy, to data breaches, to digital information quality, to the crossover between the virtual world of play to the brick and mortar one. We're thinking more comprehensively, compassionately, and creatively about the digital lives we're living.

We're at an interesting moment: we think we're in the depths of the rapids, but we are probably only at the start. The robots aren't firmly entrenched. We still have parents who remember what a VCR looked like and how to make a mix tape. We can build a better raft. Let's pause for breath, keep our heads above water, and chart the currents. True north: that goes somewhere.[21] Now where?

1 The Origins, Education, and Maturation of Tommy S.

Tom Sawyer was a creation of small-town frontier life. Our Tommy S. shares the spirit of the original—a scamp with a heart of gold. But that's where the similarities end. Tommy S. exists on the frontiers of cyberspace. He has digital data in his DNA.

This chapter tells Tommy's story, a fictional yet true-to-life portrait of childhood and adolescence today. This case study is designed to be representative, not universal. It aims to surface key modes of sharenting, some of which you may see in your own lives, some of which you may not. You may also see sharenting in your lives that you don't see mentioned in these pages.

As you read, think about what seems familiar and what seems foreign, what seems straightforward and what surprising. Do some of the sharenting activities seem inevitable, inherent in life today, while others come across as more discretionary? Where on the "Three Bears" scale would you rank the sharenting in Tommy's life: too much, too little, or just right? What are the reasons for this ranking? Might you be inclined to assign different rankings at different times of Tommy's life?

The stages of Tommy's young life have a parallel digital sequence that tracks his development. The same is true for the children in our own lives. During each of these stages, we parents, teachers, and other adults are likely to share digital data about kids and teens that create a "digital dossier."[1] These three stages are creation (which includes conception, gestation, and infancy), education, and maturation.

This chapter treats each stage in sequence. This mapping is a rough guide to the landscape of adult decisions about kids' digital data. There are two important caveats: (1) no map, including this one, could capture all conceivable actions that adults as a cohort could take, and (2) the actions taken by individual adults will vary considerably.

Why the caveats? Tech providers and tech users innovate at lightning speed. Individual users have their own preferences and patterns. Any list that attempts to capture all the instances in which all types of children's data are shared by all adults through all available and emerging digital technologies would be obsolete in a nanosecond. Adults' practices around the digital transmission of children's data involve sharing many types of information through an ever-growing array of digital products and services with a wide range of individuals and institutions for countless reasons.

The types of information include, but aren't limited to, medical, educational, social, behavioral, and psychological. The types of digital products and services involved include, but aren't limited to, laptops, smartphones, tablets, social media, text, email, sensors, and "smart" devices. Products also include the doggie drone, which supervises your kid when he walks the dog and scoops up the poop in case your kid forgets. Okay, that canine companion isn't on the market yet,[2] but you can get your child a robotic dinosaur instead of a real dog for company.[3] And you can also get a digital dog treat dispenser linked to an app so you can play with your dog while you're away from home.[4]

Digital Life Stage One: Creation—Conception, Gestation, and Infancy

Before Tommy is born, his parents have a real dog, and they want a real child to keep it company. They are older when they start trying, so they have trouble conceiving. Tommy's mom's well-meaning obstetrician recommends that she start using a fertility app to track her menstrual cycle and advise her on the best times to have sex. The app also advises Tommy's dad on where to buy flowers and when to send them.[5] When the app doesn't work fast enough, Tommy's mom adds a fertility tracking bracelet.[6]

The result is Tommy.

The app and bracelet predict Tommy's creation. The United States Supreme Court has told us that it's not its business to decide when life begins,[7] but tech companies are rushing in where the highest court in the land and others fear to tread.[8] Although the jury may be out on when life begins, the verdict on digital life is unanimous. Digital life can begin before conception.

When conception does occur, Tommy's proud parents-to-be announce it on Facebook. They follow up with all the breaking news on gestation. His first ultrasound pic pops up in the newsfeed of tens of thousands of adults around the world. His parents have their privacy settings set to share with friends of anyone tagged in the photo. In addition to tagging themselves, they also tag their parents and siblings: those proud future grandparents, aunts, and uncles.

A friend of Tommy's aunt is an ob-gyn. She notices what appears to be a minor abnormality on the scan but decides not to write a comment on the post, figuring that it would be inappropriate. She also decides against reaching out to the parents via private Facebook message. After all, the happy couple is trying to share good news, not crowdsource their prenatal care. She's not their doctor. It's possible she was reading the ultrasound incorrectly. An iPhone picture of an ultrasound printout posted on Facebook and viewed on another iPhone screen while she's getting her steps for the day on a treadmill isn't a hospital grade presentation. She has hundreds of her own patients to worry about, and she's on call tonight. It's best to get back to her workout before the next patient goes into labor.

Even though this Facebook viewer has kept her distance from the ultrasound data, Facebook hasn't. Facebook is all up in that womb. Under its privacy and related policies, Facebook can use the picture's data in a virtually unrestricted fashion.[9] Tommy's name isn't on it when it's first posted. But as soon as he's born, his parents post his newborn mug shot, complete with his full name, date of birth, length, and weight. A handful of rogue hospital employees do the same, tagging Tommy as a "mini-Satan," and causing a @#$#-storm before Tommy can soil his first diaper.[10]

Facebook and its associated service providers can likely connect the dots from the ultrasound pic to the newborn pics and start aggregating data about Tommy, including in its facial recognition database.[11] Attempts to deidentify the data prior to aggregation should be viewed with some suspicion. Experts have found that deidentification is not always an effective means of protecting privacy from tech vendors, data miners, insurers, and other third parties.[12]

To be fair to Facebook, there are some pictures of kids and teens that it does not want its users to see. According to internal company guidelines on content moderation obtained by the media, Facebook will remove "imagery of child abuse if shared with sadism and celebration."[13]

Outside of those narrow categories where Facebook or other social media companies consider content offensive and subject to removal or other action (whether based on their own decision making or legal requirements), parents are left to decide for themselves whether to share a milestone with their digital social circles. There is no Parental Social Media Association of America to give binding parental guidance to parents.[14]

Tommy's parents record his first bath. They post the pictures and get a ton of likes, which encourages them to take and share more pictures. They back up their photo library to storage space on a cloud-based server, which is helpful when they drop their phones into the tub while bathing Tommy. It's less helpful when their storage space is hacked and tubby-time pics float into unknown waters. They figure that the hackers are more interested in naked celebrities than bubble-covered, half-naked newborns,[15] so they let the missing pics be water under the bridge.

Rub-a-dub-dub, in and out of the tub, Tommy's parents are members of the digital monitoring club. They watch his every move on Nest Cam.[16] They have a scare in the middle of one night when they think a hacker has gotten into that digital baby monitor feed as well.[17] It turns out that Tommy was just snarfy. They track his sleep patterns with the Owlet bootie, a sensor-enabled sock that monitors infant breathing, sleeping, and other physical patterns.[18] They use a nanny product with artificial intelligence (AI) to help respond to and soothe him when they are unavailable.[19]

They also continue to share news of his activities on social media with exposure to thousands of their nearest and dearest. They use a free digital service to make baby books.[20] These collections are only for the viewing pleasure of Tommy's grandparents, aunts, and uncles—and whichever human or machine eyes use the images for whatever purposes now or in the future. Well before Tommy takes a single step, his digital data travels to thousands, likely tens of thousands, of human and machine users.

Digital Life Stage Two: Education

Early Childhood

Two-year-old Tommy is obsessed with *Sesame Street*, so smart Elf on the Shelf flies to the North Pole and grabs a smart Sesame Street denizen for Christmas. Okay, smart Elf on the Shelf can't really source directly from Santa's workshop. Tommy's parents didn't put in its batteries correctly.

Also, this particular product doesn't exist yet. Neither does smart Elmo. But he isn't a Christmas myth. There could soon be an Elmo available that says more than "Tickle me."[21]

Tickle Me Elmo is so twentieth century. For the twenty-first century, we need smart Elmo. Smart Elmo says, "No tickle." Smart Elmo want to read. Smart Elmo want to do math. Smart Elmo want to be Tommy's friend and give fuzzy Elmo snuggles. Drawing on the cognitive computing technology that drives the IBM Watson machine, smart Elmo would take the *Sesame Street* lessons that have provided an early education foundation for generations of children and bring them to life.[22]

So instead of learning his ABCs from Elmo's interactions with the *Sesame Street* gang, Tommy would practice his letters under Elmo's fuzzy tutelage. Elmo would show Tommy how to get to Sesame Street without leaving his parents' home. As the AI technology underlying smart Elmo grows more sophisticated, instead of watching Elmo play with other kids, Tommy would play with Elmo. But what might Elmo be learning and sharing about Tommy?

Strong, easy-to-read, and fair privacy policies need to be in place for any smart toys or smart teachers to avoid having children's data be used for an unspecified set of purposes over an indeterminate length of time. When Tommy gets sick and throws out Elmo until the fairy rescues the stuffed toy, Velveteen Rabbit–style, Tommy can also play with smart Barbie, a tracking teddy bear, and more.[23] He can go old school and play with an app: "apps meant to appeal to toddlers and preschoolers are both the most popular [type of app] and the category that has experienced the fastest growth, according to a 2012 study."[24] Tommy can also chill with Siri, Alexa, and the other home assistants that finally learn to decipher toddler speak and play *Sesame Street* on command.[25]

When Tommy does leave the house to go to daycare, his parents get real-time updates from the daycare provider on a childcare app.[26] The pictures from the provider include Tommy playing with the other kids. His favorite seems to be a little guy named Huck.

You may be wondering: are all of these digital data choices made by Tommy's parents, or are some of them Tommy's? Tommy doesn't choose whether or where he goes to daycare. Tommy does decide whether to play with smart Elmo or the tracking teddy bear. Tommy decides whether to smooch Elmo or hit him in his red furry face.

This can be a tricky line to draw. Sometimes, adults' choices around digital devices and services are about their own actions—whether to share a pic on their own social media page. Other times, adult choices directly or indirectly facilitate the subsequent choices that children and adolescents make, especially for young kids who can't express a real preference about tech decisions. The toddler can't go out and buy a smart Elmo on his own.

Other instances of adult facilitation discussed below highlight the role that parents and other decision makers play in allowing schools, camps, and other youth-serving settings to store, share, analyze, and otherwise use kids' digital data. These institutions will receive some of the data from kids' own interactions with digital devices and services. But kids are in the position to share this data because of tech choices that adults made first.

Tommy has his parents to thank for his tracking teddy bear. He's also got them to thank for starting to build his education record while he's still in diapers. In one sense, as Oscar the Grouch might point out, that proposition falls into the "There's nothing new under the sun" category. The early childhood years have long been understood as foundational for educational development. The new revelation is that these early experiences in the home that previously would have been recorded in parents' memories and scrapbooks are now digitally preserved and used by one or more tech providers, their affiliates, or other third parties outside the home—often without parents' full knowledge.

Primary and Secondary School Years

When Tommy travels from his own personal Sesame Street to the public elementary, middle, and high schools down the street, he continues to be immersed in a connected digital world. Some of these digital "educational technologies" or "ed tech" are used by Tommy himself in the classroom or other school spaces.[27] This decade is saying "Open sesame" to the floodgates of ed tech. The volume, types, and purposes of available digital products for student use in school are staggering. In many school systems, ed tech adoption has been rapid and widespread. Often, it is happening in an iterative, bottom-up way that brings a touch of that Silicon Valley "move fast" spirit into the more slow-moving world of public primary and secondary education.[28]

Many ed tech entrepreneurs try to introduce their services directly to classroom teachers or the other front-line decision makers in a given educational sphere. This is more of a side-door or back-door approach than front-door outreach to a schoolwide or districtwide decision maker, like the principal's or superintendent's office. Going through the side or back door may facilitate ed tech use as teachers and other staff quickly roll out the welcome mat for offerings they deem valuable to their students. Sometimes teachers become ed tech entrepreneurs themselves, which also can provide a window of easy access into classrooms.[29]

The protocols and formalities of the front door tend to slow down this decision-making process. But this delay can have a protective function, not just a pain in the ass one. If the front door is guarded by decision makers with a combination of technical, legal, and pedagogical know-how, a little delay may go a long way to creating meaningful educational experiences while protecting privacy.[30]

Even though Tommy is engaging directly with educational technologies, many of the devices and services that he uses are chosen for him or assigned to him by teachers or administrators, especially when he is younger.[31] Some of them his parents know about ahead of time because the school sends home a release asking for permission to transmit Tommy's personally iden-tifiable information (PII) to the digital vendor that provides the service.[32] But many others his parents will not know about, unless Tommy happens to mention how cool it is that a classmate liked his progress in an app the whole class is using.

He learns to read using a personalized learning platform on the iPad that is assigned to him through a one-to-one device program.[33] The program allows him to progress at his own speed rather than be stuck on a one-size-fits-all plan for the whole class. Tommy likes the iPad. He is already very familiar with the device because his parents toilet-trained him using the iPotty, which allows him to play while he poops.[34] He pays for school lunch using a swipe card linked to a web-based portal through which his par-ents can put funds on the card.[35] Tommy's parents sometimes get confused because the website they need to visit to reload his cafeteria card is different from the one they need to visit to see his grades.[36]

Tommy gets confused too. In addition to his cafeteria card, he has another card that uses a sensor to track when he gets on and off the school bus. He participates in a physical education program that uses a smartwatch to track his fitness metrics.[37] When he starts high school, he is given a school-issued laptop that he is required to use at school and encouraged to take home for his work there.[38] He goes online through his laptop to learn the history of the American frontier through a massive open online course (MOOC). And when he gets sent to the principal's office for trying to fake his own death so he could attend his own funeral, he is assigned social-emotional education modules from a software program as a behavioral intervention.[39]

There is a seemingly never-ending stream of digital resources to create learning experiences for Tommy. In many ways, he is lucky: his school has the financial and other resources to bring digital technologies to classrooms and other school spaces. Although most school districts in the country appear to be using one or more types of digital ed tech,[40] a "digital divide" remains in terms of access to and integration of these resources. Even within a district, the types of digital devices and services can vary considerably.

Some of them are old-school, like websites that Tommy visits from a computer that lives on a desk in his classroom. Mavis Beacon no longer teaches typing, but she's got many disciples.[41] A growing number of digital educational experiences are a post-1999 party. They rely on the cloud,[42] sensors, the Internet of Things, artificial intelligence (AI), and other emerging technologies. Some of them are designed specifically for schools, like a sensor-enabled card for attendance. Others are designed for a general audience, like a MOOC, and then integrated by teachers or other staff into the brick-and-mortar school setting.[43]

Within a school system, different ed tech types will be used by people in different roles for a range of goals. In addition to the ed tech that Tommy interacts with, teachers and administrators who work with Tommy during his primary and secondary school years also use ed tech to support their professional responsibilities. Tommy has little to no awareness of this ed tech sphere, and even his parents may not have any understanding of this space, despite the notifications about some of these ed tech choices that they receive from the school. The principal's office tracks attendance with a software program. This program sends alerts to Tommy's parents if he comes late to school or doesn't come at all.[44] The nurse's office keeps electronic health records.[45] The teachers use an online grade book to track assignments.[46] The art teacher creates a public-facing Facebook page with pictures of students' art.[47] The guidance counselor uses a predictive analytics program to assess Tommy's educational and career trajectory.[48] Do his talents lie in whitewashing fences or whitewashing the truth?

Preteen Tommy starts to test the limits around him, through fibs and more. He starts getting into trouble at school. The school's digital surveillance system sees him cutting class and smoking in the woods.[49] He gets referred to the juvenile justice system and gets a digital rap sheet that way.[50] Some of the trouble is a result of his own digital choices. In one of those adult logic moments that exasperates teenagers, schools sometimes promote science, technology, engineering, and mathematics (STEM) in one breath and, in the next, breathe fire over minor digital tech infractions. Notably, New York has wrestled over how deeply the fruits of the tech tree should take root in schools. The New York City school system has been engaged in a protracted give and take over how much latitude students should have to use their personal devices in schools. A cellphone ban spawned new brick-and-mortar business opportunities for some corner stores, which started offering phone storage to kids for a fee.[51]

City mice aren't the only ones trying to evade the trap of trouble over their personal tech. Their country cousins may also face a maze of contradictory tech signals at school. For example, in Manchester, New Hampshire, many of the old mill buildings that drove the late nineteenth-century economy have been rescued from their twentieth-century decay and are now home to a mini-Silicon Valley along the Merrimack River. STEM has some serious steam behind it. The high school is encouraging its students to jump on this tech train while also being vigilant that students' personal tech adoption doesn't go off the rails. According to a recent edition of the district's student handbook, using a personal tech device in the high school is a level 1 offense that can carry serious sanctions. Three level 1 offenses add up to a level 3 offense. Other level 3 offenses include bringing a weapon to school. Level 3 offenses lead to out-of-school suspension.[52] Out-of-school suspension separates teenagers from their phones and forces them to dial into studying. Problem solved.

Just kidding.

Out-of-school suspension increases students' chances of dropping out. It also increases their chances of being involved in the juvenile justice system.[53] Even if the underlying offense of repeated personal tech use in school doesn't violate criminal law, being out of school and likely unsupervised increases the risk that kids and teens will commit offenses that do. Also, in today's "zero tolerance" school culture, it's plausible that a student's refusal to comply with any school policy could lead to an arrest based on a disorderly conduct or similar charge.

Let's say that teenager Tommy won't stop texting his bro, Huck, about Becky Fletcher, the hottest girl in school. The teacher looms over him and says that she really means it this time: "Put that phone away this minute." Tommy is embarrassed. What if the teacher saw what he wrote? Is there any chance she'd believe that "I heart those titties" actually means "I chastely desire Becky for her superior intellect"?

He shoves the phone inside his desk so hard that his school-issued iPad falls out and hits the ground. Is it broken? Tommy is nervous. What if he broke the iPad? That @*#(is expensive. If his parents get a bill for it, they're not going to be able to pay it. He doubles down on his conviction that this mess is all his @#*($@#* teacher's fault. His teacher feels the same way Tommy does. The principal is going to run her out of town on a rail if a broken iPad turns up in her room. That @*(#* is expensive, and the big grant that the school received to buy the devices isn't going to be renewed. This is all Tommy's fault.

The following exchange ensues:

Go to the principal's office.
> No.
I'm calling the school resource officer unless you go right this minute ago.
> Don't you mean "right this minute"? How could I go anywhere "right this minute ago"? I ain't magic.
"I'm NOT magic."
> Yeah. I know. You're DEFINITELY not.
We're not talking about me. We're talking about you. You're NOT magic. NOT. Not "ain't."
> If I ain't NOT magic, then shit . . . that makes me magic!

Tommy's principal disagrees. Tommy gets a Saturday in-school suspension. His infractions and accompanying consequences are recorded in the digital database the school has for disciplinary purposes.[54] He is also assigned social and emotional learning modules on the importance of following instructions and refraining from profanity. His performance on those modules is recorded by the software program. Performance metrics include his actual answers and the data surrounding his answers, such as how long it took him to come up with each answer. Tommy's personal answering speed is less time than it takes to whitewash a fence by yourself and more time than it takes a crew of others to do it for you.

Tommy learns lessons about himself and the world outside of school as well. He attends camps, after-school programs, and community sports and activities. These informal learning spaces seem to share with their formal learning space counterpart, schools, a trend toward expansive ed tech use.[55] Tommy goes to an engineering camp where he builds a robot out of egg cartons and other recyclables. He learns how to make it move using a sensor kit and a connected app. His counselors post pics on social media. Tommy decides to start his own YouTube channel to showcase his science experiments, with a prank twist. "The Adventures of Tommy S." becomes an instant classic—especially the episode on how to teach a robotic dog to ride a raft in a backyard pool.

As Tommy grows up, he will make more of the choices about ed tech himself. Fifteen-year-old Tommy won't ask for permission to download the YouTube app and start uploading videos, whereas five-year-old Tommy had to beg his parents for Minecraft. But until he hits eighteen, the age of legal majority, his parents and, in certain circumstances, the school hold decision-making authority over whether to share his personal data via ed tech affordances. Tommy has no legal right to be involved in the decisions. Even if he did, it would likely be difficult for him to understand the terms of use to which he was agreeing. It's hard enough for his parents and teachers to do so.

Everything in the broad and ever-expanding category of ed tech with which Tommy engages is capable of capturing and storing vast amounts of data about him.[56] The extent to which each product or services does so will vary, often without Tommy or his parents being aware of the variation. Many of these digital services and devices also can analyze and share this data with third parties.[57] Sometimes, this sharing will be obvious, like a public-facing Facebook page. Sometimes, this sharing won't be evident, even to the users themselves. For example, when Tommy swipes his card to enter and exit the school bus, does he really know who is seeing his travel data and why they care? Do his parents know?

The company that supplies the sensor cards and accompanying software to the school district is likely using third-party providers to supply services such as data storage. If there are weak terms of service or poor or no contractual language in place between the company and the school, the company might also share the data with a data brokerage service or consultant who specializes in advising transportation companies of market opportunities.[58]

The company might purport to deidentify Tommy's data, but data deidentification is not always a silver-bullet solution for protecting privacy.[59]

As we'll discuss later, there are federal and state laws that limit schools' authority to share information about their students. Unfortunately, these laws are often unable to establish data-sharing parameters that promote students' success, encourage educational and technological innovation, and keep privacy pitfalls to a minimum. Tommy may only have to walk down the street to get to school. But his data may travel far and wide, which poses potential problems for him in the present as well as the future. Smart Elmo says, "That doesn't sound very smart to Elmo!"

Digital Life Stage Three: Maturation

That's not even the whole story, smart Elmo! Schools are a primary arena in which the adults in Tommy's life are going to make decisions about his digital data, often without realizing what they're deciding. As Tommy grows up, his parents, teachers, and other caregivers will make digital data choices in many other domains as well. Those other domains may be loosely grouped into four broad categories (a particular digital decision may fall into more than one category):

- Social communications with peers, including social media, contributions to parenting blogs, or the generation of other noncommercial digital content;[60]
- Familial, educational, or other interactions with the government;[61]
- Medical and behavioral interventions mediated by digital tech;[62] and
- Household and general life management through Internet of Things devices or other programs, such as a smart fridge to monitor the grazing habits of voracious teenagers or a smart thermostat to keep them from turning up the heat to sauna levels rather than putting on a @*(#@* sweater.[63]

Let's now return to the broken iPad incident that landed Tommy in his own *Breakfast Club* Saturday morning suspension. Following Tommy's refusal to obey his teacher right away, the teacher calls the school resource officer (SRO) for help.[64] The SRO is a member of the local police force who is stationed in the high school. He arrives in the classroom and arrests

Tommy for disorderly conduct and destruction of property. Tommy talked back to the teacher, and he made a scene in class. Also, the iPad won't turn on when the teacher tests it.

When these juvenile charges are heard by a judge, Tommy's court-appointed public defender puts the teacher on the witness stand and asks if the iPad was charged when she attempted to start it. The teacher doesn't recall. No one is able to locate the iPad in question. The local prosecutor drops the destruction of property charge, but the disorderly conduct charge is found to be true. This case disposition is aggregated in a court database, despite the strict rules of confidentiality that are supposed to apply to juvenile cases.[65]

Quick question from smart Elmo: why is the outcome of Tommy's case brought to us by the letter T for *true* rather than the letter G for *guilty*? According to the ABCs of juvie, when youth commit infractions that would be criminal if done by an adult, they are charged with delinquency rather than criminal offenses. The animating principle for the juvenile justice system is rehabilitation, ostensibly without the same infusion of other objectives of the criminal justice system, such as deterrence and retribution. Because the juvenile judicial process is not supposed to be focused on wrongdoing but on kids' doing better, the question isn't guilt or innocence. Instead, we're looking for "just the facts, ma'am."

Did Tommy disturb the classroom by repeatedly and loudly refusing to comply with the reasonable requests of a local government official (his teacher)? Yes or no? True or not true? There is a big exception to this "truthiness" approach: when youth commit certain types of violent acts, they may be charged as adults and found guilty with a capital G.

Fortunately, Tommy's actions don't land him in the category of teens who can be tried as adults. His parents, however, are dismayed at their son's conversion from glimmer in their eye to juvenile delinquent and go online looking for advice and support. They post on social media: "Help! How do we reform our bad boy?"[66] Tommy's mom writes a lengthy Facebook post about how difficult it is to parent a teenage boy with a wild streak and hypothesizes that perhaps he has an underlying mental health disorder. Buoyed by comments from her extended network, she sets the post to "public."[67] The post is even more successful than Tommy's YouTube channel and is viewed by thousands of people across the world. She thinks about starting her own YouTube channel, "Bad Boy Mom," and getting commercial sponsorships from companies that sell things that moms of bad boys need, like apps to track your teenager's whereabouts.

Then fate intervenes. Tommy's mom and dad have been struggling with an addiction to prescription painkillers. For her, it started with a script her doctor gave her after back surgery. Tommy's dad then decided to help himself. They have managed to keep their use from interfering with their lives until they can't anymore.

Tommy's parents pass out in the front seats of their car. Tommy is in the back seat, panicking. The police show up. While one officer administers Narcan to Tommy's parents, the other officer snaps a picture of the scene, including Tommy's face in the back seat—his worst nightmare. No wonder he was acting up in school.[68] The officer posts the scene on the police department's Facebook page. Later, when asked why he chose to share this private moment with the world, he cites the need to educate people about the evils of opioid abuse. He says that no one will remember that Tommy was there.

Tommy will remember that he was there because it is the worst moment of his life. Countless other people also will remember because the picture won't ever go away. Tommy goes to live with Aunt Polly, who will be his temporary guardian while his parents are in court-ordered in-patient rehab. Aunt Polly is concerned that Tommy might continue to get into trouble. She starts researching apps to track his whereabouts and installs a digitally networked security system in her home so she can monitor what Tommy does when she's at work.[69] Unfortunately, it's not enough to keep her from having more #teentroubles with him. Kids will be kids, regardless of who's watching.

Tommy will likely never have the opportunity, as did Twain's Tom Sawyer, to watch his own funeral and find out what his legacy would be. But Tommy and other twenty-first century kids have the opportunity, on entering early adulthood, to go online and see at least some of the legacy of their childhood. But there is a whole digital history of their childhoods that Tommy and his brethren won't ever be able to see because it's in the deep internet of data brokers and others.[70] There is also a whole range of decisions potentially being made based on or influenced by their visible and invisible digital childhood legacies about which they will have little to no knowledge and over which they will have even less control.

Put yourself in Tommy's shoes. When he is old enough to see the sharenting that has been and is being done about him, what do you think his reactions will be? Why? Do you think these reactions are justified or juvenile (in the pejorative, not descriptive, sense)?

Now walk that proverbial mile in his parents', teachers', or Aunt Polly's footwear. What do you think the reasons are for their sharenting decisions? Do you see those reasons as being solid, suspect, or somewhere in between? Might you start to realize that you already have a decision-making schema you're using to approach sharenting, even if you haven't been using the terms *sharenting* or *decision-making schema*?

Your answers to these questions might depend in part on what you understand the short- and long-term risks of sharenting to be. To equip you to explore these and other questions more deeply, the next two chapters explore the main types of risks associated with digital childhood legacies and highlight the potentially positive opportunities that flow from these legacies.

2   Not Your Grandmother's White Picket Fence: Twenty-First-Century Kid Problems

Tom Sawyer had to paint the friggin' fence. Not only does Tommy S. have to paint it, but Aunt Polly Instagrams every part of the process #bighelper #raisinhimrite. She's so happy that he's in her yard and out of trouble. These posts make it difficult for Tommy to pawn off the task on his friends. They make it even more difficult for him to explain to his boss at the pizza parlor why he said he was too sick to work at the shop yet Polly's Instagram feed showed him basking in the sun while #watchinpaintdry.

Tommy's adults are doing what most of us do, too. But whether we engage in sharenting without realizing it or with the best of intentions, we are likely creating significant risks to our children's privacy, life opportunities, and sense of self.

What do you think these risks are? Where do you see them in Tommy's tale? Where do you see them in your own life? Do some risks seem worse than others? Are there contexts in which the benefits of digital engagement outweigh privacy and related risks?

As you identify and assess both risks and opportunities, try to be aware of what your reactions suggest about your own understanding of privacy. Do you see privacy as transactional—secrets that can be exchanged for goods or services?[1] Do you see privacy as more contextual—a set of attitudes and actions designed to share information differently depending on your goals for a given situation?[2] Do you understand privacy as more fundamental—a protected zone that is necessary to develop a sense of self—or as something else altogether? There is no right answer, but your response will drive your answers to the many other questions in this book.

This book sees an identity-formation function as the core of privacy,[3] while recognizing that the process of identity formation at times necessitates the use of more transactional, contextual, and many other approaches. If you move back and forth between considering specific questions (like risks to Tommy) and big-pictures ones (like the definition of privacy), you should find that each sheds new light on the other.

This chapter begins by stealing a ray of sunshine from Tommy's day in Aunt Polly's backyard. It highlights potential positive opportunities that stem from adults' choices about kids' private digital lives. The chapter then tacks into cloudier, stormier terrain by identifying four main ways that sharenting causes current and future problems for kids and teens: (1) criminal, illegal, or similarly dangerous activities; (2) legal but opaque, invasive, and suspect activities; (3) personal reputation and other interpersonal activities and dynamics that significantly impact individual relationships and sense of self; and (4) commercial use of children's private experiences.

This chapter continues by examining the first and second categories. The next chapter begins with a thought experiment of a fictional yet potential near-future digital product that further unpacks the second category and segues into the third. The following chapter takes up category four and maps out the commercial sharenting sector, a growing multimillion-dollar industry that could also be called "sharenting on steroids."

Walk on the Sunny Side: Potential for Positive Opportunities

In her Instagram posts about the fence, Aunt Polly means well. She is proud of Tommy, and she wants to share her joy. Through her posts, she receives validation that she's doing a decent job taking care of Tommy during a tough time. She also takes joy in the act of connecting with people in her online community. She works a lot and doesn't get to see her friends much in person anymore. A social media like is no substitute for a hug, but a little dopamine hit can go a long way.

Most of us share at least some aspects of Aunt Polly's positive take on how sharenting might make us better parents, teachers, and caregivers. And we're right to think so. There are sound reasons why you may feel comfortable sharing your kids' information on social media, through educational devices and services, and elsewhere. These include greater social connection, better and more equitable educational experiences, and safer and healthier homes. Illustrations for these and related reasons are given below.

Social media can be a valuable space for building personal, professional, civic, and other relationships that are meaningful to you and your family in a variety of ways. For instance, if you're the parent of a child who has a chronic illness, you might forge vital connections through a Facebook group on the topic that can provide emotional support as well as relevant information. You can model thoughtful "digital citizenship" habits for your children by showing them how you engage meaningfully online.[4] Posting a snap of your family's holiday card can be a cute way to stay in touch with far-away friends, while a rant (about what an a@#(*@(# your teenager was when you politely asked her to stop looking at her phone and smile for the camera for just one *@(*@#)! second) would be far less cute. Your thoughtful curation of your child's digital data trail could potentially benefit her down the road. After all, if schools, employers, and other institutions and individuals will be mining your daughter's digital contacts, she may as well put her best foot forward.

Digital educational technologies may also enhance students' experiences by personalizing learning or offering new areas of study.[5] If you're teaching an elementary school class with children who have wide disparities in reading ability, for instance, you will be much better able to meet their needs if all twenty-five receive customized instruction courtesy of sophisticated algorithms. If you're teaching a high school science class, you might have difficulty getting students to appreciate the periodic table of the elements. But they may well have greater appreciation for learning the elements of coding because many have an entrepreneurial mindset and may see digital tech as key to opportunities in that area.[6]

Ed tech also has the capacity to enhance equity in many ways. Here is one of them: in a school district where many students are eligible for free or reduced lunch, using a sensor-enabled card for cafeteria purchases can reduce the potential for financial status to be on display in the lunch line. If one student pays with cash and another has a pass for a free or reduced-cost meal, the disparity is obvious. But if both pay with cards, then that distinction is reduced. In districts that serve alternative meals or no meals to children whose funds have run out, the distinction reappears.[7]

In theory, as ed tech grows more sophisticated, its equity-enhancing potential could increase. If schools rely increasingly on algorithmic decision making and the algorithm is well-designed, then these decisions could be free of the implicit or other forms of biases that impede equitable deci-sion making by humans.[8] Students then would be better able to advance and pursue new activities and opportunities without concerns about discrimination.

More sophisticated ed tech could also address areas in which there fre-quently is systemic educational inequality, such as students with disabilities or students who are given long-term out-of-school suspensions or expul-sions. Well-designed AI affordances, for instance, could be used to provide these cohorts of students with more effective and engaging learning expe-riences. Such uses of AI could include robots that work on emotional and social development with students on the autism spectrum, as is already happening in some school districts. AI could also be used to provide ongo-ing instruction outside of a brick-and-mortar school building to students who are required to stay home for a long or indefinite period, sometimes because they have been deemed to pose a threat to the school community.[9]

There are also good reasons to bring other types of digital tech, beyond ed tech, into your home. Many young people don't exercise enough. Digi-tal fitness trackers or their next-generation equivalents, like sensor-enabled workout shirts, may encourage kids and teens to exercise regularly.[10] It might be better to take this step toward using digital tech to encourage your child to take her 10,000 steps a day than to worry that her location may be monitored by a third party as she exercises.[11]

There may also be circumstances in which you as a parent have good reasons for wanting to monitor your own child. If you work long hours and can't be home when your teenager gets out of school for the day, a locator app or similar device that allows you to know her whereabouts might give you some peace of mind. To further your ability to keep your home and child safe, you might find it beneficial to rely on a digital security and lock system that allows you to let people into your home when you're not there.

The big picture that comes into focus with these examples is that digital tech can offer us and our children certain freedoms. We are less limited by geographic location. No longer is proximity destiny. If we want to connect with friends across the globe, we can do so instantly. If our children are eager to read at a higher level, they can do so. Digital tech can also offer us many efficiencies. What are you doing with the time you would have spent shopping for groceries back before an Amazon drone dropped them off?

Digital tech is also essential for most job prospects. We want our children to have skills that the robot overlords deem useful.

These and other positive points of digital tech shouldn't be hard to see. Advertising, media depictions, and many other narratives in popular culture tend to paint a rosy picture of digital tech. So you can go ahead and keep sharing digital data as you are. If you're interested in rethinking your comfort level in light of some of the privacy pitfalls discussed below, however, there are actions you can take to continue your digital life in a meaningful way while protecting your privacy.

But before turning to a potential perspective refresh, you need to take a closer look at the darker side of the digital landscape. With a more complete picture, you can better chart your own course and contribute to charting our collective one.

Criminal, Illegal, or Similarly Dangerous Activities

Let's start with the truly scary stuff. Children's data can be an appealing target of criminal, illegal, or hostile adult activities. This category includes pornography, identity theft, stalking, trolling, and other forms of cyberbullying. Some specific examples are discussed briefly below.

Because pornographers may create child porn by photoshopping pictures of children who have no relationship to the pornographer, a social media post that includes pictures of your child might be repurposed for criminal activity.[12] As soon as those Frankenstein images exist, they take on a life of their own. And they may menace your child for the rest of her life.[13]

The specter of child pornography haunts the houses of typical families and not just the lairs of monsters. When might nude images of kids, captured in the regular course of twenty-first-century life, meet the federal definition of child pornography? This question is not an attempt to expand federal criminal prosecutions of parents and other adult caregivers or to "sharent shame" parents who FaceTime with grandparents while a kid streaks from the bathroom through the living room or who inadvertently broadcast images to others, such as through a compromised video monitor in a child's bedroom.[14] Rather, it raises an observation and a note of caution.

The observation: the federal definition of child porn criminalizes depictions of real minors engaged in "sexually explicit conduct," which includes

"lascivious exhibition of the genitals or pubic area."[15] Is the traditional picture of the naked newborn lying on a bearskin rug lascivious? No. What
about a pic of a toddler getting to know her own anatomy while she takes a
bath? Is her curiosity about herself inherently lascivious? Almost certainly
not.[16] But the ubiquitous use of digital technology in the home has introduced more possibilities for capturing potentially pornographic images—or
those uncomfortably close to the line—than ever before.

The caution: current attempts to use child pornography laws to respond
to twenty-first-century norms and behaviors around intimate digital imagery that is not designed for harassment, abuse, or other nefarious purpose
have been a mismatch of Frankensteinian proportions. Consensual "sexting" between teens has led to criminal prosecutions of and sex offender
registration requirements for young people who share consensual images
of themselves or their friends and intimate partners.[17] Mainstream digital
behaviors in an intimate setting are resulting in outsized criminal consequences. There is no indication that a similar type of justice system response
is likely to befall parents who snap bearskin rug pics. A key difference is that
teens who sext are trying to do something lascivious, whereas parents who
snap family photos during a day skinny-dipping at a secluded pond are not.
Courts have said that child porn laws are not meant to end up "'penalizing
persons for viewing or possessing innocuous photographs of naked children.'"[18] But it's best to avoid being called into court to argue when a snap
is innocuous and when it is illegal.

Innocence is not the only facet of childhood that faces threats from criminal, illegal, or dangerous activities by adults. Identity also does. Even children who have limited digital data available about them are potential targets
for criminal threats. Youth might be more at risk for certain types of criminal acts than adults are precisely because they are data blank slates. A Social
Security number (SSN) belonging to an adult who has a long and legitimate
credit history may be less valuable to an identity thief than an SSN belonging to a toddler who has no credit history yet.[19] Parents are unlikely to post
their children's SSNs online. Other institutions that have children's SSNs are
also unlikely to post them online but may wind up doing so anyway as the
result of an internal security flaw or external data breach.

In their sharenting, parents, teachers, and other trusted adults post other
key personal information that can be used to steal children's identities.
Think back to Tommy's parents' ecstatic Facebook post on his arrival: all

viewers of that post know Tommy's full name, date of birth, and place of birth. This information can go a long way toward creating fake credit or other applications in Tommy's name. Viewers of the post also likely know Tommy's height and weight and the circumstances of his arrival on this planet. The bulk of commenters thought that the photo of dad eating pizza in the delivery room while mom was still pushing was #dadfail.

Although this type of information may not be central for identity theft in its most obvious forms, think about the myriad ways in which private information is used to secure digital life. For instance, many security questions for websites ask information that they assume only the real account holder knows. As more details of personal life are shared online from infancy on, however, that premise is increasingly flawed. A security question that asks a sixty-year-old to name her elementary school is more protective than one that asks the sixteen-year-old to do the same. In the boomer's case, not many people would know the answer. In the teen's case, many would know or be able to look up the school on her social media profile or another source. Given the standard practice around using this information, having it easily available in a youth digital data trail is risky.

The risk is so significant that some law enforcement agencies, such as the Utah Attorney General's Office, are creating special bureaus or task forces for addressing the identity theft of children.[20] Other stakeholders also are responding to the threat through investigations or other tools. For example, in winter 2018, the New York attorney general opened an investigation into the use of stolen identities, including from teens, to create social media bots.[21] And in fall 2017, the US Department of Justice issued a warning to school districts that hackers were increasingly targeting student data.[22] Some school districts have paid ransoms to have stolen data returned.[23]

Commercial providers of identity-monitoring services, such as All-ClearID, now offer monitoring protection for children. Following the Anthem data breach in 2015, which revealed the private information of insurance company subscribers and family members, monitoring for minors was made available to affected kids and teens.[24] There was a catch: their parents had to enroll them. There was also another catch: even after parents enrolled them, if an AllClearID alert turned up suspicious activity indicating potential identity theft, before the matter could be addressed, parents had to prove their identity and relationship to the affected child using one or more forms of personal documentation.[25] So we're being asked to protect the integrity of our children's private information by sharing more private information. What happens if there is a security breach of the protector's operation? #viciouscycle

Of the utmost concern is maintaining kids' and teens' bodily integrity. Since the early days of the internet, concerns over children's physical safety as a result of online engagement have produced both panic and productive responses. As we have driven past "information superhighway" territory and on to "digital roads running everywhere" terrain, the understanding of and approach to children's online safety has evolved as well.

We're no longer talking primarily about unknown predators who jump out like highway bandits to accost kids. This does happen. For instance, children may be subject to stalking, doxing, or other harassment based on their parents' activities.[26] We're talking a lot or even most about the bully next door and other threats closer at hand. Children may be subject to stalking, doxing, and similar dangers from their peers or even their peers' parents. This harassment can have devastating consequences, including suicide.

In "the world's first cyber-bullying court case . . . [involving] an extreme example of what might be termed helicopter parenting in the digital age," a mother faced criminal prosecution for having "participated [in] or at least passively observed the harassment of a thirteen-year-old" girl by her own daughter and teenage employee.[27] The victim of the harassment killed herself. The daughter and the victim "had had an on-again, off-again friendship; both had engaged in name-calling and spiteful actions."[28] Ultimately, the mother was not convicted.

Sometimes, the digital world can be a conduit for direct physical attacks by third parties, such as kidnapping or sexual assault. It also can be a conduit for sex trafficking and slavery.[29] Organizers seeking to traffic, enslave, or otherwise exploit children are mining social media to identify likely targets. To date, discussion of this process appears to be focused on the ways in which young people expose their own information and engage directly with predators. If parents and other trusted adults play any role, it seems most often to be by omission: kids without a strong parental or other support system tend to be more vulnerable to being ensnared by predators.

There are questions about the gatekeeping role that parents and other trusted adults may play, though. For example, one British teen's story of how she was enslaved includes a mother who lost her job and understandably cut off her allowance. The girl wound up being online more than she was with her friends, where she was ensnared by a gang leader.[30]

We don't let our kids go outside, yet we let the outside world into our most intimate spaces via digital technologies. We let our kids' data, whether generated by us or by them with our facilitation, roam free. We are inviting our own Nightmare on Elmo's Street.

Legal—but Opaque, Invasive, and Suspect

Children's data is also valuable to many individuals and institutions that operate within or close to legal limits but use this data more for their own purposes than in the best interests of children. This category includes practices that are becoming increasingly familiar to us, like "behavioral targeting" in advertising. Even digital services from seemingly safe institutions, like public school websites, often facilitate such targeting and related practices.[31]

In addition to marketing, there are less familiar uses of data that may be adverse to the current and future life prospects of kids and teens. We don't know exactly what institutions are doing in this area, and we can't really know because "when a computer stores your data, there's always a risk of exposure. Privacy policies could change tomorrow, permitting new use of old data without your express consent."[32] The broad range of data uses and potential uses includes, but is not limited to, data-driven decision making in college admissions,[33] employment, insurance, credit products, consumer transactions, and law enforcement.[34]

Sometimes, an institution uses data in-house for its own purposes. For instance, a college may run its own predictive analytics to make admissions decisions. Or it may engage in old-fashioned Googling. If Aunt Polly doesn't set her Instagram to private, what will the college make of Tommy's law-breaking activities? Other times, an institution relies on one or more third-party providers of aggregated information, loosely called "data brokers."[35] These companies comprise a growing and poorly understood and regulated industry that services many more visible sectors, like the consumer credit sector. Many of the data uses in this category remain fully or partially unknown. In part, this is by design: the data users may not want to be transparent about what they're up to with your private data. In part, this is by default: most of us don't see the matrix of data uses and consequences all around us. But the data brokers see us; the information that they "sell [includes] the names of parents whose child was killed in a car crash, of rape victims, and of AIDS patients."[36]

Recently, a research team from the Center on Law and Information Policy (CLIP) at Fordham Law School made an "attempt to understand the commercial marketplace for student information."[37] This market is a subset of the broader data broker market for data about kids and teens outside of their role as students.

The CLIP team concluded that there was an overall "lack of transparency in the student information commercial marketplace."[38] The team identified "14 data brokers who conclusively sell or advertise the sale of student information or who have done so in the past," but it flagged that this list is not comprehensive.[39] Among the offerings from these identified student data brokers, there were "data on students as young as two years old" and a "list of 'fourteen and fifteen year old girls for family planning services.'"[40] The research team reported that its members were "often unable to determine sources of student data" that brokers had available but that "educational institutions do not appear to be sources of student information for data brokers."[41]

However, even if schools' front offices are not handing out lists of student data, adults within schools are supplying information to the student data broker industry in other ways. Notably, "teachers, and guidance counselors are being used for commercial and marketing purposes as data gatherers in administering school surveys."[42] Parents and students are also supplying sensitive information through such tools as online surveys that then enters the commercial student data broker sphere.[43] This information can result in students' receiving very specific solicitations. For example, "the American Red Cross responded [to the CLIP team] that it marketed to a student as a past [blood] donor and as a potential future donor to 'facilitate special blood program matching,' which could be based on the student's blood type, ethnicity, gender, and 'test result histories like iron level.'"[44]

To help us try to get our minds around how our everyday lives are leaking data about our children such that a third party could reach out to them based on their iron counts, let's turn to a hypothetical yet realistic scenario designed to make this unfamiliar territory more familiar. This scenario illustrates how seemingly harmless everyday data gathering can have unknown and unintended consequences. Some additional real-world examples follow.

3   Beyond Narnia: More Problems Await through the Wardrobe[1]

Identity thieves and other criminals seek to appropriate children's identities. The web of "big data" analytics isn't interested in taking identities but in doing things with them.[2] Big data seeks to use children's data to affect kids' activities, opportunities, and trajectories, while also furthering the goals of the data user itself. The identity thief takes a Social Security number, date of birth, and mailing address to obtain a credit card in the child's name. Big data isn't a thief. The activities in this realm are usually lawful or at least close to the legal line. But the big data ecosystem can operate in a sketchy space. It can silently take pieces of information from children and their adults, mine them for more information, and reshare that information with an unknown number of others for unspecified ends.

At this point, what is your intuition? Do the bad actors—the identity thieves and others—seem risky enough to lead you to think differently about sharenting? Or are you inclined to see the threat they pose as more avalanche (terrifying but rare) than snowstorm (dangerous but manageable)? How does your risk assessment change, if at all, if you think more about the snowstorm scenario than the avalanche? If you live in an area with winter weather, at some point, you probably will drive in a snowstorm. And if you engage in sharenting, private information about your children will go through the big data blizzard. Time to hit the brakes?

Magic Wardrobe[3]

Let's say that the identity thief is like the stereotypical burglar who breaks into your house and takes your stuff: you're left without your possessions and harmed by this loss. The big data thief could be seen as more akin to a customer at a yard sale who buys the old bureau you inherited from your grandmother that you think is worthless, discovers a treasure trove of family photos and other heirlooms inside, and keeps the stash for herself.

That's a helpful but incomplete analogy. Let's look at where it works. Big data isn't stealing. You're welcoming it. You might be rolling out the welcome mat to big data because you don't realize it's there. You might know it's there but think it's helping you. And perhaps it is helping you or at least not hurting you.

Let's look at where this analogy breaks down. In your interactions with digital tech and associated big data, you are typically deriving immediate benefits that go beyond the removal of an unwanted possession. To make the analogy more accurate, big data might be like the yard sale customer who gives you a new dresser for free and takes away your old one. The analogy also breaks down because big data doesn't typically deprive you of the use of any of your own information that you generate yourself: it just uses it for its own purposes. To make the analogy even more accurate, our yard sale customer might leave you a duplicate set of everything she found in the dresser and then use the set she took for her own purposes. The analogy also breaks down because, in big data world, you are continually creating new data by engaging the digital tech. It's not a finite set of valuables that you leave in the form of a data trail but an ever-growing set. And it's an ever-growing set that wouldn't exist but for the digital tech that you are using.

Now we're at the point with our analogy where the yard sale customer takes away your old dresser and gives you a new one. For as long as you have it, that new dresser continues to give you new benefits, like a sock matcher so you never lose any socks again. What's so bad about your magic wardrobe? You're starting to think you might actually find Narnia after all these years! Well, you might. But it might also be that, instead of a witch waiting for you on the other side of the wardrobe, the wardrobe itself is bewitched. It starts learning a lot of things about you and your family that you don't even realize it is learning.

Let's say you're using the magic wardrobe to house your daughter's clothes.[4] The wardrobe is perfectly matching her socks, but you don't notice that it is making a copy of each sock. The wardrobe also selects your daughter's outfit for each day and coordinates the socks with the outfit. How does the wardrobe know how to produce an outfit that is perfect for the day's events? You gave the wardrobe permission, when it arrived, to communicate with your iPhone calendar via an embedded sensor in the back of the wardrobe. The sensor system is also linked to sensors in your daughter's clothes, so the smart wardrobe combines what it learns from your iPhone calendar to tell you what your daughter should wear.

Forget the Lion and the Witch: it's like Mary Poppins has taken up residence in this wardrobe! You're loving this helpful magic so much that you don't think about what else the magic wardrobe is learning about your daughter. You don't ask if it's figuring out how she's doing in school from your calendar entry that reads "Parent-teacher conference re: bullying issue @ 2 p.m." You don't think about whether it's figuring out how fast she's growing from reading her clothing tags. You don't wonder if it's keeping its discoveries to itself. Your daughter looks awesome, and you have five to ten minutes more each morning to Instagram her #girlpower pics.

What you're actually doing with your children's data in real life is a lot like this magical wardrobe. In exchange for free or inexpensive access to efficient, engaging, interactive digital services and products, you are sharing an ever-expanding amount of your children's personal information with those tech providers. You likely don't realize how much data you are sharing or how that tech provider can use your children's information and allow an indeterminate number of unidentifiable third parties to use it too. We don't need make-believe to find ourselves in a veritable *Fantasia* of spying objects.

Out of Narnia, Back to Real Life

Let's move from make-believe enchanted objects to the real-life enchanted objects and other forms of digital tech you're likely using today. Facebook can add your post about toilet training dilemmas as a data point to its own information about you, as well as whatever information it is sharing with third parties. Barbie, Elmo, new nanny: it's all data. The question isn't "Who might be interested in this kind of dossier on kids?" but "Who wouldn't be?"

Is this stuff happening already? Yes, it is. We are only beginning to understand the methods and the scope. The rapid pace of tech innovation, the lack of transparency in many major data-related markets, and other factors combine to keep us, as security expert Bruce Schneier tells it, the David to the Goliath of big data.[5]

Here's what we do know. Federal and state laws impose almost no limits on the ability of parents to share information about their kids online.[6] As soon as private individuals, companies, or nonprofits receive this information from parents, there are few legal limits on what they can do with it.

Those limits that do exist come from general bodies of law or laws that apply to the receiving people or entities, not specific statutory and regulatory schemes that address parents' legal rights to divulge their children's private information. Some significant limits include those from criminal law. Parents can't steal their children's identities, manufacture child porn, or commit other crimes against or involving their children. Consumer law and contract law require companies to follow their own terms of service and policies, best-practice commitments, and other commitments they make regarding how they will use children's data.

A federal statute, the Children's Online Privacy Protection Act, does limit what many private companies can do to collect and use information directly from children under age thirteen. The limit? The covered companies need to have a parent's permission before collecting and using the data.[7] Similar legal limits exist for teachers: they need to obtain parental consent before sharing students' private data, unless an exception applies.[8]

There are government actors and institutions outside of education where parental consent is not dispositive. For instance, a juvenile court may be legally barred from sharing information about a child's court case even with parental permission.

But we now find ourselves back more or less where we started: parents stand at the center of a largely consent-based framework for the digital distribution and use of their children's private data. After they have consented to digital data sharing about their kids, either by doing it themselves or allowing other adults and institutions to do it, the data can travel at warp speed across entities and time.[9]

Data Brokers

Data brokers facilitate this movement by aggregating and analyzing digital data. Brokers then sell this data to third parties. Data buyers then use discrete data points or larger data sets to engage in data-driven decision making for their own purposes.[10] Private companies that collect, store, and share relevant data with individuals and institutions that are willing to pay are not a new idea. Holdovers from last century include the consumer credit bureaus, real estate brokers, and employment headhunters.

We are now at a phase of data broker development where, in the words of a former secretary of defense, Donald Rumsfeld, there seem to be more "known unknowns" than there are "known knowns." We know that data brokers serve a range of constituencies. Brokers are loosely regulated, and those regulations that do exist are largely industry-specific. For instance, data brokers who are functioning as credit reporting agencies are bound by regulations on credit-based decision making.[11] Some brokers are collecting information about children.[12]

Data brokers are typically "opt out" rather than "opt in," and the process for removing your information from a brokerage firm is variable, difficult, and possibly of limited utility. We don't know exactly how many data brokers there are. We don't know how all of them gather their data, with whom they're sharing it, and for what purposes. We can't easily find out if and how we could dispute data points inside their black boxes. Data integrity is a problem, but so is data safety. We can't easily read the news to see if our or our children's data has been caught up in a data breach of a given data broker because we don't know which brokers have our data.

But we do know that children's data is a hot commodity for data brokers.[13] We have a decent sense of some key markets where data brokers' offerings are, may be, or are likely to come into use. These include credit, insurance, education, and employment.[14] We don't know what stealth, emerging, or future markets may exist for children's data. For instance, as more data about ever-younger children, even at the preconception and gestation stages, is gathered and analyzed, might there be a market for "life" insurance for the embryo or fetus before it is born? Today, parents can buy life insurance for their children. If an insurance broker can aggregate data from a fertility app and other sources, it could offer an insurance product for expectant parents that would cover medical and other costs, as well as the emotional and psychological consequences of a lost pregnancy.

Fetal life insurance doesn't seem to be a real thing. Yet. But it isn't the stuff of pure speculation. Target was able to determine which of its customers were pregnant and advertise accordingly, which outed a pregnant teen to her parents.[15] Target does this type of customer data analytics based on data from both its brick-and-mortar stores and its digital engagement.[16] Who knew that buying cotton balls meant there was a bun in the oven?

In the digital commerce sphere, there are companies whose mission is offering health and wellness services specifically for reproductive functions. For example, HelloFlo "offer[s] one-of-a-kind care packages to help women and girls through transitional times in their life. As well, we have content that will educate, inspire[,] and entertain you."[17] The company began as a subscription service that focused on delivering tampons and pads through a "reminder service that also deliver[s] the right products at the right time."[18] Its initial advertisement for a "Period Starter Kit," aimed at preteen and teen girls, was an "ever-so-slightly subversive viral hit."[19]

HelloFlo assures its users that it will protect their privacy. It follows up with broad language around product and service development that is typical of digital companies: "We may also draw upon [your] Personal Information in order to adapt the Services of our community to your needs, to research the effectiveness of our network and Services, and to develop new tools for the community."[20] With "Personal Information" that presumably contains data about a user's menstrual cycle and other health matters, there appears to be fertile ground for conceiving new commercial tools related to intimate life.

So some parts of the private market, from big-box stores to digitally based health and wellness companies, are already gathering and, in some instances, mining reproductive health data to make sales. It is reasonable to expect that private markets will develop new products and services based on this data. The pitch for prenatal life insurance practically writes itself: "A prenatal vitamin a day protects baby on its way. For one dollar more, ensure your heart won't be sore if the stork misses your door." Don Draper might cringe at the lyrics, but he'd admire the entrepreneurial spirit.

Major Markets for Mining Kids' Data Trails

Back from the plausible to the present: many of the individual and institutional decision makers who make key choices about kids' futures already use or are likely to start using some form of digital data–driven decision making to inform their decisions. The scope and types of data tools vary. Some may purchase profiles from data brokers, while others run their own in-house or even ad hoc operations. But the general takeaway is unambiguous: the gatekeepers to services and opportunities that are likely to matter most to young people's futures are using digital data trails to decide whether gates open or stay barred.

On the education front, we know that colleges look at the social media profiles of applicants. They certainly look at applicants' educational records. And the "use of predictive analytics [in college admissions] generated from big data sources such as social media postings, test scores, and demographic data faces few legal limits. No law prohibits colleges from gathering information about students from social media or other publicly available information."[21] Employers seem to be increasingly "integrating the screening of social media profiles [of job applicants] in Applicant Tracking Systems."[22] And "there are currently no restrictions in place to protect against discrimination on the basis of one's personal [social] network."[23]

So are schools and employers looking at what parents say publicly about their kids? Most likely. Do we know how educational and professional decision makers will react to such information? No.[24] Your kids could be flagged as better or worse candidates depending on the profiles you have created for them on public-facing websites, like blogs. The potential impact of your social media content is less clear if that content is not publicly available. But even if we don't currently have data brokerage of kids' information from their parents' private social media posts, if social media companies change their policies, we could.

We know that some insurance companies already use smart technologies and other predictive analytics to help calculate risk and premiums. This practice is likely to expand as kids who have been using "enchanted" items like the Owlet bootie from birth come of age and apply for more insurance products.[25] We know that the consumer credit industry is looking at ways to score you based on your social media engagement.[26] Your kids might not yet be applying for credit cards, but when they do, will what you said about them on social media be part of the card issuers' decision-making process?

We are also seeing evidence that actors in government and politics increasingly rely on digital data in their activities. These activities carry potentially far more serious consequences than getting into a certain college. They strike at the heart of young people's ability to participate in democracy and enjoy the protections of democratically created and maintained civil rights and liberties: "A society that permits the unchecked ascendancy of surveillance infrastructures cannot hope to remain a liberal democracy."[27] As kids come of age and vote for the first time, what digital content will be served up to them, and how will it be determined? We know that there is a growing role for personalized, microtargeted content that is related to democratic participation.[28] Imagine the precision of the microtargeting that could be done on Tommy S. and his cohort: kids conceived during a full moon respond favorably to ads showing furry people or furry friendly monsters, preferably red.

We don't need to look into the future to find an interplay between kids' personal digital data and the public sphere. Governmental actors' use of digital data also has consequences for kids during their childhood. We know that governmental actors use various forms of surveillance, including facial-recognition software, and predictive analytical tools to engage in digital monitoring and policing.[29] We don't know if kids and teens are exempt from or subject to special protections in this realm.[30]

We know that schools and law enforcement agencies are relying increasingly on digital tools to effectuate and track discipline. A misbehaving student isn't just sent to the principal's office; instead, his data is may be sent to the court system to follow him as he pursues future opportunities.[31]

We know that law enforcement monitors social media and uses data from it in their policing.[32] Information you share could implicate your kids in wrongdoing. It could also stigmatize them or otherwise make them vulnerable if you are engaged in lawful yet potentially unpopular activities.

There is an argument to be made that sometimes parental inclusion of kids in social media accounts of unsafe situations may play a protective function for the kids that outweighs any privacy harms. Parents who have live streamed hostage situations, for instance, might help law enforcement monitor and try to protect the well-being of the children involved.[33] Although parental social media use might help provide a window into some tragic situations that require governmental intervention, it also appears that social media use might play a role in setting up a portion of those situations. If the hostage taker is a mentally ill parent, did the lure of momentary social media fame contribute to her decision to take those acts against her children?[34]

We also know that law enforcement is using social media themselves in new and surprising ways that can result in making your kids' private data public. Take the sheriff in Ohio who posted pictures on Facebook of a woman and man passed out from heroin overdoses in the front seats of their car. The woman's young grandson was in the backseat of the car. The grandson was also in the picture. The sheriff didn't deidentify him. When asked to explain his decision, the sheriff cited the importance of raising public awareness about the tragedies of opioid addiction. He reasoned that no one would remember who the toddler was anyway.[35] Unfortunately, the national discussion over whether his action properly balanced the child's privacy with public safety has likely ensured that many more people will remember.

And we know that law enforcement and the broader justice system are increasingly relying on digital data collection and analytics to inform many high-stakes activities. These data-driven decisions may include where to establish a police presence, how long to incarcerate a convicted criminal defendant, and what terms to require if that defendant goes out on bail.[36] Tech company employees have started signing pledges not to build certain types of law enforcement databases, like a Muslim registry.[37] These types of statements reflect the growing reality of data-driven governmental action. But such declarations may be largely symbolic.

Governmental actors are unlikely to need to build new databases or programs to gain access to information that allows people to determine religious affiliation or features of identity that are sometimes related to religion, such as ethnicity. For example, school districts keep detailed records on kids and families. Under the current presidential administration, the US Immigration and Customs Enforcement (ICE) agency has increased immigration enforcement near schools. It's not a stretch to think that ICE could ask schools to share digital data with its agents so that ICE could attempt to mine the data for information related to immigration status.[38]

Third-party tech providers also handle student and family data from schools because they provide services for schools. It's also not a stretch to think that ICE could ask these third parties for such data.

How a given school or vendor would respond to these requests is not a given one way or the other. Either way, as a parent, such transactions would be largely if not completely out of your line of vision. Big Brother today is part of an extended family network that often makes you digital data offers you can't refuse—because you never receive the offer in the first place.

Personal Identity: Reputation and Sense of Self

We've reviewed how digital information about children might expose them to criminal or hostile activities, as well as how this information might be used by third-party decision makers to assess children's merits and access to opportunities. Let's think now about a more old-fashioned type of risk— interference with or harm to kids' interpersonal connections and personal lives. People of all ages that kids meet now or in the future will go online and learn things about them.

This category shares some of the same concerns as the third-party risk category. It looks at the implications of lawful (or not clearly unlawful) use of kids' digital data trails to make judgments about them. But it is distinct in its focus on how this data can affect nondigital interpersonal interactions that kids have in their youth or adulthood. In turn, these interactions impact children's and teens' reputations (both now and going forward) and their sense of self (kids' understanding of who they are and will become). We're done talking about Big Brother in the metaphorical sense. Now we're talking about brothers, sisters, and all other types of humans in the actual sense.

Reputation

Reputation is comprised of the narratives and expectations that others have of you. It's about the narrative they see and hear, not the one you understand yourself. This perceived narrative is a key component of your relationships with others. Some aspects of it might be grounded in truth, and other parts might be extrapolations, assumptions, or even errors. Reputation is something you can cultivate or not, but either way, you will have one. It reaches people you've never met and may never meet. It also reaches people whom you actually know.

The key here is that it is an interpersonal story, not an arm's-length, robotic, number-crunched transaction. We are moving from "What will the data analytics program used by the college admissions officer at a teen's dream school make of the social media profile his parents built for him?"

to "Congrats! He's admitted into his dream school! What will his freshman roommate say when he sees the same profile?"

Let's put ourselves in the shoes of this first-year college student. Maybe the admissions officer thought it was adorable that you used to dress up as Peter Pan and stage impromptu musical performances. But your new room-mate is a jerk and makes merciless fun of your five-year-old self, and he has the video footage to prove it. Your parents' Facebook privacy status is set to "friends of friends," and his cousin's girlfriend's aunt's dog-trainer's assis-tant is your mom's BFF. Even in the predigital age, jerks found ammunition for mocking people, but in that age, private, playful, childhood moments stayed protected in the past. Back then, your roommate would have been able to mock you only for things you did at school, such as puking in the stairwell or other collegiate missteps: "Baaaaaad night omg #pukeface #nofilter" with a Snap attached. That makes him an a#$^%^, although he might still look like a saint compared to what some eighth-graders did with the Peter Pan video when you were in the sixth grade. You were too embar-rassed to tell your mom what happened about so she never took down the offending footage. Actually, your classmates' parents were more vicious than your classmates were.[39]

Your peers aren't the only ones who have access to the internet. The adults you encounter also make their way to Google, even if they get there typing with their thumbs on BlackBerries. So instead of having the oppor-tunity to introduce your new boss to the young adult version of yourself, your presentation of your present-day self is filtered through digitally avail-able information about your past selves.

For instance, the human resources (HR) department at your first post-college job likely will tell your boss not to Google you. HR doesn't want your boss to uncover sensitive information (like a blog post in which your parents referred to the times in your tween years when you questioned your sexuality) that you could later allege informed your boss's attitude toward you. Your boss probably ran the search anyway. Humans are curi-ous mammals. And Google is a resource that is impossible for our mammal selves to resist.[40]

Even in the predigital era, your boss would have been curious about you. But learning about your adolescent angst would have been diffi-cult unless she knew your teenage self or knew someone else who had known you. And if she had known you or someone who had, she would have more robust context for understanding the information about your sexuality struggles. She likely would have some degree of affection or at least good will toward you from having watched you grow up or knowing someone who did. She likely would feel bound by more long-established norms around interpersonal interactions with children in brick-and-mortar communities.[41]

What do behavioral norms dictate when an adult who didn't know your childhood self encounters this self for the first time in its digital record form? It's complicated. That adult is looking at information about you that is out of date, not presented by you, and not contextualized. You will need to navigate the extent and impact of her knowledge as you get to know her.

Here, there is no clear set of norms. Should you assume that everyone will Google you before meeting you? Should you assume that everyone can find your parents' Facebook profiles through social networks? What about Twitter? Instagram? Parenting blogs? You don't know what they've seen or haven't seen. You don't know even how to bring up that question because although using the internet to learn about someone is widespread, it would strike an awkward note if your conversational gambit was something like, "You probably know that I wet the bed until age ten because of my mom's blog post about it."[42]

Instead, you are left with a free-floating sense of unease. You know that your reputation will be shaped significantly by the digital data that exists about you. You can't know what all this data is or who has access to how much of it and when. You have no reliable, meaningful way to have input into how these data points are integrated into the stories that other people develop about you. Frustrating, isn't it?

Now let's go back to being our adult selves. We can't handle the truth of the teen brain. But we do need to keep looking at the range of reputation-related acts in which we as adults engage. Perhaps more insidious than the "meeting a new adult" category are the ways in which parents and other trusted adults can use social media to mediate our children's relationships with their other loved ones.

Think of parents who are locked in a vicious custody dispute.[43] A mom might Instagram a picture of a Valentine from her six-year-old daughter with wobbly block letters that says "You're my #1 parent." But what if her former husband, her daughter's father, sees it and is angry at both mom and possibly daughter? This mom may have told her daughter to write it to support her case for sole custody. But the daughter is put in the position of having to explain it to dad during one weekend visitation, even though she has no idea how dad saw the card. And if dad tends to have too many beers while watching the football game on Sunday, then he might not listen to her. He might see her as playing for the opposing team, and she might come to see herself as unworthy of being on his team, a negative dynamic that inflicts both immediate and long-term damage.

For the writer Pam Houston, our lives are shaped by the stories we tell ourselves about ourselves, but the stories we tell also can "put walls around our lives."[44] The stories that other people tell about us can do the same. It's not only children who are affected by storytelling in the digital world. For adults, aspects of digital life seem to be re-creating, in perpetuity, some of the worst dynamics of middle school and high school.[45] This pressure is likely influencing how we talk about our kids. Do we feel more compelled to share information about our kids and families because the digital world makes us feel as though we're at our lockers again, waiting to see who's cool and who's not? (Do schools even have lockers anymore?)[46]

As adults, we're asked whether we like a post or not like it. If we like it, we can like it, share it, or retweet it. For nuance, we also can laugh at it or get angry about it. This is taking the ethos, the mentality, the pecking order of adolescence at its worst and putting it in our pockets, homes, cars, and more. Fears that the popular girls are whispering about us in the locker room or the popular boys will lock us in lockers are enacted time and again with each swipe and status update.

Status update. Think about that for a minute. It's not an "activity" update. It's not a "thought or feeling" update. It's a status update. In the offline world, we don't tend to ask people "What's your status?" in every-day conversation. We use it technically (as in marital status, occupational status, tax-filing status, delayed flight status) and colloquially ("Hey hon, what's your status? Working late? Or can you pick up kitty litter because the Walmart digital delivery human duo got locked out?").

But even in these situations, it tends to be precise, focused. It's not a general "How's it going?" And it's certainly not a thoughtful "How are you feeling about the inevitable stressors and ephemeral pleasures of your day? What have you learned about yourself and those close to you? What mean-ing are you making out of your failures and frustrations?"

Status. We go here or we go there. We feel good or we feel bad. We get dopamine hits or we get dissed. We are sixteen again, secretly afraid that everyone will forget our birthday even though we know social media will remind them.

In some ways, our daily predicament is worse than Molly Ringwald's in the 1984 homage to adolescent oblivion and redemption, *Sixteen Candles*. Everyone she knew forgot her sixteenth birthday! But it's not like they had digital reminders everywhere, so she could forgive her nearest and dearest for their memory lapses. Plus, the hot guy with a heart of gold finally found her! Screw everyone else. She was seen by the one person who mattered, at least for that moment.

We are all Molly Ringwalds now. We "dwell in [the] Possibility" of rejection and recognition.[47] Such is our status pretty much all the time, although we try to maintain perspective. We enjoy those moments when Throwback Thursday makes us just the right dash of nostalgia, offering the perfect swirl of milk into the cup of tea of daily life. We can ignore those moments when no one likes the pic of our cat curling up next to the teapot. Forget tea cozies. This cat is more like a tea kitty, am I right?! LOL?! Anyone? Anyone? Bueller?

The next time, we will post a picture of the baby next to the cat next to the teapot because everyone loves cat pictures.[48] It will be like a twenty-first-century Mary Cassatt! Or a real-life illustration of "The Farmer in the Dell." The farmer takes a wife, the wife takes a child, and they both take pictures of the child. They share those pictures and much else about the child, in part because it's a form of social status currency. To the extent that we are using our kids like those stone-washed jeans we just had to have circa 1985, we should knock it off. Or should we?

That's a hard question for each of us to answer for ourselves. We may try to answer it from the mature part of our selves, but we're pulled in many directions. The simultaneous existence of multiple stages of self that digital life demands, this "never forgetting" functionality of the internet, is impacting adults too. Although our past selves weren't born and raised online, they are being resurrected there. We're lucky, compared to our children. Presumably, we are more established than they are. We've earned degrees, gotten jobs, been married, had children, and generally gotten along in our lives. We've also dropped out of school, been downsized, been divorced, had miscarriages. Status update: we've been there and back again. "Roads go ever ever on."[49]

When we're sharing our own adventures—whether which tea we brewed for elevenses/second breakfasts or which dragon we fought that afternoon—we're the ones hitting Post. When we're tracking how many steps it takes to outrun that dragon or jumping into our driverless car to speed up our escape, we're the ones buckling on the watchband or seatbelt. We are consenting adults, hooking up our devices and putting out our own information. But we don't understand exactly what data we're sharing, with whom, why, and what they will do with it. The same general confusion over privacy policies, terms of service, and other parameters of our digital tech engagement arises when we're transmitting our own data instead of our children's.

The two harms, though, are distinct in origin, scope, and impact. Even though there are limitations to informed consent as an effective framework for personal data sharing in the digital world, adults should be allowed to choose what they do or don't do with their information. Otherwise, the autonomy and agency principles that structure our legal system start to wobble. Have we identified the "X marks the spot" perfect point on the treasure map? Certainly not. There are many compelling reasons to think about digital privacy and related reforms here too.

But the reasons for thinking about reforms related to adult usage are less compelling than those that prompt us to look at how we share information about our children. The law allows adults to smoke, drink, gamble, sleep around, and engage in all manner of other behaviors that are of questionable benefit to personal and public health. The law does not permit our children to do these things, and it makes adults the chief guardians of their well-being. It's not a perfect system, but as discussed below, there is a core of ethical, emotional, and pragmatic value in this framework.

We adults have a heightened legal and ethical responsibility not to @#$@ around with our children's lives. We have greater latitude when it comes to @#$@ up our own. We also have had much more time on this planet than they have. We've had time to figure out ourselves, more or less, and time to build credentials and connections that will help us get to where we want to go regardless of what our digital dossier says about us. There's less we can @#$@ up for ourselves than we can for our kids and teens. They have so much more road ahead.

We certainly can and sometimes do hit road blocks in our own digital lives that affect our everyday realities. A common way this happens is when we exercise our own misguided or poor digital judgment. We hit bumpy spots in our marriage when we respond flirtatiously to a high school girlfriend or boyfriend who messages us out of nowhere. These and other digital dalliances with people who "knew us when" may be more about wanting to find our past selves and view alternate visions of our lives than about being attracted to the old flames themselves.[50]

But the potential for these detours from our domestic routines to bring us into dangerously uncharted territory seems much greater now that we can transcend time and space with clicks rather than the cloak and dagger machinations of yesteryear. Whitman says we contain multitudes.[51] Maybe the digital world is simply delivering on nineteenth-century transcendental promises of the infinite self.

Our digital lives also can hit the skids and smash through the guardrails into our "real" lives through other people's digital choices rather than our own. We can fall victim to criminal, illegal, or unethical decisions by others, much as our children can. Some of those actions are identical, or nearly so, to those that befall kids and teens. We can have our identities stolen. We can be doxxed or trolled. We can be turned into pornography through the distribution of real intimate images or the creation of photo-shopped ones.

When a digital transgression happens to us, the law regards it as a less serious offense than it does when it happens to children. The US Supreme Court has ruled that it is constitutional to criminalize the possession of child pornography, even if the person in possession did not create the images.[52] These images are themselves a crime, the Court explained, rather than mere proof of a prior crime. It violates a minor's bodily integrity for such an image to exist and be looked at. It is legally impossible for a minor to give consent to the creation or distribution of such images. In contrast, it is perfectly legal to take or share an intimate image of another adult with that adult's consent. The crime arises when there is no consent.[53]

Unlike our children, we adults can legally give or withhold consent to a wide range of digital activities. Like our children, however, we often have limited control over mean-spirited or thoughtless choices made by others. An angry coworker rants about us on Facebook, taking public a private mis-understanding. A flighty friend Instagrams a drunken bikini pool party pic of us, circulating a moment that was supposed to stay in Vegas. A well-meaning doctor prescribes a "smart" pill, giving us a spoonful of surveil-lance to help the medicine go down.[54]

These and similar choices threaten our privacy. They also affect our existing and potential future opportunities. Does our boss believe our colleague and pass us over for a promotion? Does the uptight chair of the charity anniversary gala planning committee eject us for unbecoming conduct? That one might go in the "Who cares?" category, but others will not. Will our health insurance premiums rise if we find the new "smart pills" our doctor prescribed too bitter to swallow and stay away? What stories are other people and institutions telling about us based on what we do or don't do in our digital lives?

Sense of Self

Shakespeare admonishes us to be true to ourselves.[55] Fair enough, but this is easier said than done with the parental creation of a childhood digital data trail that may affect the child's developing sense of self. A four-year-old is unlikely to Google herself or even to look at her parents' Facebook feed for her own image. However, even young children are growing accustomed to having their pictures taken, and requests to post or not post information may come at very young ages.

Tech vendors are also aggressively marketing to all youth, with "infantainment," smart devices, and other types of tech and content.[56] Many of these programs or devices collect data about kids from the kids themselves.[57] Toddlers don't yet have credit cards, though, so it's up to parents to set the terms of young children's digital access.

Parents thus shape kids' digital sense of self, which in turns shapes kids' overall sense of self, from a very young age. Some parents take this practice to a whole new level by monetizing kids' stories in the commercial sphere, which is the topic of our next chapter.

Adults' choices about kids' digital data can intrude into the space of childhood and adolescence, shape those spaces, capture data from those spaces, and transform the data in terms of audience, purpose, and longevity.[58] Childhood moves from being a protected time for play and exploration into a phase that is surveilled, tracked, and analyzed by countless third parties. Adolescence, already a period of tentative and turbulent transition toward autonomy and more personal responsibility, finds new limits on a phase meant for making new choices and making mistakes. Without having developmentally appropriate opportunities to try activities and take on responsibilities, youth find it difficult to develop an authentic sense of self.

Without having opportunities to make and then learn from mistakes, youth find it difficult to become open-minded, flexible, and resilient.[59] Knowing that they might find it difficult to move past their inevitable mistakes or foolish choices, youth may become overly rigid. They also may become more reckless than they would be otherwise. Either way, Neverland, interrupted, poses an existential threat to youths' future selves.[60]

This is when a hand is raised and a voice from the back of the classroom asks, "So are you saying that you want the Lost Boys to stay lost the rest of their lives? Wouldn't they be kind of pains in the ass?"

No and yes.

We do want Peter to be able to leave Neverland. But we want him to do so when the time is right and when he has the right reasons. We don't want the pirates to push him out, walking-the-plank style. We don't want the Lost Boys to mutiny or to follow Wendy blindly back to civilization. We do think they could be more helpful around the Wendy house: do they not notice that their dirty dishes are everywhere?

The transition from youth to maturity inevitably involves some loss. But all is not lost. Joni Mitchell hits the mark when she sings, "Something's lost, but something's gained, in living every day."[61] Naiveté is replaced by knowledge. Being rocked to sleep gives way to rolling on toward your dreams. There is no set map for when, why, and how to leave Neverland. Ideally, both the destination and the journey bring meaning and promote mastery. Hopefully, an innate sense of self is nurtured in childhood and is part of the gravitational pull that leads us on. Unfortunately, there are many reasons to think that the "tectonic shifts"[62] of the digital world are shocking if not razing this identity core.

Is this the wrong warning to issue? Is it possible that the 7.0 earthquake we're experiencing is less likely to blow open childhood and adolescence than trap people inside of it? Is technology infantilizing us to the point that we'll heed Peter's call and "never grow up, never grow up"? Some argue that tech companies are increasingly giving us robo-parents—digital products and services that "fall into the category of 'things that I, a 25-year-old-man, wish that I could still get my mother to do for me.'"[63]

Building on this view, the argument becomes this: the digital world isn't destroying childhood and adolescence but is letting childhood and adolescence cross traditional boundaries and reshape the landscape of adulthood. The real threat around youth today and for the foreseeable future isn't that grown-ups will demolish what it means to be a kid. It's that a certain child-like mentality will erode what it means to be an adult. We'll abdicate personal responsibilities and let the robots and other digital tech figure out the hard questions and the easy questions alike for us. Then the only real grown-ups in the room will have artificial rather than actual intelligence, and we'll conclude that we "really don't know life at all."[64]

This argument has some solid ground beneath it. One need look no further than the "bro'" mentality of much of the tech ecosystem to see a valorization of some of the less praiseworthy and principled aspects of juvenile existence.[65] "Build fast and break stuff" sets a certain tone and arguably shapes the products and tech that result, although this entrepreneurs' culture is the province of only a fairly small number of people. We can let the hoodies and suits duke it out, Sharks and Jets style, on a street corner far away from us. Let's look at the rest of the map, where most of us live.

Increasingly, all of us grown-ups are living in a world of enchanted objects, adorable monsters that fly down the street,[66] and cars that drive themselves. Have we crossed the great divide into adulthood or Willy Wonka's factory? If we can't quite locate ourselves on the frontier between maturity and make-believe, won't it be that much harder for our children when they come of age?[67] How are we going to teach them to take out the trash when there is an Oompa Loompa robot to do it for them? Already humanoids are programmed to respond to digital directions to bring the goods we order into our homes and put the goods where they belong. We don't give them an allowance. Instead, they allow us to become ever more removed from the logistics of daily life.

The digital service industry and its human accomplices are more about execution than design, however. We still need to place an order, either manually or on an automated basis, to receive the goods in question. We still need to think about what we need and when we need it and share that specific set of data points with the appropriate digital service provider. Perhaps the rise of AI will allow us to teach a robot to be mission control for a household birthday party for Huck next week (take one mom brain and combine all the data from a calendar)—with the next generation of Harry Potter–style "house elves"[68] seeing that the perfect birthday gift is selected, wrapped, and delivered automatically.

Some retailers are moving in this direction by combining digital technologies with human capacities to integrate a more convenient and customized shopping experience into your normal routine. These hybrid services are coming both from traditional brick-and-mortar stores as well as digitally based companies. They are offering and developing various combinations of digital/human mammal interaction.

For example, Walmart is already "testing new delivery ideas . . . like delivering packages inside customers' homes and putting groceries away in their refrigerators" through a partnership with a "smart home" service provider.[69] In this model, digital shopping will be combined with a human delivery person who gains access to your home through digital means: you will control and be able to monitor the delivery person's home access through an app on your phone.[70]

Other companies are focusing their digital technology use on getting you the products you want rather than getting them inside your home. Popular clothing delivery services "curate" a shipment of shoes, clothes, and accessories based on your stated preferences, thereby taking some of the decision-making burden off you.[71]

But this is only a small step, albeit one taken in perfect alligator-print stilettos, toward an AI that can do executive functioning rather than function as an executive assistant. You still need to do a lot of personal data input. There is still some human involvement in making style selections. Indeed, that sense of getting a bargain-basement deal on an elite service is part of the allure. When there is AI that can organize our schedules—note that we have an upcoming presentation at work, figure out what outfit we need and when we need it, order the outfit, and have it altered and hung in our closet in time—then we really have stitched together a fix for that category of household administration that moms often supervise. And we'll have put the magic wardrobe out of business before it ever began. Sorry, Aslan. Nothing personal. See you at the next VC pitch-fest.

When we have AI that approximates a mom brain or household mission control, will it render the human denizens of the house less mature? What will executive functioning AI or other emerging, ever-smarter digital technologies do to adulthood? AI undoubtedly will remove certain tasks and decisions from our regular repertoire of things that grown-ups do.

For instance, presumably you can't have your robot give your consent to a marriage proposal that came out of a Tinder hookup, even if your robot has all the relevant data. But the impact of that change on some overall maturity quotient for the eighteen and over crew is a far more complicated equation. Just because some tasks and decisions have been accepted as part of what grown-ups do does not mean that these are the only actions and responsibilities that connote adulthood. We used to expect the lady of the house to churn butter or embroider. Are today's women any less adult because they don't do their own dairy or doilies? AI changes the equation somewhat away from a linear "We outsource X set of life tasks to Y" to "We outsource X set of life tasks and life decisions to Y." But as long as we still have some degree of agency and oversight in choosing and teaching our robot staff, it seems unlikely that we will suffer from perpetual Panism to the point where we are no longer "adulting."

Another key variable in this calculus of whether digital technologies might lead us all into a throwback further than Thursday is what the rising generation of adults will choose to do with the additional time that is likely waiting for them before too many more "revolving years" are through.[72] If the answer is "play more videogames while my robot does the laundry, pays my taxes, and puts the kids in the driverless car that takes them to school," then it's difficult to see digital innovation as maturity-enhancing. If the answer is "get in my thirty minutes of daily cardio, spend more time playing in the dirt with my kids, and volunteer at the local soup kitchen" while the robot cleans up, then it's difficult to see digital innovation as infantilizing. To be mature adults, do we need to do our own dishes by hand? Could we instead simply take responsibility for ensuring that our dishes are done in an efficient, equitable, nonexploitative manner? No, Peter, leaving them out for Wendy to do doesn't count.

Whether our kids grow up to do their dishes by hand or by robot, they will need a robust sense of self to engage these and other questions about what it means to be an authentic adult. And the questions won't keep for eighteen or twenty-one years. At every step along the way, some iteration of "What does it mean to exist meaningfully at this point on the journey?" presents itself. What does it mean to be a capable eight-year-old? Do you need to know how to ride your bike? Is cursive optional or optimal? What about a truly sweet sixteen? Car wheels have replaced cartwheels and also bike wheels. Should the guy with the coolest car be your new best friend, or should you still be riding shotgun in Archie's old jalopy, sticking with the friendship that is as reliable and comfortable as the car itself?

Without space in childhood and adolescence for unencumbered experiences, it is difficult to lay the foundation for an authentic self. Without a sense of self at your core, it is difficult even to begin to answer all the questions, never mind reaching any conclusions.

There is a seismic disturbance at the center of our beings being caused by the digital tech disruption of youth. And yes, there are also fissures arising in our grown-up landscape from the digital tech infantilization of adulthood. But the damage there is surface level, not structural.

As between the dueling threat models of adults to childhood and aspects of childhood to adulthood, the first is the bigger threat. Adults' decisions about children's digital lives are disrupting childhood such that individual youth and the life stage of childhood itself might not recover. Digital tech does enable some encroachment of childhood's "Let mom take care of it" attitude into adulthood. However, adults who have been able to cultivate a sense of self-understanding, self-efficacy, and internal accountability will know how to seize the constructive opportunities digital tech affords and decline the destructive ones.

Are all children given an equitable opportunity for such personal development? Our country has heartbreaking inequalities in childhood opportunity[73]—poverty, abuse and neglect, sexual assault, discrimination based on identity including race and sexual orientation, discrimination based on immigration status, lack of access to health and mental health care, lack of access to dental care, weak education systems, parents and caregivers caught in opioid and other addictions, gun violence, bullying, environmental toxins.

These and many other deep structural problems deprive too many children of a secure foundation from which to begin their lives. The deprivations arise in countless ways. Notably, the risks from engaging in activities that could run you afoul of law enforcement are heightened for kids and teens of color. Most pressing: the consequences are lethal. They are also developmental. Kids and teens need to be able to explore a range of choices and even make mistakes in order to learn and grow.

Is it a fake gun or a real gun? Twelve-year-old Tamir Rice never had a chance to answer this question for himself. Tamir was playing in a city park when he was killed by a Cleveland police officer. When his fourteen-year-old sister ran over to him after the shooting, police "tackled her to the ground and put her in handcuffs."[74] The gun was fake.

Tamir's death is one of many. Too many kids and teens of color, especially African American youth, die when their ordinary behavior is met with deadly force from law enforcement or private individuals. Even going to school is proving unsafe for children in families with mixed immigration status. Federal immigration officials are detaining immigrant parents when they take their children to school.[75]

For these kids and teens and their parents, it doesn't matter that they are US citizens. It doesn't matter that the US Supreme Court has made clear that public schools must educate all youth within their jurisdiction, even those who lack legal immigration status.[76] Facing a choice between keeping their families together and keeping their education on track, many families with mixed immigration status are keeping their kids at home. Schools are moving from the heart of our democracy to a potential hell, through no fault of the schools themselves.

Sources of fear and loss in our public schools go beyond the current immigration policies of the federal executive branch. Significantly, gun violence, by both youth and adults, is killing both youth and adults. It's also killing our collective faith in schools as a protected space. Firearm drills are the new fire drills. Sheltering in place, under your desk, is likely to be about as effective against this threat as it would have been against the nuclear bombs of the Cold War era. At least those nightmares never became reality.

So why should we advocate for an ideal of childhood and adolescence as the foundation for an authentic self if that prospect is out of reach for many? Doesn't that minimize the obstacles and marginalize the already vulnerable among us?

The goal is to deepen and broaden our collective commitment to respecting and protecting childhood for all kids and teens. In its current form, that commitment is deeply broken. Rethinking our relationship to digital tech will not fix the fault lines that leave some kids with security and others with instability or trauma. Our kids won't have cleaner water if we post less on Facebook. In fact, we might move less quickly toward collective goals if we remove entirely social media or other digital tools from our advocacy toolkit.[77] But if we engage in rethinking, we might move more quickly toward such goals in a more privacy-protecting way that is healthier for our kids.

All such rethinking needs to take place with an awareness of the structural problems that plague us. Saying that adult use of digital tech needs to be reexamined doesn't mean that adult choices in other areas don't also need to be put under the microscope. In fact, a process of adult self-reflection and transformation toward greater protection of and respect for childhood in one sphere (digital tech use in daily life) will hopefully strengthen rather than weaken the odds of that process happening in other spheres as well.

Let's turn now toward a sphere where parents are focused on the positive value of youth experience and are measuring that value in terms of money—"commercial sharenting." On first glance, this "commercial sharenting" sector might seem to be galaxies away from the disheartening set of societal failures that are leaving children hungry, abandoned, and dead. Monetizing children's and families' experiences turns on making those experiences so appealing to viewers that marketing, sponsorship, and other dollars follow.

This process results in a lot of fairy dust and sparkles, literally and metaphorically, being put on display. But it also results in a surprising and, at times, disturbing display of the pirate side of Neverland. Commercial sharenting content can get dark. It can get predatory. People are watching. Let's take a look at what they're seeing. And let's take a look at how the commercial sharenting sector reflects truths and trends about adults' digital use of children's private lives even when no money explicitly changes hands.

4 My So-Blogged Life: Commercial Use of Children's Private Experiences[1]

Let's shine on a spotlight on some kids and teens who are subject to an especially intense form of parental intrusion into their private lives—the stars of the relatively new commercial sharenting sector. Commercial sharenting is sharenting that is undertaken for financial gain. This gain could be immediate compensation, development of business interests for future compensation, or other forms of current or potential revenue generation. Revenue may come from a variety of sources, including marketing agreements with businesses to promote a given product or service and other partnerships or deals, such as the YouTube Partner Program.[2]

Lawyerly caveat: commercial sharenting refers to actions taken by parents or other primary caregivers, not by teachers or other trusted adults. Teachers and other adults can and sometimes do engage in commercial sharenting or activities similar to it[3] but far less frequently than parents themselves do.

Through YouTube channels, blogs, Instagram accounts, and other digital platforms, commercial sharents use their families' everyday experiences to create revenue-generating content that is available to the public. This form of entertainment may be thought of as reality TV 2.0. It doesn't require a Hollywood studio or even a television, although successful commercial sharents typically have some corporate connections, structures, or platforms. Parents can make their own videos, pictures, written stories, and other depictions to capture everything from that first poop in the potty to prom night. They can join the growing ranks of "microcelebrities" who live in "a state of being famous to a niche group of people, but it is also a behavior: the presentation of oneself as a celebrity regardless of who is paying attention."[4]

Within the commercial sharenting sector, there is tremendous variation of practices and outcomes. Some sharents make millions through endorsements and other deals.[5] Many more are engaged in what scholars call "hope labor"—free work done with the hope of future compensated opportunities.[6] This sector also has a supporting cast of third parties available to help with marketing, branding, and other digital strategies. Kids and teens typically have top billing, however, whether they like it or not.

As you consider commercial sharenting, check in on your privacy paradigm. For instance, do you still think of privacy as being transactional—that secrets can be traded for services or goods? Whatever perspective you have on privacy, try strength-testing it by seeing if your reaction to commercial sharenting is in line with what your paradigm would predict. Do you see risks to youth privacy, opportunity, and sense of self in commercial sharenting? Why or why not? Are your answers here similar to or distinct from your risk assessment of noncommercial sharenting? When points of tension emerge between your answers to these questions and where your paradigm points, you might use them to guide reflection. Can you articulate an understanding of privacy that would comprehensively and consistently explain your answers to the questions in these chapters?

The same query applies to your understanding of childhood and adolescence. After looking at regular sharenting and now looking at commercial sharenting, what is emerging as your conception of childhood and adolescence? What do you think of the vision the book is advancing—that these life stages should promote playing, making and learning from mistakes, and developing a sense of self? If this resonates with you, why does it? If it strikes an odd note, what would hit the right one? If you find yourself thinking that privacy intrusions and related risks are justified in the context of successful commercial sharenting, there are implications for your conception of youth as well as your conception of privacy. Perhaps you would define childhood and adolescence in pragmatic terms, as life stages to prepare kids and teens to provide for themselves in adulthood. In this conception, commercial sharenting is cause for celebration, not concern.

This chapter begins by having some fun, lawyer-style. It challenges the basic premise that commercial sharenting is best understood as a new phenomenon of our digital world. Satisfied that it is (or at least accepting that it could be, for the sake of continued argument), the chapter goes on to describe several main narrative categories of commercial sharenting. During and after this description, the chapter surfaces some key legal, ethical, and practical risks and opportunities that can arise when the family business is turning personal business into everyone else's business.

This discussion also shines new light on regular sharenting. In the commercial space, money takes center stage. In the noncommercial space, it lurks offstage, seemingly invisible. This chapter's spotlight on commercial sharenting can help us start to see how financial considerations shape all adults' choices about children's digital lives. It also helps us to see how these financial considerations interact with our understanding of what it means to be a parent, especially a mother. Further, it raises some uncomfortable questions: Are we coming to accept an element of cyberbullying as part of today's parenting? Are we encouraging children to be actors instead of their authentic selves as we create the digital stories, both commercial and noncommercial, of their lives?

Is Commercial Sharenting Even a New Thing?

Before we go further, let's play a lawyer's favorite game. This is how it works. Someone says something, and you say, "You're wrong." Then that someone says something else, and you don't even listen. It doesn't matter what he or she says. You just say, "You're wrong." It's fun, and it can last forever—especially if you do it with your uncle at Thanksgiving dinner or the stranger sitting next to you on a red-eye flight.

We'll make the game short and sweet in the hope that it actually will have some value. The statement: commercial sharenting is a distinctly twenty-first-century enterprise that is designed to monetize children's private experiences in unprecedented ways through new and emerging digital technologies. The response: you're wrong! Commercial sharenting simply brings together two familiar parental practices—commiserating and running a family business.

Parents have always shared stories about their kids. Parents talk to other parents. They talk to professionals, like teachers and doctors. They talk to the cashier at the grocery store to commiserate when their kid has just pulled all the candy off a shelf. Parents need to connect with peers, get advice, and maintain perspective. So all that commercial sharenters are doing, it could be argued, is using newly available modes of connection to build a wider circle of support.

To the extent that some of them make money, isn't that a good thing? Family businesses have long been a vital part of the United States economy. Look no further than *Little House on the Prairie*: Laura and Mary had responsibilities for keeping the family homestead up and running.[7] Successful sharenters are just doing a modern version of what Pa and Ma did— asking kids to make contributions to the family livelihood in limited and appropriate ways.

This argument is not frivolous, as a lawyer might say, but it's not convincing. Commercial sharenting isn't just another form of communication or family business. It's different in type and scope. This type of sharenting trades on personal experiences, not tasks like milking cows, and it can instantly broadcast these experiences to the world. In the recent past, more widely accepted privacy norms sheltered these experiences from public scrutiny. Think back to 1990. You would have found it bizarre if a parent had paid for a billboard by the highway that said, "My daughter just got her first period!" How is it different to make a YouTube video about that same experience?[8]

Essentially, it's the same. Both YouTube and the billboard broadcast a personal coming-of-age moment. The key differentiators underscore how far removed commercial sharenting is from more established forms of interpersonal communication or family business. YouTube is free to use; the billboard has a fee. YouTube has global reach; the billboard has a local audience.

To be fair, YouTube does invite interaction and education beyond what a billboard or other brick-and-mortar options would offer. But those opportunities to develop community and learn about content, while generally positive, do not mitigate the privacy violations taking place. We have zoomed right past the potential billboard phase of sharing our children's private stories, which would have been less privacy-invading, and are speeding down the information superhighway route of doing so.

Commercial Sharenting Scripts

Commercial sharenting is a new phenomenon. When commercial sharenting hits a small screen near you, you can see first periods, family pranks, more extreme content that YouTube's algorithms suggest you watch next,[9] babies playing with kittens, and teens playing with tigers.[10] The broad picture presented here of the major categories of narratives in commercial sharenting today might be seen as a fuzzy series of screenshots taken from a phone while walking. This description is not a panoramic picture of the entire commercial sharenting space at present, an analysis of its evolution over time, or a taxonomy of all the variables that shape its content.[11] Instead, these screenshots aim for just enough clarity on commercial sharenting narratives to keep the conversation going without losing days of our lives conducting research.[12]

There are three main types of narrative categories: life stages, activities, and cause-based communities.[13] The lines between them are "cellphone pics while walking" blurry. A particular instance of commercial sharenting may encompass more than one narrative framework.

Within each type of narrative, there are subgenres. For example, family prank videos may be understood as a specific type of activity. Suggestions of how to craft with kids are yet another activity subset, although there appears to be room for a crossover prank and craft toddler star who replaces coffee with dirt and calls it art.[14]

Across narrative types, sharents usually look to strike a balance between a "just between us" authenticity and the polish of performance.[15] This approach holds true for all parent narrators, although they fall at different places along its spectrum. Indeed, this mode is the heart of commercial sharenting's appeal—crafted moments in a family setting. This could be your family, the narrator effectively says, yet we're way cooler than you. Winky face emoji.

The main narrator's persona often will impact the nuances of this balance, as well as throw other variables into the mix. The new mom discussing postpartum weight gain is likely to use the cadence of a best friend meeting you for a cup of coffee. In this narrative, intimacy is most important. Staging is subtle, designed to hide rather than highlight that the presenter is on the other side of a screen, not the other side of a café table. The single dad playing a trick on his adolescent daughter[16] will take the opposite approach. The set-up is visible. The tone invites the viewer to join in the joke but is more about delivery of the punchline than dialogue. Fortunately, digital technology does not yet allow whipped cream pies to be hurled across cyberspace and emerge from your computer.

Life Stages

The first narrative type of commercial sharenting script is life stages. This is largely the province of so-called mommy bloggers who create web logs called blogs. This term is used expansively to include vloggers (people who video log their content), Instagrammers, and creators of other types of digital content who are presenting in their role as mothers. Some women who create such digital content find the term disrespectful.[17] Others embrace it and make it their own.[18] Here, it is intended to be understood descriptively, not pejoratively.

A life stage encompasses both the chronological age and developmental phase of the children in the family. The experiences and emotions of a parent (typically a mother) are made visible primarily as they relate to whichever life stages her children inhabit.[19] Commonly chronicled life stages include[20] conception, gestation, labor and delivery, newborn, infancy, early childhood, childhood, preteen, and teen.

Within these stages, bloggers discuss topics familiar to most parents. A conversation about conception, for instance, may include the logistics of trying to become pregnant or the heartache of infertility. Often, these conversations include details about cervical mucus and other bodily functions that previously would have been known only to an intimate partner, medical provider, or a trusted circle of friends and relatives.[21] An entry about early childhood may focus on a toddler's transition to becoming a big sibling when the new baby comes home.[22]

Many of these topics could have been on the table back in the 1950s when mothers met for a neighborhood coffee klatsch. But many have a distinctly twenty-first-century flavor, such as which baby monitors offer parents the most peace of mind or which fertility tracking devices will help them produce tiny humans who need said monitoring.[23]

Whether dishing about the traditional or the digital, commercial sharenting about life stages frequently contains a generous side helping of advice for other parents. This advice may come dressed in medical or scientific glaze, be served up as personal experience, or lie somewhere in between. Either way, the narrator typically lacks formal qualifications in the field in which she blogs, such as reproductive medicine.[24] This new capacity for nonexperts to give parenting advice to millions of people is a dramatic disruption of two more established channels for such information—a personal network (which includes relatives, friends, and community members) and credentialed experts using traditional platforms (such as print publishing). The actual and potential impact of this shift in both personal and public lives is vast and complex.[25] Much of it is beyond the scope of this discussion.

But let's chew on a few morsels of food for thought. A self-reinforcing cycle seems to be emerging in which successful commercial sharents are incentivized to share more and more about their children and their families. When a parent has become recognized as a parenting expert based on her identity and actions as a parent, she enhances her status by showing more and more of her parenting. To an extent, whether a given parenting choice succeeds or fails is irrelevant. If it fails, she can present that failure as a helpful data point: "do NOT try this at home!"

Parents outside the commercial sharenting circle appear to consume this content at least in part because it is understood as a source of expertise. The more they consume and engage with the content, regardless of whether they are convinced by it, the more it is shared across digital platforms, bolstered by the additional dollars from advertisers and the heightened display by algorithms. The more it is shared, the more it is believed by parents and other viewers. This entrenched believability likely boosts the commercial sharenters' credibility, deepening their reach and encouraging still more sharing.

In this cycle, there are few or no points at which informational accuracy is the primary focus of content creation. It may not be a meaningful variable at any point. There are no final exams in parenting. There is no peer review of tips offered online on how to make your child sleep better. No license from any governing board is required to share your own experience of infertility, with some purportedly medical data in the mix. If you claim that you have an MD when MD actually stands for "Mama's Dishin'," you're violating multiple laws and regulations, including those against the unlicensed practice of medicine and truth-in-advertising requirements.[26] But there are likely no legal violations if you share your own experiences and reflections on relevant medical, scientific, or similar sources without misrepresenting your credentials, telling lies, or engaging in similar nefarious conduct.

The Federal Trade Commission has begun to take more of an interest in the digital commercial activities of social media "influencers," a category that may include some commercial sharents. Its focus, however, is on the need for transparency in marketing endorsements when an influencer is being compensated to promote a product or service.[27] Whether or not there may be anything unfair or deceptive in the content or impact on consumers of a commercial sharent's allegedly "expert" advice itself appears to be on the periphery of the regulator's radar.

This may be in part baked into the typical commercial sharent narrative's focus on recounting personal experience that viewers or readers can then generalize from and apply to themselves if they so choose. This narrative amounts to "Here is my experience. I hope it will work for you, too!" This type of claim is different than one that promises a potential purchaser a certain outcome. For example, if a mattress company promises that all babies will sleep 100 percent better if you use its mattress and that claim is false, then the company's actions are likely unlawful.[28] If a mommy blogger says that her sleep advice worked for her own child and that she hopes it will work for yours, that doesn't appear to be unfair or deceptive. (But if she recommends the 100 percent better mattress because that company is paying her to do so and she doesn't disclose the financial arrangement, then she would be violating truth-in-advertising requirements.)

The life stages sector of commercialized sharenting seems to be trending, at least in part, toward becoming a space for transmitting expert information that is largely from noncredentialed and unregulated parenting experts.[29] Given the wide reach that recommendations from sharents have, inaccurate, incomplete, or even misleading information about parenting topics can spread like a virus and may contribute to the spread of actual, dangerous viruses.[30]

Activities

The second narrative type of commercial sharenting script is activities. The topics in this category run from arts and crafts to zany pranks, typically with a focus on doing activities with kids or guiding kids as they engage in such activities themselves. Some activities land on the quotidian. For example, the founders of WhatsUpMoms YouTube channel identify the search for travel tips for families as a key impetus to start creating content.[31] Still other familiar activities include holidays,[32] sports,[33] and household decor.[34]

Sometimes these pursuits move beyond quotidian concerns into inspiration. Do more than get through the holidays: accessorize your home into transcendence!

Other activity categories are less common across households. Many moments in family life unintentionally create humor, as when you put laundry detergent in a dishwasher. Oops. But the laughs that bubble over from mistakes or spontaneous play are distinct from those that arise from elaborate plots to "put one over" on a family member. When that family member is a child, the prank may be no laughing matter.

The dark side of the family prank space requires zooming in beyond the screenshot level. This side reveals how commercial sharenting can result in the total exposure of children at their most vulnerable. At its most extreme, such sharenting reveals to the world parental conduct that meets the legal definition of child abuse or neglect.

Recently, a court determined that a Washington, DC, area couple had neglected two of their children after a series of videos posted on the father's YouTube channel, DaddyOFive, showed what to "most onlookers . . . looked a lot like abuse."[35] In an especially disturbing sequence, the parents spill disappearing ink in their son's bedroom, swear and scream at him about how much trouble he's in for the mess, then mock his justified indignation when he is told, "It's just a prank, bruh!"[36] This basic script repeats itself in a number of episodes: they put a child in an inappropriate or unsafe situation, capture his understandable emotional reaction, reveal that it's "just a prank," then document and ridicule his inevitable meltdown.

The court ordered two children removed from this family's home and placed in foster care. The parents themselves had already suspended their YouTube channel, which had roughly three-quarters of a million followers. Viewers alerted authorities about the dangerous household.[37] This development could suggest that the family's YouTube postings, although a privacy intrusion for their children, were justified because they allowed outside eyes to witness the inner workings of this house of horrors. It could also suggest that the incentives to generate new and sensational content to capture viewers' eyeballs contributed to this vicious and dangerous conduct in the first place.

Regardless of where you come down on these complex questions of causality and consequences, two general points about privacy and pranking are straightforward. First, after a prank is loose in the digital world, it is pretty much impossible to scrub it from the internet. The DaddyOFive YouTube channel is gone. Its content is the digital equivalent of real ink, however, rather than the disappearing kind. Its stain remains. The internet hosts per-petual reruns, whether the "actors" like it or not. The DaddyOFive content is readily available through other online sources, such as the YouTube chan-nels of the viewers who have commented on it.

Even when that commentary is a respectful and thoughtful analysis of the "many ways to abuse your kids" and the reasons they're all unaccept-able, as one leading YouTube commentator put it, that commentator is still facilitating viewers' access to the videos.[38] Cody, the boy who was the butt of most of his parents' so-called jokes, appears to have lived through a nightmare in the DaddyOFive household. In some ways, he will continue to live through one as long as that footage has an undead perpetual exis-tence on the internet.

For Cody, decision makers about his current and future opportunities will not need a data broker to dig for or an algorithm to analyze intimate information about his childhood. His humiliation, fear, anger, and so much more are there in plain view. You would have to be heartless to hold any of his experiences against him.

But how about reasoning that goes something like this: "Of course, it wasn't Cody's fault, but given what we know about the potential for child-hood trauma to have lifelong adverse impacts on survivors, maybe I don't want to let my child have him over for a play date. Maybe I don't want him in my class. Maybe I don't want to give him a summer job." Such questions are rational. They are also unfair to Cody. Depending on the role of the decision maker, they could shade over quickly into unlawful discrimination against him based on an assumption of disability.[39] Perhaps more import-ant, from a child's perspective, they likely will make it hard for him to make friends and be himself, whoever that self turns out to be.

The second general point about privacy and pranking is that many kids today are subject to parental pranks. But there is a difference between so-called pranks that actually constitute abuse or neglect, like Cody experi-enced, and pranks that do not. A prank that is in poor taste or just not funny typically will be lawful. Today's digital sharenting culture, however, does have an uncomfortable subplot of parental pranking to it even among commercial and noncommercial sharenters who avoid crossing the line into abusive or neglectful behavior.

Kids are natural comedic geniuses. Toddlers find it hilarious to repeat the old "throw the spoon on the floor, shriek for dad to pick it up, repeat" routine. Parents are also funny: they can make the spoon start to talk, flirt with the fork, and elope with the dish. Mazel tov! Maybe the family is the only one laughing, but it's a spoonful of sugar to help real life go down.

The sweetness starts to sour, though, when we get laughs at our kids' expense rather than laughing with them or at ourselves. Take the annual trick or treat prank that late-night television host Jimmy Kimmel sets up every year. Parents pretend they have finished all of their children's Halloween candy, film their children's response, and share the recordings digitally.[40] The YouTube video of the 2017 "I told my kids I ate all their Halloween candy" challenge put out by the Jimmy Kimmel show has more than 2.8 million views.[41] Kimmel gets contributions from sharenters everywhere. Spoiler alert: taking candy from a baby may be easy for the adults, but there's nothing easy about it for the babies. These kids take it hard. Some of them have epic flipouts, and others struggle to remain calm while falling apart inside. The trick cuts deep, upending the immediate promise of Halloween mirth and the fundamental one of parental reliability.[42] It generates a cheap and even sadistic laugh.

That so many parents play along raises a disturbing question about the adult appetite for humor: how much of it is based on behavior that should be understood as bullying?[43] It's a loaded word, but *cyberbullying* might be the right term to describe the dynamics underlying certain instances of commercial and noncommercial sharenting.

In the last decade or so, there has been a growing focus by educators, lawmakers, and other decision makers on how to address bullying behaviors between youth, as well as to protect kids and teens from the harms that result.[44] In many ways, the digital world has exacerbated these challenges and risks as children and adolescents engage each other around the clock across a range of devices and platforms.[45] A common response by decision makers has been to pass new or update existing state statutes and regulations to require educator and law enforcement intervention when bullying occurs.

Let's look at one such antibullying state law, which defines bullying as "a single significant incident or a pattern of incidents involving a written, verbal, or electronic communication, or a physical act or gesture, or any combination thereof, directed at another pupil which . . . causes emotional distress to a pupil."[46] The law specifies that bullying covers "actions motivated by an imbalance of power based on a pupil's actual or perceived personal characteristics."[47] This law is binding only in the school context, hence the use of the term *pupil*. It is a law about how kids treat other kids.

Thought experiment: what happens if you swap in the word *minor* for *pupil*? The law then would prohibit a single significant incident that causes emotional distress to a person under age eighteen, including when that incident was motivated by an imbalance of power based on that person's age. Publishing your children's suffering—by taking Halloween candy from them, recording their reactions, and sharing the results with the world—seems to fit that adjusted definition. It is a significant incident that causes emotional distress to your child, however that distress is measured. An imbalance of power is inherent in the set-up of the incident. The parental role affords the adult "prankster" access to the candy. The child role puts the child in a place of dependence on the parent. What recourse does she have to get her candy back if her parent says it's gone? The child role also virtually guarantees that the incident will garner a response that the parent sees as worthy of filming because, from a developmental perspective, the child is likely to have a strong and complex reaction to the "prank."

Is it time to call in the parenting police? No, an antibullying law that covers parents and other adults won't be written.[48] Such a law likely would be unconstitutionally vague and overbroad. Especially as applied against parents, it could prohibit positive parenting conduct that keeps your child safe, like making your thirteen-year-old cry when you tell him he can't drive your car because he's underage. If the government proscribed even one "significant incident" of parental conduct that causes "emotional distress" to a child based on the respective parent and child roles, then the government would be intruding too far into constitutional protection for the liberty to parent and raise a family.[49]

The rights to other adult-child relationships, like teacher-student or coach-athlete, are not entitled to the same level of constitutional protection as parent-child. However, these other roles do carry with them certain legal responsibilities that require adults to make decisions, based on the child's age, that are necessary to keep them safe but may still cause the child emotional distress. Thus, an antibullying law that covers nonparent adult caregivers also likely would be too vague and overly broad to survive a legal challenge.

Although law enforcement won't be opening a file for the case of the missing Halloween candy, we adults can and should still be thinking about the norms we adhere to in our daily lives.[50] We don't need a law to tell us that bullying our kids is wrong. We do need to think about how we explain the following to our kids: it is fine for us to take their candy, make them cry, film their crying, and share the video, but if they do the same thing to a younger pupil, they will get in trouble at school and perhaps with local law enforcement.

Is the right explanation similar to the one we give about drinking beer and driving cars? That explanation goes a little something like this: "You can't do it now, but you can do it when you're older." Can we come up with a sound explanation here, one grounded in common decency and upholding the spirit of the antibullying laws our elected officials have passed for the schools that teach our children? If we can't, then we should rethink the Halloween prank, both participating in it and watching it. More fundamentally, we should rethink our current acceptance of sharented "prankster" content by amateurs or professionals that makes kids the butt of jokes. There's a lot more that is ghoulish than grown-up about it.

Cause-Based Communities

The third narrative type of commercial sharenting script is cause-based communities. Let's see what happens when the better angels of our nature prevail. Many commercial sharents are trying to lift up their own and other people's children and families. A snapshot of this major narrative type reflects an ethos of bonding and triumphing over adversity or rallying around shared affirmative goals that go beyond beating hardship.

As with the other two categories, there are many variations on this broad theme. One common subcategory responds to adversity, such as children or families living with serious or terminal physical illness[51] or living with disabilities of all types.[52] Their content may include blogs that aim to destigmatize experiences of chronic health conditions by sharing both the "normal" aspects of daily life as well as the burdens of illness.

Another subcategory is situated between an adversity-based perspective and an affirmative goal-based perspective. The content here comes from kids or families that might be nontraditional or unconventional in some regard within their community, state, or country. They tend to be subject to unique pressures and difficulties in their lives, which are grounded in interactions with other individuals and institutions rather than in a physical or mental health condition. Commercial sharenting here includes

LGBTQ families and interracial families.[53] The child's or family's experience is offered as motivation for those watching and reading, as well as for the content creators themselves. At its core, this is the familiar buddy system: if you're trying to reach a goal, find a buddy. Or find a million.

Sometimes, the real goal is to find a million dollars (or close to it) to pay for a sick or disabled child's medical treatment and other needs.[54] The requests for money for this purpose or a similar one may make this category of commercial sharenting more explicitly financial than other categories are. At first glance, this focus on the monetary in the caused-based community space might seem counterintuitive or somehow inappropriate. Why try to "make it rain" (in the sense of introducing explicit monetary goals) on a parade where everyone is marching toward an uplifting, nonmaterial goal? What about letting in the sunshine of shared goals, without a price tag? Isn't this commercial sharenting at its most exploitative—cashing in on other people's pity for your child?

These are fair questions, but they ignore the category five hurricane for the drizzle. Making it rain money is an attempt to get to a sunny day. The real storm comes from the excruciating financial and related pressures that face many families whose child is seriously ill or has a disability. Often, even with health insurance, families face insurmountable costs and agonizing choices. Do they use their resources to pay their mortgage or buy a service animal for their child that insurance and other sources won't cover? These types of tradeoffs strike at the core of parents' duties to their children to provide for their well-being in the present and future. The law sets a floor for these responsibilities.[55] Parents tend to aim for the stars, as well they should.

Thus, the financial request is commercial only in a technical sense: it uses the digital marketplace to generate income. At its core, it's likely to be about survival. If comprehensive and accessible resources were available for families with sick or disabled kids, then families would have less need to share their children's private medical information with the world to educate others and motivate them to contribute financially to the care and success of their children and others in similar situations. The price of privacy is too high when health and life are on the line.

Will this amount to a "borrow now, pay a lot more later" situation? Our consumer credit realm is replete with such offerings, although money rather than privacy and opportunity is at stake. A familiar example is the payday loan, where the borrower gets a short-term loan that must be repaid, with interest and fees, on the borrower's next payday. The borrower writes a check for the lender to cash on this upcoming payday or gives electronic bank account access to withdraw the funds.

This lending product offers borrowers who lack good credit, savings, or other resources a way to bridge a financial gap and satisfy time-sensitive obligations like rent or car payments. Unfortunately, it also tends to trap them in a cycle of additional borrowing when they predictably can't afford the three-figure annual percentage rate (APR) plus amount borrowed they must shell out on their next payday.[56] So pernicious is the payday loan that Congress has banned it for members of the armed forces.[57] And Google has blocked payday lenders from advertising the product through its search engine.[58]

Defenders of payday loans say they are providing a necessary survival mechanism for borrowers who lack other options. Critics say that the solution creates bigger problems by exacerbating financial instability and increasing the likelihood of total financial ruin. The legal system's response to weighing these and other considerations varies significantly by state, although the potential for a more uniform federal regulatory solution remains. The bottom line, especially with internet-based payday lending that transcends state boundaries, is that would-be payday loan borrowers need to decide for themselves how high a price is too high. The same is true for would-be borrowers of other high-cost, relatively short-term loan offerings, like auto title loans, payment-optional adjustable-rate mortgages, or medical loans.

And the same is true for parents of kids with serious illness or disabilities. There are far fewer legal and regulatory oversight mechanisms in place for commercial sharenting than there are for consumer lending. There is also much less information about the sharenting space available than there is about the consumer lending industry. Because the children whose private medical information is shared in this way are still young, the cost-benefit analysis is difficult to do. Will a child whose struggle with cancer is on public display be bullied, be denied access to educational or other opportunities, or face other negative consequences down the road? Even if she does, are those downstream impacts still preferable to losing her home because her parents choose to pay for her treatment rather than their other bills?

One potential point of comparison is with children whose health struggles have been shared through a nonprofit organization as part of a campaign to obtain services for them or other children in a similar situation.[59] These campaigns seem to enhance children's lives overall rather than detract from them. Such a comparison may be limited by the layers of decision-making and governance structures that legitimate nonprofits have that families lack.

But is a board meeting at which trustees direct an institution to carry out such a campaign better than a kitchen table session where two parents, who know their own child better than anyone else knows her, start a blog or GoFundMe campaign? On the one hand, the professionalism of a board and staff might result in a better analysis of costs and benefits than the understandable emotionality of parents. On the other hand, if your child needs life-saving medical treatment immediately, the deliberative pace and the multigoal nature of an organization likely would be an obstacle to your financial goal. Here, arguably more than anywhere else, commercial sharenting is all about caring and caregiving.

The Gender Lens

Zooming out from the three narrative types, let's consider the familial caregiving role itself. In many two-parent heterosexual families, mothers fill this role more often than fathers do.[60] Single-parent households are disproportionately headed by a female parent, making mothers the only caregiving parent.[61] And in a household with two mothers, by definition, a female parent is playing this role. Across the board, then, more women than men inhabit the family caregiver role.

Commercial sharenting trades on domestic doings. Even narrative types that focus on topics other than caregiving are likely to originate from or at least involve primary caregivers, who are closer to children's and families' experiences than are nonprimary caregivers. Because primary caregivers are often women, the roles and responsibilities of mothers in commercial sharenting are complex.

Right off the bat: major props are due to any parents who combine career with caretaking, and special props to women who insert themselves into the traditional ways that companies reach customers. These women are adding another layer of gatekeeping. Why trust company jargon when you can hear a real person talk about how a product or service worked for her, even if she is being paid? Extra special props go to the people who have found ways to use this addition to the commercial sphere to create space for additional authenticity—or at least for new topics of discussion. Would we see such a booming market in menstrual product services, fertility trackers, and other women's health products if female commercial sharents weren't out there talking about these topics?

But one of these new areas of discussion is children. In addition to an ethical analysis of how maternal sharents influence female empowerment, feminism, and consumer culture, the unavoidable reality is that being a commercial sharent involves your child. Maybe you are thinking about having a child, trying to have a child, expecting a child, parenting a child, or coping with the loss of a child. You are in one or more of these categories. Otherwise, you are not a parent in any sense of the term.

By definition, then, doing commercial sharenting successfully means that you are sharing your private life to some extent.[62] It also means sharing your children's private lives. It's a family business, but the product is not hardware sold in the family store: it's your self—your experiences, thoughts, emotions, and struggles. Being a primary caregiver doesn't rob you of the ethical right to sell your own self in this way. But it also doesn't give you an open license to do so for your children, simply by virtue of their dependence on you and your investment in them. The line between mama and baby may be hard to draw, especially for infants and children. We need to be mindful of drawing it for them, even when every minute of our waking hours, and many of our resting ones, are consumed by their care. Motherhood is a life-changing role. Can we talk about that transformation and its elations and frustrations without overexposing our children's fledgling selves?[63]

Playing a Part or Being Yourself

It's time for another fun lawyer game: the objection! This question about motherhood and the overexposure of children cannot be answered because it rests on a faulty foundation—that commercial sharenting portrays children's real selves. If kids are playing parts rather than being themselves in commercial sharenting productions, is there still a privacy problem?

This objection is sustained, as a judge would say. This ruling allows an objection to redirect the course of a courtroom or, in this case, a written conversation.

To respond to the objection: it is difficult to determine how much commercial sharenting content is sparkle and how much is substance. In a sector where the transparency and relatability of the presenters are part of the construct, it may be impossible.[64] Maybe all the worldwide web is but a stage, and all the kids merely players. Maybe just part of the webpage is a stage, and all the kids more than players. It seems most reasonable that commercial sharenting productions fall on a spectrum ranging from fantasy to fact and that there is some performative element involved in most of them.

Accepting the premise that there is at least a dash of fiction in most content, does this mitigate or even eradicate the privacy problem? It is tempting to say yes. After all, the audience doesn't tend to watch the lucky child who scored the lead in the school play and think, "He's such a good Peter Pan that he must have huge issues with his parents and wants to avoid adulthood." The audience recognizes that the kid in the green tights is playing a part in a narrative written by an adult. If there are mommy and maturity conflicts, they are those of the playwright. The performer can connect with the audience through a shared emotional experience even as he keeps his personal feelings to himself.

However, this protective coating of fiction fails to translate from the auditorium to the app. There are several significant distinctions between these two settings that erode the privacy-protecting functions that acting out a fictionalized role might provide. First, there is a difference in audience. Viewers of the school play are limited in number. Also, they presumably are part of the same brick-and-mortar community as the performer. Viewers of a blog post of a big brother meeting his baby sibling for the first time may number in the millions and lack the community connections.[65]

Second, there is a difference in authorship. A playwright makes visible her creative contribution and ownership. A commercial sharent typically seeks to downplay her role in shaping her child's actions. She may function as a reporter, documenting what her child does, or as an analyst of the child's actions or her own reactions. Her responses often include those of caregiving, but even though these actions are centered on her child, they are still portrayed as separate from the child's. The narrative trope is that the child is the creator of his own contributions rather than the parent.

Third, there is a difference in accessibility. A character in a play is written to belong to all actors who step into that character's shoes, although the belonging ends when the curtain falls and is always bounded by the author's rights. By contrast, a character in a commercial sharenting production is meant to represent one person and one person alone. That one person just so happens to have the same name in real life that he has on the digital stage.

And that one person is sometimes too young to understand that he is being asked to play pretend, no matter how much a commercial sharent may try to design a fictional alter ego for him. The newborn whose trip down the birth canal is recorded offers the most obvious example of a participant with no ability to appreciate the subtle difference between being yourself and playing the role of yourself. But even kids and teens who weren't born yesterday may have trouble understanding this distinction. Such a challenge is both a function of their developmental stage, as well as the genre of commercial sharenting itself.

The commercial sharent wants her audience to experience the portrayal of her child as authentic, so the domestic scene is set accordingly. Presumably, she recognizes that savvy blog consumers will not experience every detail of the blog as genuine. Every parent knows that baking with kids is 90 percent mess and 10 percent success on a good day. It's definitely not 100 percent #blessed. But she is trading on some sense of identification, even as it mixes with voyeurism over the stainless steel appliances and spotless faces.

Trying to explain to a child that he is at once himself yet not himself as he sits in his own kitchen with his own family is an existential challenge worthy of a Shakespearean soliloquy. The explanation grows even more difficult if and when the child becomes aware that viewers, advertisers, and other stakeholders are responding to his performance in the form of likes, comments, and capital. Because there's an incentive to play to your audience, the "art imitates life" origins of the sharenting production are likely to evolve to where "life imitates art." The part played in commercial sharenting seems likely to move toward the heart of who the child is.

Being true to thine own self is a challenge across life stages and performance stages.[66] It is a challenge even in the quotidian performative arena of digital life. Even parents who aren't seeking to monetize their digital lives may stage them for viewers' consumption. You don't need to care about making dough you stash in the bank to want baking pics that show dough becoming cookies rather than going up the dog's nose. It seems likely that the noncommercial space would be subject to less staging than the commercial. In this space, parents lack access to the same supporting cast and crew of make-up artists, marketing consultants, and others. They also lack the same entrepreneurial goals. Thus, they are likely to prioritize other goals, like forging interpersonal connections or old-fashioned venting, which would seem to bring with it more of a premium on authenticity. But even the noncommercial space isn't #nofilter all the time.

The same fundamental question arises in the noncommercial space: how can there be a privacy problem if the lives on display are not fully real?[67] Can you have any sort of privacy interest in a depiction that is part fiction rather than all fact? The short answer is that there is a privacy problem when the portrayal draws significant material from real life, is held forth as real life, and in some fashion loops back in to inform real life.

The longer answer is that the same factors around audience, authorship, and accessibility are salient in the lay sharent realm, just as they are in the commercial sharenting space. The impact and emphasis of each differ when we're talking about millions of viewers and a paycheck as opposed to mom's friends from college and "playbor" (activities that blend play and profit motives).[68] But there is a financial dimension even in the noncommercial realm: parents, teachers, and other trusted adults receive free or lower-cost digital services by "paying" for them with children's data. The rise of the child digital day laborer, both in commercial and noncommercial spaces, is examined further in the following chapter.

Here's the basic equation for both commercial and noncommercial sharenting. Parents are inviting in a wide and uncontainable audience whose members may lack any actual connection to the family or children.[69] Parents are holding out their child's actions as authentic, eliding their own role as creator. And parents are giving their child a part that bears his name, that lives in his house, and that is understood by the child to be him. At some point, he will likely become aware of the viewing public's reaction to this portrayal. Regardless of any explicit financial stakes in the commercial realm, there is likely to be a "life imitates art imitates life" cycle that develops in which the child's choices, experience of the world, and felt sense of self are filtered through the sharenting lens.

What do you think that children's and adolescents' sense of self should be worth? Would you farm your kids out to a warehouse to work for free so you could get all the DVDs you want? Clearly not. So why are you comfortable sharing their toilet-training dilemmas online to generate revenue for your sharenting enterprise or in exchange for ostensibly free access to all the social media services you could want? And why does our legal system let you make these choices? The next chapter looks at the dominant myths that our legal system holds about children, parents, families, and other adults that make adults' stealth digital attack on childhood and adolescence possible.

5   Leaving Neverland: How Did We Get Here?

The child is father of the man, according to the poet William Wordsworth.[1] The belief that we contain the blueprint of our essential selves from infancy and that those young selves should enjoy some form of heightened protection is deeply felt in both poetry and the law. Without taking sides in the chicken-and-the-egg debate that is the nature or nurture question, it's safe to say that the adults we become hatch from the baby bird versions of our selves. Quack.

More provocatively, Wordsworth's line suggests that kids do some of their own parenting. They bring up themselves without as much shaping from parents or other adult caregivers as we might like to believe. If Wordsworth had meant simply that the child preceded the man, he could have said so. "Father" connotes agency, responsibility for the function of parenting. It implies that a certain amount of benevolent ignorance or even benign neglect might be beneficial for kids. We're not looking to go full *Lord of the Flies* here.[2] We're thinking more of a Peter Pan or Charlie Brown situation where the grown-ups leave the nursery unattended or just go "mwa-mwa-mwa" in the background.[3] The kids make the magic happen.

Today, though, what happens in Neverland doesn't stay in Neverland. Children's private lives—so often characterized by imagination, experimentation, and exploration—seem less their own than they have ever been before. Neverland is under attack. There is no coordinated pirate plot. The attack flows from a constellation of outdated, conflicting, and flawed assumptions that the law holds about the nature of youth development, family life, and education and about the civic, commercial, and other spheres in which kids and teens engage. These assumptions are grounded in a mix of fact and fiction and are so deeply entrenched that it makes sense to call them legal myths. This label doesn't mean they can be ignored; rather, it means they have a staying power that makes them impossible to ignore.

Before we turn to these myths, let's return to our ongoing conversation with some new questions. How do you think the law understands childhood and adolescence? Does the law see kids and teens as vulnerable, in need of protection by parents and the government? Does the law see youth as volatile, in need of control whether they are in school, on the streets, or somewhere else? Or does the law regard them in another way entirely?

Based on your paradigm for childhood and adolescence, where do you think the law's understanding is correct? Where do you think it fails? How have you seen the law's understanding of childhood and adolescence in general manifest itself in the lives of individual youth? Do you think there might be areas where there are gaps between the law's design and its implementation? Do such ruptures tend to be positive, negative, or circumstance dependent?

How do you think the concept of privacy informs the law's perspective on kids and teens in general (not specifically related to the digital world)? Is your sense that the understanding of privacy in the law here is similar to or divergent from your own privacy framework? Where you see disconnects, does it concern you? Do you think the law should have a single or small set of privacy concepts? Might it be inherent in the idea of privacy that individuals should be free to develop their own definitions of privacy, within the outer bounds set by the law?

As you read this chapter, think about whether the legal myths it identifies resonate with your paradigms for childhood, adolescence, and privacy. This chapter identifies three legal myths that have led to the siege against Neverland and that impede attempts to restore the realm of youth to its rightful owners. These legal mythologies address kids at home, in the public sphere, and in the marketplace. In unpacking these myths, you'll see that the law often gets childhood and adolescence wrong. At best, it is schizophrenic on the topic.[4]

Through error and an erratic approach, virtually all sharenting is legal or, at least, not clearly illegal. This wide-open playing field gives adults a lot of room to maneuver without leaving kids much room to defend either themselves or the life stages of childhood and adolescence. Where are Peter and the gang when you need them?

Myth 1. Home Is Where the Heart and Head Are: Protecting Parental Control over the Family Protects Kids' Privacy and Opportunities.

The law provides superprotection for parents' decision-making authority over their children's lives and futures.[5] The assumption is that parents are in the best position to make choices for their kids and, thus, that protecting parental control protects kids too. The family unit is treated as inherently private[6]—a safe space where kids can be the parents of their adult selves. Parents get to decide who enters. They also get to determine (more or less) the activities kids engage in outside of the home. And they get to decide which intimate information about what happens in the home gets shared outside the home. The law assumes that they will do a good job.[7]

The government gets involved in familial decision making only if the family breaks down through abuse, divorce, or similar circumstances.[8] Non-governmental third parties, like private companies, are allowed into the family fold only by invitation. There aren't any realistic circumstances in which a nongovernmental third party could lawfully force entry.[9] Parents are supposed to stand sentry over the castles that are their homes.

But kids today no longer live in a world of brick-and-mortar places with definite boundaries. This transition marks the fundamental change of our digital world.[10] It may well account for some of the so-called helicopter parent phenomenon[11] that has developed as the privileged set tries to extend the brick-and-mortar boundaries of Tom Sawyer's America.

Wireless tech rolls right over whitewashed fences. Through digital devices and services, sales promotions, opinions, and other forms of connections outside the home are a constant feature within the home.[12] Some are visible, like the ad on the lock screen of the Kindle before you enter your passcode to let your toddler watch *Daniel Tiger's Neighborhood* ("Dann-eee Tig-ee, Tig-ee, Mama, I wan' Dann-eeeeee Tig-eeeeeee NOW!").[13] Some are stealth: just how much audio is the Amazon Echo recording, and who is going to hear this showdown over "Dann-ee Tig-ee"?[14]

Today's parental gatekeepers often wind up like Nana,[15] the dog who is tasked with watching over the Darling children's house on the night Peter Pan takes them away. Nana tries her best but is no match for outside forces. Peter Pan is charming. What else is he: shadow or boy? The night sky beckons. Star maps promise infinity. The children don't care what Peter is. They follow.

Nana is locked up and can't be in the nursery on that fateful night. But we adults are free to move. That freedom is part of our problem. Perhaps we are just as much the Darling children as we are Nana. We are as intrigued with the digital universe as the Darlings are with Neverland.[16] Play a game on our smartphones where we stalk imaginary monsters in the real world? Stalk our high school boyfriend on Facebook? Post supercute pics of ourselves with our babies so our ex can see what he let get away? Yes, please!

Because we adults are still struggling to grasp the digital world, we are often lousy gatekeepers. When we use digital tech to enhance our own lives, young people's needs and preferences may take a backseat or be invisible. We prioritize our own needs, whether consciously or not. Even when we intend to use digital tech to enhance our kids' lives, we may not understand what we are doing. And our children may not want us involved in their digital lives.[17] But the law treats us as if we do understand and should be involved in our children's digital lives. We are our children's watchdogs-in-chief, so the law holds us responsible for making informed decisions about whether, when, and why to share our children's personal data online.[18] And the legal regimes around digital data privacy don't make our task easy.

Privacy law is a hodge-podge,[19] like the potion powders in Snape's classroom.[20] The law doesn't equip parents with Harry Potter's "cloak of invisibility" so that we can wrap it around our children's digital selves.[21] In general, we are asked to operate on a consent-based system.[22] We are expected to find, read, and understand the relevant privacy policies, terms of use, or other legal instruments that define what a third party wants to do with our children's digital data. Then we are asked to give informed consent to this third party's proposed actions.

Most of the time, we don't take all these steps. Could we read a bit more of the fine print? Sure, but we are largely set up for failure here. Reading and understanding all the fine print are difficult if not impossible.[23]

We agree to "clickwrap agreements" to join social media sites or connect a baby monitor we want to use without reading the fine print.[24] Even if we try to find the fine print, we might not be able to locate it.[25] Even if we find the fine print and try to read it, we probably don't understand it.[26] Even if we understand it, we may never know if the company violates it.[27]

In the event we do find out about a violation, we might not care about it. After all, if we're willing to share pics of our kids in diapers with ten thousand of our closest friends, how much do we really care if the company decides to let advertisers take a peek?

If we do care, we could turn to state tort law for potential remedies[28] or notify the Federal Trade Commission to encourage enforcement action for that company's violation of its own stated privacy policies or other terms of service.[29] Yet even if we succeed, our victory is likely to be slow and costly and still not give us a way to put the genie of information sharing completely back into the bottle.[30] They just don't make genies like they used to in the predigital age.

Some sectors have privacy law regimes that offer stronger built-in safeguards to keep children's private digital data under wraps. A familiar example is the federal Health Insurance Portability and Accountability Act (HIPAA), which controls information sharing about patients in the healthcare system.[31]

A similar but likely less familiar example is the Family Educational Rights and Privacy Act (FERPA), which prohibits schools that receive federal funding (almost all schools nationwide) from sharing "personally identifiable information" (PII) in students' "education records" unless they have written parental consent or the particular form of sharing falls into one of FERPA's enumerated exceptions.[32] Of all the federal statutory privacy regimes, FERPA comes the closest to imposing robust and comprehensive limitations on adults' sharing of children's personal digital data.

However, FERPA suffers from some of its own serious limitations. First, it was written for the brick-and-mortar world, where an apple on the teacher's desk meant a fruit, not a phone. FERPA did not anticipate today's world of ubiquitous digital tech and digital data collection. "FERPA's regulatory mechanisms rely on the assumption that it is not easy to share student [education] records without individual or institutional action," writes privacy scholar Elana Zeide; however, today "intention and knowledge are no longer required to disclose information."[33]

There are just too many devices and services collecting too much data for too many reasons for schools to have an easy time getting a handle on what data is being collected, by whom, and why—threshold questions for determining whether the data being collected is PII in an "education record" subject to FERPA protection. Students' data can be collected through digital devices that schools honestly don't understand to be creating "education records" with PII that are protected by FERPA—even if they technically are.

These devices may include "wearable fitness devices for physical education classes"[34] or digital surveillance cameras.

And some data collection in schools may fall outside of or at least not clearly within FERPA's control. For instance, is metadata (data about data) an education record? In these and many other ways, key privacy problems that arise when students' data is being shared with digital tech and service providers are not fully addressed by FERPA's requirements.[35]

Second, FERPA is built on a parental consent framework. Under the letter of the law, parents typically are expected to have the final say in judging the complex potential trade-offs between privacy risks and educational benefits.[36] This is unrealistic, even fantastical. It's difficult enough for parents to try to read and understand privacy policies and terms of use for digital tech in their homes. It's essentially impossible when parents lack easy or any access to information about the digital tech being used in their children's schools, which is often the situation parents find themselves in.[37]

Third, FERPA fails to rely completely on a parental consent framework. The exceptions that exist for schools to share PII without parental consent or even for parents to have the right to opt out of sharing mean that there often is a fair amount of PII sharing taking place over which parents have limited to no control.[38] The most frequently used exception is the "legitimate school official" exception, through which schools can share PII with a third party—as long as that party is doing something that the school otherwise would do itself, is under the control of the school, and doesn't reshare the data.[39]

When schools (or well-intentioned individuals within schools, like teachers looking for new resources) rely on clickwrap agreements with providers instead of negotiated contracts, these requirements are unlikely to be met—meaning that the schools are in violation of FERPA if they have not gotten parental consent to share the PII.[40] More important than the technical legal violation is the actual danger: without a negotiated contract in place that is actively monitored by the school, how do schools and their staff know what these third parties are doing with students' data? Are the third parties mining it to make predictions about children for marketing or other purposes? Are they selling it to yet other third parties who will do so? Sometimes the answer to these questions is yes, which could allow PII to get into the hands of data brokers and beyond.[41]

FERPA has an often forgotten cousin: the Protection of Pupil Rights Act (PPRA), another federal law about student privacy that has its origins in allowing "parent access to federally funded experimental instructional materials."[42] PPRA was created before the digital age and amended during it.[43] Its amendment, although awkwardly drafted, does address today's challenge of dealing with private information about students that digitally departs from schools and winds up in the hands of third parties that may use it for noneducational purposes.

Under PPRA, public K–12 schools "must offer parents an opportunity to opt-out from having their child participate in any activity involving the collection, disclosure or use of students' personal information for the purpose of marketing or selling the information '(or otherwise providing that information to others for that purpose).'"[44] PPRA defines "personal information" as "individually identifiable information, including a student or parent's name, home address, telephone number or a Social Security Number."[45]

So before a school engages with an ed tech provider that collects personal information, the school should determine whether the provider will use this information for marketing or related purposes and whether the provider will pass it along to data brokers or others to use for such purposes. Parents then must be given the ability to opt out. However, the right to give consent prior to any action is stronger than this opt-out right after notification of pending action. Essentially, PPRA is creating another layer of (required, if not actual) notification that may be difficult for parents to understand—if they even see the email or find the note underneath the week-old banana in their child's backpack.

Although parents are far from perfect gatekeepers with respect to their children's privacy in the digital era, the law assigns the lion's share of those guard-dog duties to them. Performing those duties grows ever more complicated when there are too many animals trying to mind the farm, which heightens the risk that no animal is really on top of the situation. Ask George Orwell: animals aren't supposed to mind the farm themselves anyway.[46]

With today's parents not fully on top of watchdog duty, are there other people or institutions that could and should play that role? The next myth unpacks the misunderstood nature of youth vulnerability and the rise of the childhood surveillance state.

Myth 2. Childhood and Punishment: Keeping Kids on Track Requires Surveillance and Consequences.

Jack and Jill do not go straight up the hill. Jack falls down. He breaks open his head. Jill falls down. The nursery rhyme doesn't tell us what happens next. But we can guess: they get fixed up and go on their merry way. Then they fall down again and again.

Growing up is not a smooth uphill climb. There are bruises. These are literal and metaphorical. They are self-inflicted and caused by others. Most of them are well within the range of normal. Neuroscientists,[47] psychologists,[48] and other experts broadly agree.[49] Maturation from child to adult is not linear. Childhood is a series of different developmental stages and struggles, many of which require learning through "mistakes."

The law purports to take into account the nature of childhood. It recognizes that kids are less mature and therefore less accountable for their actions than adults.[50] And it forgives them for their mistakes more readily than it forgives adults. But it fails to recognize fully the distinct and positive qualities that set childhood apart from adulthood. It doesn't see how kids and teens can sometimes be more than adults rather than just less.[51] It doesn't promote play as a positive pursuit—the true "work of childhood"[52] (and arguably of adolescence as well, although the manifestations of play are different from three to teenager).[53]

Today, childhood is a surveillance state.[54] The theory is largely one of protectionism.[55] Kids need to be protected from their own immature impulses by being put on the straight and narrow. The rest of us need to be protected from the crazy $%$ that kids do.[56] Parents,[57] schools,[58] and law enforcement[59] tend to be hypervigilant about monitoring youths' lives. In order to protect against danger, you need to be able to see it. With a large and growing industry of digital products and services to support such surveillance efforts, adults today have more ability to access data about the inner workings of Neverland than ever before.[60] And the data collected by these surveillance products is unlikely to stay completely within the data repositories of a given tech provider.[61]

The surveillance state isn't curious just for the sake of curiosity alone. It leaves curiosity to little monkeys.[62] As soon as they learn what the Lost Boys are up to, the adult captains of the surveillance state ship step in to mete out justice. The result is that routine juvenile mistakes and mischief are met with consequences that may be well meaning but make it harder for kids and teens to learn from their mistakes. Digital tech is available to help with the consequences piece too.[63] As with the surveillance piece, this sensitive data is unlikely to stay on total lockdown.[64]

On paper, our legal system doesn't "punish" kids. When kids and teens commit acts that would be crimes if done by adults, they are charged with "delinquency" offenses, not criminal ones.[65] These offenders are processed through a separate juvenile justice system. States have some exceptions to this approach for murder and similarly heinous acts done by older kids and teens.[66] In these limited circumstances, the juvenile perpetrators can be charged and tried as adults in criminal court. In general, though, minors are processed through the juvenile justice system for misconduct.

What counts as misconduct worthy of the juvenile justice system's attention? The list is long: "pushing and shoving has become battery . . . talking back to staff has become disorderly conduct or obstructing."[67] The list gets longer still for minority and disabled youth.[68] Schools pay especially close attention to making this list and checking it twice. Each time they check, they find more students naughty than nice. The school-to-prison pipeline sends hundreds of thousands of students each year into the justice system for infractions committed in school.[69] Often, these offenses are minor.[70] Often, this trip is in addition to consequences imposed by the school, such as out-of-school suspension, for the same infraction.[71] There is a tension here: schools want students to learn from their mistakes, yet they kick them out of school when they make mistakes.[72] So where is the learning supposed to take place?

In theory, some of it could take place through the court system.[73] Juvenile courts assign minors found "true" of delinquent acts to undergo activities and receive services that are meant to "rehabilitate" rather than punish.[74] But rehabilitation often looks and feels a lot like punishment.[75] Consequences can include placement in a group home or a secure facility. They can include community service, restitution, therapy, drug counseling, and strict curfews. They can include "do not contact" lists.[76]

The consequences also pile on. When a young person is under the close monitoring of a juvenile parole and probation officer, that officer is likely to find some additional infraction of the court's "terms and conditions of release."[77] Kids will be kids. They fall down and try to get up again. Courts will be courts. They want to stop the falling down and make the getting up happen by the book. So judges assign more and more "rehabilitative" measures to address the misconduct.[78] Kids fail "fast, early, and often"[79] to fulfill the courts' orders. Even the most thoughtful rehabilitative measures transform themselves into Sisyphean tasks.

The ironic result is that we are often "protecting" children out of their childhoods and their futures.[80] There are certainly times when schools, law enforcement, courts, and others in positions of authority need to step in to protect kids and society. A kid threatening to use an actual gun should never have the opportunity to make and learn from that mistake. But a kid with a fake gun shouldn't be treated like public enemy number one. He should not be shot and killed.[81] He needs to play, mess up, get some thoughtful and proportional adult feedback, then go play and mess up some more. The teenage girl who texts a picture of herself in her bra to her boyfriend should not be prosecuted for manufacturing and distributing child pornography and required to register as a sex offender.[82] She needs to understand the consequences of such self-exposure, mature more into her own understanding of her own sexuality, and continue to explore sexual and romantic relationships. Take away that process, and Neverland looks pretty bleak. The prospects for developing into an autonomous adult who is able to self-regulate and evoke self-efficacy look even bleaker. We might be raising adults who lack self-trust and imagination.[83]

We're also plundering this stash of kids' private experiences for our own commercial transactions. The next myth looks at how we're transforming our kids as digital day laborers even as we purport to protect them.

Myth 3. Children Should Not Be Seen or Heard in the Workplace: Parents Will Protect Children from Labor Markets.

Huck Finn decided to "light out for the territory."[84] He wasn't alone. From the mid-nineteenth through the early twentieth centuries, many real children headed west. But these kids didn't typically travel under their own steam. Some rode on "orphan trains."[85] Sent from crowded urban areas to the western frontier and other parts of the country, these kids headed to new families and new lives.[86] They found adventure, but they could also be taken for quite a ride.[87] They were commodified, often exploited.[88] The gold rush era generally did not make childhood into a golden life stage.

Today, we are seeing unexpected echoes of the pre-twentieth-century conception of childhood. We think of the twenty-first century as an age of "helicopter parents" engaged in kid-glove handling of kids.[89] Yet every day, parents, teachers, and other trusted adults also place kids in the commercial sphere from within the comfort of their homes, schools, and other community centers. Private childhood experiences are captured, transmitted, stored, and used as digital data through which adults themselves, as well as kids and teens, receive free or low-cost digital goods and services. Unlike the nineteenth century, when commercial engagement was explicit, it is largely hidden today. Kids' labor is invisible, even as their value to their households, their schools, and the commercial sphere more broadly grows.[90]

We wouldn't let parents, teachers, or other trusted adults send children to work each day in a factory, around the clock, where the children's activities were monetizable for the adults' benefit. But effectively, we are doing that now with children's data. Parents, teachers, and other caregivers are engaged in the large-scale "sale" or exchange of their children's labor, in the form of data, with third-party institutions that span governmental, non-profit, and for-profit sectors.

Today's kids are also making their way through a wild west frontier of sorts: digital life.[91] At first glance, our current legal approach to the role of children in the marketplace seems to be the polar opposite of the orphan train era. Our system generally aims to keep kids out of commerce and to protect them when they do engage.[92] Federal and state child labor laws restrict the ability of employers to hire minors, with certain important exceptions that will be unpacked further below.[93] In most circumstances, contract law does not permit minors to enter into binding contracts.[94]

There is even a specific federal law that applies when kids who are under age thirteen go online. This law is one of the "few comprehensive privacy regulations" at the federal level in the United States.[95] But it does not prohibit sharenting. In fact, it implicitly condones sharenting because it is based on a parental consent framework for most digital activities by younger children. Called the Children's Online Privacy Protection Act (COPPA), this law requires for-profit tech providers "that either target children or knowingly collect personal information from children under the age of 13" to obtain parental consent before kids under age thirteen can use the companies' services.[96] The consent of a child under age thirteen is not legally sufficient. For educational technologies used in the classroom, teacher consent can replace parental consent if certain requirements are met, including that the data collected and used by the ed tech company is for use within the school system only—and not for external purposes, like marketing.[97] And data that is collected with parental consent is not supposed to be used for "profiling (e.g. behavioral advertising) or cross-device tracking."[98]

COPPA itself is twenty-years old: "Before 1998, no federal law restricted collection of personal information from children online."[99] And the federal regulations that implement COPPA were updated in 2013.[100] This update reflects a positive, productive federal regulatory response to "the increased use of the Internet by children in the mobile and social networking era"; the significant changes included "expanding COPPA's reach to mobile application developers and third-party vendors," entities that interact more with children than they did when COPPA was written.[101] Such specific, nuanced attention to the realities of youth engagement in the digital world demonstrates the capacity of administrative rulemaking to respond in a flexible, effective manner to complex privacy challenges and opportunities.

However, even those protections that are on the books do not always translate to real-world protections. Notably, a 2018 study of roughly six thousand Android apps aimed at children found that almost three-quarters of them "transmitted sensitive data over the Internet," without having "attained verifiable parental consent" prior to transmission.[102]

Is this website safe for my two-year-old? How about my twelve-year-old? What data is being collected about them, and where is that data going? What is being done with it? And what about my thirteen-year-old, where COPPA is silent about my ability to consent to or even know about the data collected from her? Often, not even parents are being put in their legally entitled position to know and to choose whether to consent.

And kids and teens have no legal rights when it comes to the choices their parents make, either about their own digital engagement or their parents' sharenting behaviors. The frontiers of digital life are largely wide open for parents and many other adults to share and use private information about children. These federal and state marketplace laws and others like them essentially do nothing to stop parents from sharing anything and everything about their kids online. They limit teachers and other caregivers more so than parents but still not significantly.

The weakness of marketplace laws here rests on two primary founda-
tions. The first foundational weakness is that these laws have an outdated
understanding of what it means to perform labor in the twenty-first century. They do not recognize adult digital transmission and use of children's
private data as drawing on child labor that is subject to marketplace regulation. The laws understand companies that offer digital services to be market actors and regulate them accordingly. The laws understand adults who
engage these services by sharing their children's information to be consumers of the services. The laws further understand children who engage these
services directly to be consumers. The laws do not understand these adults
or these children to be somehow supplying labor to these services.

This oversight is understandable. You think you are purchasing the services of a magic wardrobe. You don't fully realize that the magic wardrobe
is owning you. It is acquiring information about you, generated by your life
activities, in an ongoing way. The magic wardrobe can be understood as a
thief, as we've previously discussed. It can be understood as a product that
was sold to you with some amount of deception or at least not full transparency. The wardrobe also could be understood as a type of boss, making
you work for it without your full knowledge or consent. If you're a child
and the wardrobe is introduced by your parents, your parents could be said
to be making you work for the wardrobe, Narnia Incorporated. It's easy to
miss the potential "labor" variable in the equation. You think that you and
your children just are going about the business of your daily life.

Current marketplace laws would reject any approach that sees the magic
wardrobe and the parental purchasers as relying on child labor. Indeed, the
legal system does not yet uniformly recognize people as being consumers
and as somehow purchasing so-called free online services with their private
personal data.[103] Under today's existing legal schema, then, it would be a
stretch to understand parents, teachers, or other adults as somehow serving as "employers" of minors within the meaning of labor laws when they
are sharing data about minors or even giving minors digital technologies
to use through which the minors will wind up sharing their own data.[104]
Thus, even for nonparents, as long as they are sharing data about children
or giving children devices to use in the context of education, athletics, or
other nonmarketplace pursuits (rather than having children manufacture
such devices or similar activities), their actions do not legally amount to
having children perform labor.

However, if we understand work, in its most general sense, to be tasks that we perform so other individuals or institutions will give us money, objects of value, or services of value, then we are working hard for our magic wardrobe and other digital services. We're doing other things too. Those other things, like being consumers, are more central to the arrangement. But they are not the only things. The legal oversight that fails to see the role of labor by users in the arrangements of daily digital tech life risks ignoring the full range of complexities of generating, using, and controlling private data in the digital age.

The second foundational weakness of today's marketplace laws as applied to the sharing of children's digital data applies to parents in particular. Even if the law were to accept that the transformation of children's daily activities into data gathered and used by digital technologies somehow constituted labor, parents would enjoy broad exemption from labor law regulations. Under the federal Fair Labor Standards Act (FLSA), parents can employ their own children to engage in almost all types of work even if the children are under the legal minimum age requirements.[105] State child labor laws tend to mirror the federal approach to this practice.[106] Because parents are serving as the gatekeepers when it comes to sharing their children's private lives, if children are "employed" by anyone to put their digital data to work, they are employed by their parents. Here again, parents enjoy their familiar broad autonomy to make these employment decisions.

What happens when the family business involves sharing the family's business for money? The analysis of marketplace laws does get more complex when we turn back to the child stars of the commercial sharenting sector. Acting and performing receive special treatment under federal and state child labor laws and regulations. When a parent goes from letting a toddler play with an app to filming the toddler playing with the app, posting the video online, and receiving sponsorship revenue from the app developer, we've moved into commercial space.

The federal FLSA "permits minors of any age to work as an actor or performer."[107] These child stars are performing the part of themselves, however, so it is not clear that they are even "working" as an "actor or performer." Legal scholar Kimberlianne Podlas has analyzed the status of child reality TV stars under the FLSA and concluded that the federal law does not apply: "either the FLSA does not cover children appearing on reality TV because their participation is not equivalent to work [they are simply being themselves] . . . or, the FLSA does not cover children appearing on reality TV because they qualify as children performing in a television production who are exempt from the FLSA's child labor prohibitions."[108]

This analysis would seem to cover children appearing in the commercial sharenting sector because the legally relevant variables are the same: children are appearing on a screen playing the role of themselves. In addition, in the commercial sharenting space, parents, not a production company, are typically running the show. And the FLSA permits parents to employ their own minor children—if commercial sharenting even were to be recognized as "employment" within the meaning of the law.

There does appear to be a possibility that some state labor laws could regulate commercial sharenting.[109] In the absence of uniform regulation of child performers on the federal level, state statutes serve as the primary legal framework for ensuring the well-being of child actors and for setting expectations for the child's end of the bargain on which their entertainment industry adult colleagues can rely.[110]

Even though these statutes step in where the federal FLSA is absent in order to regulate the terms and conditions of child performance labor, it is unclear that commercial sharenting stars would count as performers or actors within the meaning of many state laws. They are playing themselves and thus might not be considered employed as an actor. If they are legally deemed to be employed, they are employed by their parents in their own home. State labor laws typically mirror the federal permissive attitude toward parents' employing their minor children in a family business. And when it comes to state regulation of minors in performance, the law typically vests primary responsibility for decision making with parents, subject to certain standardized requirements around hours of work, the necessity of education, and the use of trust accounts (in some jurisdictions).

But the possibility for regulation does exist in statutory language such as Pennsylvania's Child Labor Act: under the "Child Labor Act, a minor is engaged in a performance if the minor models or renders artistic or creative expression . . . over the Internet . . . or via any other broadcast medium that may be transmitted to an audience, and any person receives remuneration for the performance."[111] The law makes explicit that "a minor is engaged in a performance if the minor participates in a reality or documentary program that expressly depends upon the minor's participation, the minor's participation is substantial, and any person receives remuneration for the minor's performance."[112] Many commercial sharenting activities would meet that definition: the minor is playing himself, the minor is the star of the show, and the parents are getting marketing or other revenue from the activity.

Assuming the law does apply to commercial sharenting, mom-agers and pop-roducers are still left with considerable leeway to put their children in the spotlight. Key requirements include a permit for the performer, a limit on the hours worked, an education for the performer, and a trust account where parents or guardians deposit a certain amount of money. However, the delineated categories of prohibited types of performance activities are narrow. Almost all of the familiar commercial sharenting activities would be permitted. Even the DaddyOFive "pranks" seem potentially permissible under this statute, although barred by child abuse and neglect statutes.[113]

We return to the familiar point discussed above, then, that the only real legal obstacle to sharenting—commercial and noncommercial—is criminal law.[114] Even in a state like Pennsylvania, where there might be legal limits on commercial sharenting, the practice is still lawful if done properly. Teachers and school officials are more limited in what they can share without parental consent. But even they enjoy considerable latitude if the sharing is done with a third party to which the school has outsourced educational or related tasks.

The language and scope of the federal and state labor laws thus fail to recognize that work in the digital era is no longer limited to the factory floor or the family dairy farm. Today, many of us work by creating data and exchanging it for the use of digital services. We create data virtually all the time, without realizing we are doing it. We exchange it without necessarily realizing it is being taken. We put our own and our children's data to work, at least in the colloquial sense of the term, when we engage in commercial sharenting or, in the noncommercial realm, get a free educational app in exchange for letting the app provider learn about our kids. By failing to recognize this twenty-first-century type of work and by leaving much of the decision making about kids' engagement with this type of work in parent's hands, current labor laws largely fail to keep child's play out of the labor force.

Data is a valuable product.[115] Nonprofit institutions, like universities, are increasingly engaged with it.[116] Private-sector businesses are increasingly focused on collecting and using it.[117] The government and other major sectors are as well.[118] Individuals use and exchange their data all the time but are typically less aware of its value than their institutional counter-parts are. Some of this information asymmetry seems intentional on the part of institutions. They get a damn good deal when the fine-print terms that users are agreeing to give the institutions virtually unlimited ability to use and share users' data. Some of the asymmetry reflects a limited toolkit on the part of users to understand or care about the terms of the deal.[119] We can't directly use our data to put a roof over our heads or food on the table unless we are engaging in commercial sharenting. But we can use our personal data to obtain free or low-cost digital services of unprecedented strength and scope.

Just by virtue of being alive, we generate information about ourselves. We work to produce data. The same is true of becoming alive; just think back to Tommy S. and the digital edifice that was constructed around his conception and gestation. The same even holds true after death: our digital selves outlive us, and their beyond-the-grave grip can be powerful.[120]

That the ghosts of lives past can continue to be productive suggests another way of thinking about data that is related to yet subtly distinct from seeing the labor of daily life as working to produce data. We might also think of our personal data as a type of currency. It's a currency we spend freely, often invisibly. After all, the currency seems to be limitless.

Even when we don't have money in the bank, we can access the search functionality of Google, the social networking of Facebook, and much more by exchanging our data for these services.[121] As the oft-used phrase tells it: if you're not paying for a product, you are the product.[122] Under this frame-work, parents, teachers, and other adults are spending the currency of kids' data. We're spending it without kids' knowledge, without their consent, and without a full or thoughtful understanding of why we're spending it and what the consequences of spending it might be.

Whether we're looking at a framework where we might understand the relationship of parental, educator, and other trusted adult use of chil-dren's data as constituting child labor or as spending children's currency, a thought experiment might help us understand whether and why we might be uncomfortable with this type of arrangement.

Let's suppose that a friend confided this to you: "I let an unknown num-ber of unknown people from these private companies come over to my house and take pictures of my kids everywhere, all day long. They take pictures of the kids when they are playing outside, eating meals, and washing in the bathtub. Don't worry, though, in the tub pics, the bubbles cover the genitals! And then I let these companies use the pictures for an indefinite length of time for whatever purposes they choose. In exchange, these companies give me free access to their services."

You probably would find this situation to be really creepy. Now let's take it one step further: your friend tells you that she does all of these things and that, in return, the company gives her money. You would likely find it even creepier, and she possibly would be in violation of child labor laws, depending on the state in which she was located.

There are some important differences between these hypothetical scenarios and the business models employed by social media and other digital companies. These distinctions include that, in the actual model, children's experiences of the physical world are unconstrained by a visible external presence. There also is a core similarity. In both the hypothetical and real-world scenarios, parents, teachers, and other adults are exchanging data about their own children or children under their care for access to services that these adults want.

Let's take one step further still and go to a realistic near future. Today, adults freely use the currency of their children's data to obtain free or low-cost commercial services. Are government services next? All levels of government use a "pay your own way" model for certain services we may think of as "public," such as criminal justice and fire prevention.[123] But poor people are disadvantaged when they are forced to use or choose to use "pay to your own way" services (such as some public defender services) because they don't have the funds to pay. Sometimes, being unable to pay means you don't get a service. Other times, it means that this "captive market" of "service" users is required to take out loans from the government.[124] They get the "service" (such as a public defender for themselves),[125] the government foots the bill up front, and the users are required to pay the government back, typically with interest, late fees, and a range of governmental "super creditor" tools (like wage garnishment) that regular creditors don't have.[126]

"Pay your own way" is already used for juvenile delinquency and other court proceedings involving parents and children in states around the country. Here's how this approach works in a juvenile delinquency case. As a parent, if your child is found "true" of a delinquency offense and placed out of your home for rehabilitation or other services, you are given a bill for the cost of the placement, services, and more. If you can't pay that bill in full and on time, it becomes a loan that you need to pay back over time. If you don't, you can face contempt of court proceedings and become incarcerated yourself.[127]

So we have a "pay your own way" model. We have surveillance technologies in wide use in the private and public spheres, such as by car insurance companies that offer a discount for safe driving and digital tracking of adults on parole or probation.[128] What happens if a state government says to a poor parent who is facing a massive "pay your own way" bill for a troubled teen's stint in juvie, "You can use the currency of your child's data as payment for this bill?"

The government is already collecting a lot of data on the child and the family as part of the juvenile delinquency proceeding. But let's say the government wants to use this data collection power to support what it sees as further rehabilitation of the child in the family context. The government says, "You can pay the bill with dollars, or you can pay it with data." The dollar option is some amount of money each month that you can't afford, with stiff financial and other penalties if you fail. The data option is have your child wear this sensor and video-enabled watch twenty-four hours a day. If the data tells us that your child is going to school on time, eating three well-balanced meals, not watching more than thirty minutes of screen time each day, doing all his homework, and going to bed by 8 p.m. every day in a given month, we will accept that data in lieu of your financial payment for that month.

We, the government, also will review the data we receive to see if there are other, more customized requirements that we could impose on you, parents, as part of your child's terms of parole and probation so that you can better support your child's rehabilitation. So if the watch tell us that you smoke, drink, or eat saturated fats, we're going to order you to stop doing those things if you want to receive the data credit for that month's payment. Oh, and we are also going to use your child's and family's data for anything and everything else we think could be helpful to us, now and in the future. Is that cool with you? To use this option, you need to waive any constitutional or legal objections to anything we ever do with your child's and family's data.

Think of this hypothetical situation as a warped version of the old MasterCard commercial: it's priceless![129] It's priceless on a lot of levels.

It's priceless because the parent can give away something that seems free instead of giving up money or acquiring debt. For the parent, this exchange can seem like a huge bargain. It's priceless because the government, if this works right, will save a lot of money on other forms of parole and probation monitoring and prevent recidivism.

We might also say it's priceless because it seems ridiculous, but it's not far-fetched at all. Data is dollars. That is, data translates into and is used as dollars already. Slap a "Digital Data–Driven Home Rehabilitation Program for Youthful Offenders" label on this scenario, and you've got yourself a brand-new governmental initiative. You could probably get some grant funding behind it and hit up a private company to donate the watches in exchange for access to the data.

It is ironic that kids risk being turned into digital day laborers on the internet. In its infancy, the internet was an open, playful frontier. In many respects, it still is. But the playground ethos that kids, more than any other demographic, need is increasingly unavailable to them in digital life, even as digital world purports to offer limitless possibilities. Is there a way to create a mechanism to stop turning kids into digital day laborers and let them play?

Just as the child is the parent of the adult, our flawed legal mythology contains some grains of truth that can grow into a path forward. The next two chapters lay out this thought compass of guiding principles to help us chart our course toward a childhood that protects privacy and—by extension—opportunity, agency, and autonomy within our current and future digital worlds.

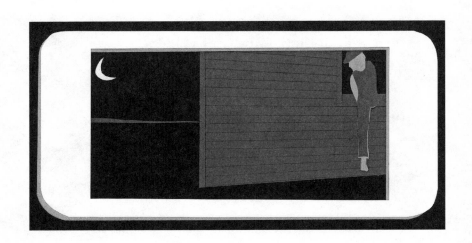

6   Drones and Growns: Navigating the Digital Era

France is training eagles to attack drones.[1] The eagles are good at it. In the twenty-first century, chivalry may be dead. But medieval practices are not dead yet. There is a lesson here, but it's not as straightforward as you might think. At first glance, the lesson might be that older eras can conquer the digital one. Now take a closer look. The sky has plenty of room for both the machines and the birds. The lesson is that the layers remain. Eagles hunt drones now. They still also hunt small mammals. They don't need an app for that.

All of us parents, teachers, and other adults who care for kids and teens are a lot like those eagles. We inhabit a new world filled with digital creatures. And we have the instincts to do the same fundamental things that our parents, educators, and other caregivers did for us.[2] We feed, shelter, nurture, and train our young. We leave our nest to find food for them. We take out a second mortgage to put a new roof on that nest and then a home equity line of credit to send our big chicks to college.

Our challenge today is this: how do we train ourselves to take our parenting, teaching, and other caregiving instincts and adapt them to navigate today's digital landscape? The lesson is this: we can do much more than we think we can. We can keep our own young out of the way of drone attacks, metaphorical and potentially literal, and set them up to soar.

Where have your instincts been taking you as you parent, teach, or otherwise engage with youth? Have you observed others around you proceeding in similar ways? Do you see key public institutions—such as public schools, legislatures, courts, executive branches, and regulatory agencies—exhibiting positive, negative, or neutral instincts around how adults should treat children's private digital data? How about key private actors, including private schools, tech companies, and other business interests? Are there changes you would like to see in your personal life, our shared public life, or the private sector to chart a different course for the relationship that parents, teachers, and other trusted adults have to shaping children's digital lives and the attendant current and future opportunities? Do you understand those changes as animated by big-picture principles, pixelated details, or somewhere in between? Asking these types of questions, regardless of how you answer them, makes you the proverbial early bird when it comes to recognizing and reflecting on sharenting.[3]

This chapter begins with a thought experiment so we can better explore our instincts and those of the people and institutions around us. Next, this chapter and the following one outline a "thought compass"[4] to reorient our approach to our children's digital lives. Childhood and adolescence should be valued as unique life stages that are anchored in play so that agency and autonomy can be developed through bounded experimentation—making and learning from mistakes.

This compass is not a complete to-do list for personal best practices, legislative or other structural reforms, or any other checklist. Rather, it's a navigation device grounded in overarching principles.[5] These two chapters do offer a few suggestions about potential reforms—some of which are new, some of which may be familiar—to illustrate how some of the compass principles might be implemented, but those are not the main feature. The goal of these chapters is to help us find our own and a collective true north for nurturing a playful, meaningful, and self-affirming coming of age in the digital era.

We have more building blocks at our disposal than the Darling kids did in their nursery. We have legal protections for the home and family. We aspire to rehabilitate rather than punish misbehaving youth. We have some understanding within the legal system of the need for kids and teens to explore and test limits, although not (yet) a robust understanding of a play-based paradigm. And we aim to have meaningful consumer participation in our capitalist markets.

As detailed above, these and related commitments are experiencing complication and erosion, but they are by no means gone from the picture. Digital content is perpetually mashed up. We need to get more comfortable remixing the legal and other principles that shape the institutional and individual decisions around parental and other adult disclosure of children's data so we can respond effectively to scenarios like the one below.

Thought Experiment: A Near-Future Hypothetical Scenario

In this near-future hypothetical scenario, you're helping your seventeen-year-old daughter finish her college applications. The applications require her SAT score, SAT 2 scores, AP scores, and Tyke-Bytes "personal capital" scores. What the heck is Tyke-Bytes? Siri tells you that Tyke-Bytes serves as "your child's passport from her past into her future." You ask Siri to stop reading the Tyke-Bytes sound bites and do some digging. The response: Tyke-Bytes is a commercial database that serves as a repository of childhood data and a clearinghouse into adulthood. Tyke-Bytes aggregates as much data about each child in the country as possible and then packages the data for purchase by different types of institutions and individuals. The most popular product is a set of scores that rates children's likelihood of future success in a range of areas, including education, athletics, and employment.

Tyke-Bytes will share these "personal capital" scores with any individual or institution that pays for them, isn't legally prohibited from having them, and demonstrates what is, in Tyke-Bytes' opinion, a legitimate need for them. You and your daughter don't need to do anything to have these scores sent. All colleges that receive applications from her will request and receive these scores from Tyke-Bytes at no cost to individual applicants. Tyke-Bytes does allow parents and youth age eighteen or over to opt out of having Tyke-Bytes collect and share their information. But the Tyke-Bytes website warns you that opting out risks your child's future. "After all," the perky chatbot in the "Click here for help" section tells you, "an applicant without Tyke-Bytes scores is like a car without airbags: you could take it for a spin, but why risk it?"

Tyke-Bytes doesn't exist. Yet. But its potential existence is far from the "Clap now if you believe in fairies" scenario.[6] Some services exist already that reduce youth skills in a particular domain to a number, such as the Universal Tennis Rating system.[7] And a cross-cutting data-aggregation and analytics service that uses sensitive digital data about kids to generate scores across the board to inform decisions by gatekeepers about kids' future opportunities is not far from what is happening already.[8]

For example, a recent study from the Center on Law and Information Policy at Fordham Law School on the student data broker sphere found that higher education institutions use data gathered by commercial brokers for recruiting.[9] This data is sold broken down into specific lists or "selects" ("attribute[s] that can be used to filter a subset of a mailing list"), including "ethnicity, religion, economic factors, and even gawkiness."[10] Some currently available lists or selects include: "Home School Oriented Christian Families," "Jewish Households with Children Nearing High School Graduation," and "Rich Kids of America."[11] There doesn't appear to be a score attached by the data broker. Yet.

The hypothetical Tyke-Bytes business plan would suffer from some holes, notably the lack of data in the specific areas that the law protects from disclosure, such as juvenile justice (although there are plenty of holes in those holes through which ostensibly protected data does get out). These holes are unlikely to tank the entire project.

What's so bad about receiving a set of scores based on your childhood experiences? We have credit scores. Insurance providers assign scores using proprietary formulas to which we have limited or no access. Admissions offices for colleges and universities use models to predict student success and make admissions decisions. Judges and probation officers assign scores to predict future dangerousness and help set bail conditions.[12] Painting with a broad brush, the practice of various institutions and individuals using data-driven predictions to inform their actions is well established.

Are we troubled by the prospect that a parent's blog post about a toddler's toilet training fiasco in 2016 might play a role in determining where that now toilet-trained teenager gets into college in 2031? Likely your answer is yes. Let's reorient ourselves and our institutions using four principles: play, forget, connect, and respect. In order to mitigate the toilet training and similar threats to privacy and opportunity, the digital world needs to return to the internet's more playful, iterative roots. It needs to set up a protected place for childhood play the same way we try to protect brick-and-mortar playgrounds and classrooms: experimental, iterative, inclusive, equitable.

To do this right, the digital world needs to be forgetful. It needs to let go of much of what it knows about our kids and teens in order for them to develop the autonomy and agency necessary for thriving youth and meaningful adulthood. And when youth are engaged in digital spaces and relationships, the people, businesses, and other entities with which they interact need to show them respect. If their data is going to be commodified, they are entitled to more agency as economic actors rather than objects.

Play: Making Room for Make-Believe, Mischief, and Mistakes

We may be the hypocrites our teenagers think we are. We use digital technologies to enhance our own lives without thinking enough about the impact that sweeping up youth into our tech use might have on them.[13]

This book is focused on the impact of our sharenting on our children. Briefly: many other dimensions of our relationships with our children are likely impacted by our digital tech use. We need to ask whether our bonds with our digital devices are interfering with the parent-child bonding necessary for healthy child development.

This isn't a sharenting question. For this question, it doesn't matter whether we are using our phones to take pictures of our kids (and then posting them online) or to pay parking tickets. It matters only that we are using a phone or other digital device. Academic inquiry into the developmental impact of adult digital tech use on parent-child and other adult-child relationships is still in its early stages. Notably, a study published in the journal of the American Academy of Pediatrics cautions that despite some positive potential from digital tech, "mobile devices can also distract parents from face-to-face interactions with their children, which are crucial for cognitive, language, and emotional development."[14] Presumably, a study is forthcoming that concludes it is better to direct the inevitable frustrations associated with parenting into a snarky text thread with your friends rather than be snarky toward your children.

Back to the hypocrisy allegations: we use tech to create opportunities for ourselves and to control young people's digital and nondigital lives. For example, we encourage our kids and teens to use ed tech in their classes and activities in order to put down roots in STEM. Yet many schools have "zero tech tolerance" policies for students' use of their own devices on school grounds, and a student caught texting too many times can wind up with an out-of-school suspension.[15] We value "entrepreneurship." We applaud start-ups that "think big" and "fail early and often." Yet we are often intolerant of that same iterative process in childhood, even though it's necessary developmentally.

We're letting the grown-ups play and making the kids pay.[16] We have it backward. The digital world needs a protected place for childhood to play in the same way we try to protect brick-and-mortar playgrounds and class-rooms—by making them experimental, iterative, inclusive, and equitable. We can't have play be the province only of those privileged enough to build private forests for their kids.[17]

So how do we head in the right direction? The near history of the development of our current frontier, the digital one, offers some inspiration. In its origins, the internet had a Wild West ethos that allowed individual participants, including kids, a lot of room to play.[18] That playful spirit is alive and well, but the terrain has shifted. Increasingly, the Wild West ethos seems to be manifesting itself in a gold rush for data.[19] Institutions in the private and public sectors have a "grab data now, figure out what to do with it later" mentality. That adventuresome spirit certainly brings some societal benefits with it. Technological, entrepreneurial, and other forms of innovation are powerful drivers for economic, educational, and other key areas of growth—but not if they come in the form of individual or institutional decisions that keep the gold for the grown-ups and give kids lumps of coal.

We need to let kids have their own Wild West. Protecting the frontier of childhood requires that adults make conscious choices to impose limits. We need limits around those types of childhood experiences we track digitally.[20] We need limits around how we share and use the data that we do collect.[21] Playing requires room to experiment within reasonable bounds, without too much attention from or accountability to others. There is a tension here: without bounds, play becomes more *Lord of the Flies*, less *Peter Pan*. But with too many bounds, play loses its essence of exploring, making mistakes, learning from mistakes, and then doing it all over again.

The focus of this analysis is on experiences that adults share or that adults set up children to share, like giving a toddler a smart toy. But this same principle of play would certainly apply to situations where older kids and teens are making their own choices about which data to share and why. Here's a concrete example: a parent chooses not to use a toilet-training app with unclear privacy policies. We also need to limit the potential negative consequences from those experiences we do track. So the potty programmer flushes its old privacy policies and replaces them with a guarantee not to reshare toilet-training data with any third parties, including data aggregators.

There are plenty of other examples. A summer theater camp decides not to take digital pictures of campers until opening night to avoid making the teen performers nervous as they rehearse. When the curtain rises and the flashes go off, the camp puts pictures on its website only after the teens themselves and their parents give consent to publication of specific pictures. For its part, the admissions office at the local community college agrees not to Google applicants or, if it does, to notify applicants of any results that surface that give the office pause and give the affected applicants a chance to explain the content. That way, if a picture of Lady Macbeth from that summer camp production, dressed in black and holding a bloody knife, is made into a meme, it won't raise concerns about the applicant's mental stability. She'll explain: "This is not a sorry sight. It's just a spotlight on my future stardom!"

Social media and other tech platforms frequented by parents, teachers, and other adults could develop more features to encourage choices that protect play, such as a feature that asks, "Are you sure you want to post this about your child because it could have the following consequences?" We could also look to companies for parent versions of kid-focused platforms. We have YouTube Kids and new Google services for kids.[22] But what about YouTube Parents or Facebook Parents: ways for parents to connect without these platforms tracking, aggregating, or otherwise using data about the parents' kids?[23] For example, Facebook could leave up a post from a parent about toilet training with the privacy settings that the parent picked but couldn't pass that information through to third parties in any way or use information from it for its own internal market analysis or product development.

These are just a few examples of human-centered and tech-centered solutions to protect play,[24] but implementation of the same principle could be pursued using laws or regulations. A legal toolkit seems best suited to regulating governmental, commercial, or other institutional conduct rather than monitoring parental conduct directly.[25]

For instance, the federal Department of Education could pass rules requiring colleges and universities that take any funds from the Department of Education to adopt some version of the "don't Google or explain the Google results transparently" privacy-protecting approach outlined above. Government agencies outside of the education realm could also limit the uses to which they put private data about kids. An agency in charge of public benefits might commit to use family data to make public benefits decisions but not to engage in predictive analytics around any sensitive (yet arguably relevant to public benefits administration) life events, such as trying to determine which kids in a family might become teenage parents themselves.

We could think bigger than the rules or policies promulgated by individual federal agencies. We could have a federal law that prohibits all federal agencies, as well as state and local agencies that receive federal funds, from making sensitive predictions or decisions—around education, public benefits, and job training programs, to name a few—based on all or certain types of digital data collected about kids and teens, whether directly from them or from adults about them. For example, we could allow the use of data to determine the grade in which a child should be enrolled but not allow it to be used for third-party data analytic software that attempts to determine which children will be truant from school.

This type of federal law could also be written to apply to private companies engaged in interstate commerce. It could be broadly written or more sector-specific. Here is a valuable example: in 2014, California passed a law limiting what ed tech companies can do with the digital data they collect about students. Under the Student Online Personal Information Protection Act (SOPIPA),[26] these restrictions on ed tech companies include a prohibition on using student data for "targeted advertising" or the "creation of a profile of data on an individual student unless the profile is 'amassed' for 'K–12 school purposes.'"[27] This state law aims to fill gaps in the existing federal legal framework for student data privacy by regulating companies that collect digital data directly (rather than looking to parents and schools to be gatekeepers for youth data privacy) and specifically delineating activities prohibited by companies that the legislature found to be threatening to kids and teens.

Congress could follow California's lead for ed tech companies nationwide and prohibit marketing, profiling, or other high-stakes activities based on student data. Congress could go beyond ed tech companies and require the same of all companies that know or have reason to know that they collect digital data about youth—whether from youth directly or parents, teachers, and other adults on behalf of youth. Congress could also look to regulate earlier on in the digital data acquisition cycle and intervene at the stage of data collection, rather than waiting to the stage of data use.

As effective as it could be, the prospect of broad federal legal reform around youth digital data privacy seems as far away as the stars that guided Peter and the Darling children. In recent years, even more limited efforts at federal law reform around youth digital data privacy (for student privacy specifically) have failed.[28] And given the tech sector's focus on digital data as a profit source, the many other sectors (both public and private) that rely on digital data for various purposes, and our collective reliance on digital devices, comprehensive federal statutory or regulatory reform around youth digital data privacy will likely continue to be light years away.

At the moment, perhaps that's just as well. Federal legislation and regulation can be cumbersome and overbroad, running the risk of stifling innovation by state legislatures, regulators, and other actors in the public and private sectors. Let's play around ourselves. What would it look like to think about play as a positive motivator for legal reform, whether at the federal or state level?

So far, the suggestions we have explored around potential legal reform are protectionist. Privacy is used to protect childhood and adolescence as a space for play. Through creating virtual boundaries around these life stages—in terms of what can be done with information about those humans in those stages—we are enabling experimentation, the process of making and learning from mistakes. But protection is, as lawyers like to say, a floor, not a ceiling. Let's blow the roof off the ceiling. How could law be used to promote childhood and adolescence as life-stages-grounded play in our digital world?

We could spend money, offering public funding to companies or other entities that create "digital content and services of social, civic, artistic, cultural, educational and recreational benefit to all children."[29] This language comes from recent guidelines issued by the Council of Europe's Committee of Ministers on how its member states can "respect, protect and fulfill the rights of the child in the digital environment."[30] These guidelines recognize a "right to engage in play."[31] Although these guidelines are not binding on the United States, we could look to them—and we could one up them.

We could spend public money to incentivize the creation of these types of digital content and services that include both youth and their parents, their teachers, and other trusted adults. We could think about a massive investment in building the digital equivalent of neighborhood playgrounds or national parks. What would the new city-level Digital Parks Advisory

Committees design?[32] Could they build hybrid outdoor digital spaces where kids and adults alike could play in actual and virtual sandboxes? What would a future federal Digital Wilderness Act give us?[33] Could a digital space be created that is secured for the online equivalent of hiking through pristine mountains: no advertising, no surveillance, no trace left of the experience? We have no idea. Yet. That's the beauty of it: we can start to build it, and the playing will come.

In part, it will come because we will play in the process. Just as our kids do, we will need some room to experiment in the digital realm. These suggestions illustrate some ways the legal and regulatory toolkit could be used to foster youth digital lives that are protective of play and the benefits that flow from exploration, experience, and learning from mistakes. They are not the only, the best, or even necessary ways. We will doubtless have some false starts as we try to foster play in the digital realm. We will try again. We will have partners. New questions about digital life are giving rise to new collaborations on new projects. Many of these collaborative ventures represent what Urs Gasser, a leading scholar of digital governance, terms "multistakeholder" digital governance:[34] different sectors joining forces to tackle complex, unprecedented, and rapidly evolving challenges. In a sense, there is an element of play—in a pure, noncommercial sense of the term—to this approach. Let's dump our toys out together and see if we can make this pig fly.

It's not all fun and games. Each sector has its own values, goals, and other structures. Sometimes, there is conflict between or within sectors. Sometimes, in order to achieve a certain principled outcome, one sector needs to have the final say. It's important for the market sector to contribute to the fight against child pornography. It's imperative that the government have the power to prosecute and incarcerate child predators. It's crucial for leaders and employees in the market sector to pledge not to create a "Muslim registry."[35] It's essential that the court system remain open to address the violations of core civil rights and liberties that would arise from a government attempt to contract out such a registry. It's beneficial when the government makes grants to get new types of tech businesses up and running.[36] It's bedrock that the market sector produces based on private innovation and investment, within legal limits. As in many play spaces, sometimes one side is stronger than the other. Red rover, red rover, send the government right over. Psych! I want to play with the tech sector instead! Just kidding. No take-backs.

What is the team of grown-ups going to look like that helps put the play back in the internet? The eagles and the drones are available. Countless other combinations of players are as well. Much like the eagle and drone saga, it's too soon to tell who will win this particular race. In part, the crystal ball is murky because it's unclear what winning would look like. Would it mean that kids and teens are taught how to play so that they can monetize their creations? Would it mean that they are taught how to play without concern about entrepreneurship? Somewhere in between? There are normative value judgments at work in all proposed toolkits. Sometimes, these are explicit. Other times, they are implicit. When assessing attempted solutions, it's important to think critically about what those are and whether you agree with them.

Many stakeholders are rushing to innovate at this intersection of the internet and play. Much like the eagle-drone match-up, some of these innovators are arising at the intersection of the digital and the traditional. For example, traditional brick-and-mortar toy companies are starting to think more outside of the proverbial shrink-wrapped box. In summer 2017, Mattel debuted a new figure: a chief technical officer (CTO). The good news: the CTO doesn't need batteries. Now for the bad: you can't find him in any store or app near you. The CTO lives only in Mattel's headquarters, where he is in charge of creating "digital physical" experiences for children.[37] At the moment, the CTO is rare enough to be a collector's edition. You won't find that he has many counterparts in corporate toy headquarters across the country.[38] He's unlikely to be lonely for long, though. Making and selling toys aren't child's play. The toy and game industry is a huge market and creative force. Toy manufacturers are realizing that they need to transcend the online-offline divide to engage children where the children dwell. A CTO can help lead the way to Interland.

Wait, where's Interland? Why hasn't Siri given you directions yet? Siri, you @#$# piece of !@#$@#.

Stop screaming. Everyone in the world will be able to hear you when your meltdown gets filmed and posted on YouTube.

You can find Interland courtesy of another recent adult addition to the collective project of reimagining the internet as a place for more and better child's play: a new "Be Internet Awesome" curriculum from Google and the nonprofit iKeepSafe (iKS).[39] It contains a lot of lessons that take place in Interland, a designation that evokes Neverland. The curriculum seems to present this realm as simultaneously real and make-believe. The real part is that kids can get to Interland anytime, anyplace, anywhere. It's a real destination, a few clicks, swipes, or simply steps, if you're taking the sensor or wearable route, away. The pretend part is that you go there to play games, tell stories about your and your friends' lives, and generally get away from the "here" of everyday life.

It's a fair portrayal. The digital world is a liminal space. But is it a space that should displace or even replace Neverland? Not the Disney version but that frontier of unfettered childhood play for which Neverland is a general signifier. Digital Neverland should respect the original. It should integrate principles of the original. It should not destroy or co-opt the original.

The Google-iKS curriculum is a massive undertaking designed to help teach kids how to develop safe and rewarding online lives. This is a map that needs to be drawn, with a destination that is broadly accepted as desirable. However, this and all similar educational ventures should empower kids to do more than navigate the digital world as they find it. Our children need to feel they can change the digital world: often, "young people themselves are the ones who are best positioned to solve the problems that arise from their digital lives."[40] Finding Interland is not enough. We need to make sure that kids can build a new world and that we can too.

At its core, play pushes boundaries. It creates new worlds. Sometimes these are internal. Other times, they are interpersonal, institutional, or virtual. A map can get you started. It can't get you all the way there. Play on![41]

Forget: Creating Clean Slates and Room for Reinvention

What happens when play fails? What happens when we're not playing and we do something thoughtless, cruel, or embarrassing? Can we just sweep the mistakes into an old toy bin and forget about them?

In the early 2000s, New York City's Metropolitan Transportation Authority put up posters in its subways that said more or less, "Sometimes you have to go backward to go forward." This public service campaign was intended to make riders feel less grumpy about subway repairs, but the same basic concept applies to growing up. You have to go backward to go forward. You have to make mistakes in order to grow. You have to remember your past in order to leave it behind.

Kids and teens today do not have the good fortune of actual ignorance or benevolent amnesia on the part of people and institutions they encounter as adults. There is too much remembering and not enough forgetting.[42] Today's youth are the digital superstars of their own existence, from womb to dorm and beyond. They leave a trail, much of it not generated by them. Even as recently as the 1990s, the only computer-based trail young people were likely to have associated with them was their time playing the video game *Oregon Trail*. For Generation X and even some of Generation Y, the identity of your high school boyfriend might be something that only a few people in your adult life know. Maybe that data detail is enshrined in hard copy in your senior yearbook gathering dust in your parents' attic. But only the moths know.[43]

To kick it old-school media style for a moment, think about *Say Anything*, a classic teen movie from the 1980s.[44] When John Cusack's character, Lloyd Dobler, holds up his boom box to blast a Peter Gabriel song to his beloved, no one live streams a video. Today, that iconic exchange would live far after the first love faded. And Lloyd probably would just AirDrop the song anyway. Or maybe Diane's father, who hates Lloyd, would film the whole thing, put the video on YouTube's "Jerks who want to date my daughter" channel, and then turn the footage over to the police for a trespassing prosecution. And then either that video would be played by the best man at their wedding in the "happily ever after" version, or in the version where they break up after high school, it would be played furtively by each of them.

The digital world remembers. It's set up to remember. But it needs to learn how to forget the silly, stupid, and insensitive things kids and teens do, especially when adults are choosing whether to record them. We need to think more about how the digital realm could forget childhood. Right now, we're thinking more about how to make sure all remembering is done consensually and safely. So we're thinking about up-front consent by parents or protection from unauthorized third-party access. We do think about data destruction, but more as a security measure than as a principle of limited use.[45]

The European Union (EU) is doing more than thinking about forgetting. It is creating new, robust, and still evolving legal protections for individuals that empower them to require certain holders and users of their digital data to forget about them—if certain criteria are met. Under the new General Data Protection Regulation (GDPR), which went into effect on May 25, 2018, EU "subjects"[46] have a legal "right to erasure," more commonly called the "right to be forgotten."[47] Erasure is like taking one of those old-fashioned pink rubber erasers from school supplies circa 1990 to the digital data that a given data controller has about a person: under certain circumstances, following a request from that person, the controller has an "obligation to erase personal data without undue delay."[48]

Among the many reasons this right can be invoked are that the "data subject has given his or her consent [to personal data use] as a child and is not fully aware of the risks involved by the processing, and later wants to remove such personal data, especially on the internet."[49] However, this basis for erasure does not appear to apply when that child's parents shared the data themselves, or even when those parents gave consent for the child to share the data directly: "The GDPR has been partially inspired by COPPA [the US Children's Online Privacy Protection Act]," which is a parental consent-based framework.[50]

For children under age sixteen and, in certain EU member states, under age thirteen, parental consent is now required in most circumstances before digital data can be collected from children themselves. It is unclear how much erasing young adults in the EU can do of data that their parents gave consent for them to share. And it does not appear that this right reaches data that was sharented about them in their youth because it was not their consent that was required to share it in the first place. It was their parents' decision rather than theirs.

Even if young adults in the EU are able to force the forgetting of previously sharented information, young adults in the United States have no such legal right. In the United States, we don't have any type of federal legal right to be forgotten for kids or anyone else.[51] The law—on the state level—mandates such complete forgetfulness only when the juvenile justice system is involved. Those records are confidential, often remain sealed, and can't be ported over into adult life in many situations.[52] The rehabilitation rationale in the juvenile justice realm requires both real-time and future protection from disclosure. This protection allows rehabilitation to take place and allows the adult that the child has fathered to enter adulthood unencumbered by any stigma or other life-altering consequences of child-hood actions.

The penalties for disclosure of juvenile justice records can be severe. It may be a criminal offense for a party to a juvenile justice case to share records from that case outside of the other parties.[53] A post from Aunt Polly that reads, "Court today for Tommy. Tommy testified that Huck made him do it, but Judge still slapped him w/ two years in juvie for faking his own death. Here's a copy of the court order #injustice" would be criminal con-duct. But a post that reads, "Tommy faked his own death today. Damn Huck. Grateful for his return but want to wring his neck!!" would be fine. We find ourselves in a strange situation where juvenile misbehavior that leads to involvement with the juvenile justice system triggers the strongest possible privacy protection. In contrast, misbehavior that stays out of the system is entitled to little or no privacy protection.

The takeaway isn't to get rid of the privacy protections for the juvenile justice system or to place even more situations into this system. We need to import the animating insight from this system (that learning from mis-takes requires a clean slate going forward) to our treatment of childhood experiences more broadly. We need to explore whether and how children and teens deserve a "right to be forgotten" or "reputation bankruptcy"[54] with respect to those pieces of private data that parents, teachers, and other adult decision makers capture, create, and use about them without their knowledge or consent.

There would need to be plenty of carve-outs for appropriate medical, educational, governmental, and other uses. Such a right wouldn't require a doctor's office to dump a childhood vaccination record. But it might require Instagram to remove a picture a parent posts of a child's face covered in a rash, if the child reaches age eighteen and goes through an appropriate pro-cess with the social media company that posted the picture. Indeed, social media companies already provide a way for parents to request the removal of or impose limits around certain information about their children.[55] It gets trickier, however, when we start to think about an eighteenth birthday as bringing with it a legal right to have content previously shared by par-ents, teachers, and other adult caregivers removed.

The First Amendment looms large here. What about the scenario where a child breaks from an evangelical Christian family in adulthood and requests that all family photos involving the child be removed from social media because the photos demonstrate the prior religious affiliation of the child? For the law to require a social media company to remove that post or to require parents themselves to take down the posts raises serious free speech and free exercise problems that the parents may well assert,[56] even if the company provided prior notice about granting the removal right for young adults when they come of age.

The parents have constitutionally protected rights to their freedom of conscience and speech. These rights include the freedom to practice and talk about their religion. The Fourteenth Amendment joins with the First to supercharge those rights when it comes to childrearing.[57] As discussed above, parents enjoy heightened protections of domestic privacy to guide their children's religious upbringing.

However, parents can't use religious freedom as a shield to avoid compliance with criminal law or most other laws of general applicability to protect public welfare and safety. They can use it as a sword, however, to pierce almost all barriers to private worship and public dialogue about this devotion. Taking their kids to an evangelical church is private worship. Taking a picture and putting it online transforms this private moment into public engagement about religious belief. It's a lot like giving your kids a bunch of flyers to sell on street corners to spread your family's understanding of the gospel. Such an arrangement is so last century and likely also illegal.

Why isn't it a #1stamendment #foul for the government to make parents keep their kids off the street but not off the information superhighway? Is it reverse digital discrimination? On first glance, it might appear that the odds of a First Amendment victory rest with whether the speech is happening online or off. But look beneath the surface. Whether the road is pavement or fiber optic is irrelevant. What matters is whether the activity that is happening on the literal or digital sidewalks is legally defined as one that can be regulated under public welfare and safety laws.

Having kids stand on street corners to sell religious literature? That's child labor, according to the Supreme Court, so state laws that regulate children's employment to protect them from unsound and unsafe practices can be enforced. Enforcement may occur even when the labor implicates the free exercise of religion and other constitutional rights. When the aunt of a nine-year-old girl let her ward offer religious material for sale on the street corners of Massachusetts, in contravention of the applicable state child labor law, the US Supreme Court held up a stop sign: "Neither rights of religion nor rights of parenthood are beyond limitation. Acting to guard the general interest in youth's well being, the state as parens patriae may restrict the parent's control by . . . regulating or prohibiting the child's labor, and in many other ways."[58] The aunt's criminal conviction stood.

What about when kids are pictured online? Let's return to our hypothetical evangelical family. Let's say that the posted picture of the kids in their Sunday best showed them holding open copies of the New Testament, with this caption: "Know the truth." The posting of that picture isn't considered to be child labor under existing federal and state child labor laws. Posting the picture does not result in kids' offering any items for sale or performing any service for compensation. There are situations in which a picture posted of a child online could implicate child labor laws. For example, when a child participates in a photo shoot for a fashion designer and the resulting pictures are put up online, child labor laws apply to regulate the duration and circumstances of the photo shoot itself. But in this and similar instances, child labor law is concerned with the circumstances of the acts captured in the picture, not the posting of the picture. Even though kids' private data is being used by parents and other trusted adults to obtain free or low-cost digital services, the law does not tend to see transactions of this data as a form of child labor.

Forget the law. (Isn't forgetting fun?) Let's think instead about what social media and other digital tech companies might offer in their privacy policies and terms of use. As a matter of private contract between the company and the user, why couldn't the companies reserve the right to remove any data an adult user transmits about a minor after that child turns eighteen, subject to the child-turned-adult's request? Such provisions would put the adult user on notice of this reasonable limitation on its rights to control private data about children. The adult user could choose to use or not use the service with this understanding in mind.

You might hear Silicon Valley screaming: "This would take too much work!" (Insert angry emoji faces here.) Yes, it would take a lot of work. However, there would be plenty of ways to make it less work than it might initially seem. The companies would need to put a process in place for the requesting party to prove that she is the child whose data was shared. The companies then could limit the types of data subject to removal to content that might harm privacy or cause embarrassment to a reasonable person. The companies could require that the requesting party make a credible showing of why the data requested for removal falls into one of those categories. The companies could put some categories of data completely off limits for removal, such as data more than a decade old or data that has been irrevocably mixed in with the adult user's data such that it would not be possible to disaggregate. Data picked up from smart home appliances, for instance, might well fall into that second category.

It seems unlikely that this type of private-market solution would be offered by companies. In addition to the legitimate concerns about workload, which likely could be mitigated through thoughtful tailoring, there is a more fundamental problem: where is the market cohort that would push for this new privacy or terms-of-use provision?

The companies could come up with some type of market-based partial solution to the problem of digital forgetting. But we adults are unlikely to want it. Even if we recognize that we may need to rethink our tech habits, we're unlikely to push tech companies to give our future adult children a contractual right to revise our tech decisions. Kids and teens might think it's a great idea, but they are still not the market force their parents are. And a legal framework that requires this type of child-turned-adult revisionist history risks running afoul of constitutional requirements and spirit, as discussed above.

It's probably best, then, to forget about a childhood "right to be forgotten." Perhaps the more appropriate right to consider is the "right to respond." As long as data brokers and other third parties continue to aggregate and use private information, federal law or regulation could institute one or more centralized bureaus for the oversight and handling of this information. As part of such a comprehensive data broker, social credit, reputation bureau scheme,[59] teens could be entitled to a credit report–type disclosure of the digital data about them that is out there when they turn eighteen.[60] The bureau could have in place a mechanism for youth to respond or provide a counternarrative to the picture of their youth that is available in the digital space and to request corrections of specific information that the brokers and bureau themselves are storing.

Even painting with purposefully broad-brush strokes, many tensions and issues come into focus with such a scheme. Chief among them is that such an approach would add yet another layer of data aggregation and surveillance. Existing credit bureaus operate with a business model that could be described as letting the fox mind the hen house. Expanding that business model beyond financial data to other personal digital data would be like letting that fox open a restaurant and dish out eggs Florentine.

The following colloquy between Senator John Kennedy (Republican of Louisiana) and the former CEO of Equifax at a federal legislative committee hearing in fall 2017 lays out the heart of the credit bureau model with the precision of a four-star chef.[61]

Kennedy: You collect my [financial] information, without my permission. You take it, along with everyone else's information, and you sell that information to businesses. Is that basically correct?

Former Equifax CEO: That's largely correct.

Kennedy and his colleagues in the Senate went on to discuss the tensions inherent in this model of data collection and use. Credit bureaus, which are private businesses, collect sensitive financial data, like how much debt you have and how well you're paying it back. They don't ask your permission. They aggregate that data and analyze that data. They sell the data to other private businesses. Those businesses use that data to make monumental decisions about your access to essential opportunities, like getting a mortgage. Sometimes, those opportunities go beyond consumer purchase transactions, like whether or not you're qualified for a certain job.

And when the credit bureaus fail to safeguard your data, like the massive Equifax data breach that Senator Kennedy was inquiring about, they offer you data monitoring and related services. These services may be free, but the chickens will come home to roost. For the credit bureaus, doing a crappy job may be the goose that laid the golden egg. They acquire a captive market of new customers who wind up paying them extra to do what they were supposed to be doing in the first place: serving as responsible and effective data stewards.

This business model is rather like an unscrupulous tow truck company that is hired by businesses to remove illegally parked cars from their lots. The car owners haven't asked for their cars to be moved. And it's not clear that removing these cars is the best way to free up access to these businesses or achieve any other commerce-related goals. But let's stipulate that removing these cars is authorized by law and is essential to the free flow of commerce.

The towing company scoops up the cars but leaves them in the middle of the highway, where the cars get hit by other cars. The towing company tells the owners that it will tow their cars to safety free of charge. It won't fix the cars because it doesn't know how. (It's a towing company, not *Car Talk*.[62] *Car Talk* knows everything about cars and about talk.) But the towing company will get the cars out of the highway, preventing further destruction. The company takes those cars to a parking lot in the middle of nowhere.

The cars have crossed to safety, but as novelist Wallace Stegner has told us, the story isn't over so quickly.[63] If the owners want to regain full use of their cars and ensure their cars won't be whisked away again, they need to pay the towing company for additional services. Indefinitely. That's right: the company that you never asked to work with in the first place and that has led to the wreckage of your car, now has the chutzpah to ask you to pay it to do more work with your car. You don't trust this company, but you have few or no other options for getting the work done. And the work needs to be done. Your car might keep running without the repairs, but disaster could strike at any moment. You'd rather not go from sixty to zero the hard way.

The car in this scenario is your credit history and all the personal information it contains—Social Security number, date of birth, addresses, debts. The towing company is the credit bureau, collecting this and other information without your explicit consent and often without your knowledge.[64]

A free-market capitalist system does need mechanisms that facilitate fair, efficient, and productive matches between borrowers and lenders. Lenders find money trees hard to grow, and borrowers find them hard to climb. For lenders, having a standardized screening for borrowers' creditworthiness helps them run their businesses. For individual borrowers, having this system helps them access loan options quickly. The digital data system of the credit report and credit score seems like everyone has struck pay dirt.

If the hen house of consumer lending needs to be guarded, why are the Senators on the hunt for the credit bureaus? Because the bureaus are doing a rather lousy job, and the current legal and regulatory landscape offers few incentives for improvement. Credit bureaus lack transparency and accountability. They mess up a lot. They take in inaccurate information. They fail to fix it. Consumers need to request copies of their credit reports, review the information, then make a written request for any changes.[65] That's right: an industry designed to be a data broker isn't worried about how broken its own processes and quality control are.

The bureaus know where we live. They know where we used to live. They probably can predict with a reasonable degree of certainty where we'll be living ten years from now. So why can't they drop us a note and let us know when something is inaccurate? And use our credit card information to book the movers, while they're at it? If that's too much trouble, could they at least let us know when someone steals our credit card information to book movers, move books, or pay bookies?

Well, they could. Sometimes, they actually do. Often, they make us pay them for the privilege of telling us when this theft has occurred. Take the Equifax data breach, which is believed to have resulted in the theft of private consumer data from over half of adults in the United States. Equifax's failure to take straightforward data security measures made the theft possible.[66] As soon as thieves have this information, it can be used for a variety of purposes that cause concrete harm to us, the rightful owners of the information, such as obtaining new credit or a fraudulent income tax return. Harm can also manifest in less tangible forms, such as the stress that comes from anticipating the possibility of future harm.[67]

Equifax told us all about the breach free of charge. Then it offered us monitoring and notification services to let us know if our stolen information was used for unauthorized activities. It also offered us the ability to lock our information so that it couldn't be used at all. These offers initially were made on a "freemium" basis: free of charge for a period of time, after which payment was required.[68] Even though Equifax backed down on some of its proposed charges, it still stands to benefit financially from the mess it created.[69] Last one to sign up is a rotten egg.

Back to our hypothetical social credit and reputation bureau scheme. Let's say it's possible to establish a bureau that works effectively and fairly. Even with effective and fair functioning, such a bureau still would require a high level of digital literacy for young adults to navigate. There are other potential interventions in addition to or instead of this one that could promote forgetting. For instance, social media companies could offer an "auto-forget" option that applies to all content in an adult feed that is demonstrably about kids. This auto-destroy option would have a few advantages over current privacy settings, mostly that you could "set it and forget it" rather than having to go back through and manually remove or change the privacy settings for certain content as your kids get older.[70] And it wouldn't suffer from the problems of the childhood "right to be forgot-ten" scenario where kids have removal rights after they come of age.

Here, adults could make a decision such that they could enjoy the bene-fits of social media or similar digital technologies at one point in time and have their engagement with these technologies develop along with their children's development. App developers could also get in on the action. There may be an emerging market for an app that is interoperable with major social media, retail, and other heavily trafficked sites that would opt out of posts about kids from any data aggregation and set an auto-destroy function.

There could also be legal limitations on the specific uses of childhood data over time. For instance, just as negative information on a credit report drops off after seven years, a schema for a data broker bureau could include a mandatory erasure of certain private and sensitive data about a juvenile after the juvenile turns twenty-five, which is seven years after the legal age of majority. Other tech, legal, and other types of devices could achieve sim-ilar or complementary results. Here's the key direction: if the child is going to father the man, after a certain point, the child needs to fade away for the adult to enter stage left. Sometimes, you have to stop looking backward to go forward.

7 Second Star on the Right: Taking Flight in the Digital Era

The internet needs to forget. We need to remember. We need to remember our earlier selves and our current selves. We need to remember to connect with both of these so that we're making thoughtful decisions that empower our children and also our own lives. We need to connect with our kids, our partners, our families, our friends, and our communities in more mindful ways.

Connect: Caring about Our Selves and Our Children

"Only connect!" implores E. M. Forster.[1] Well, Aunt Polly is going to follow that mandate. But how? Aunt Polly is going to blab. She can't help herself. She *wants* to. She *needs* to. She's fed up. She's mad as hell, and she's not going to take it anymore. This teenager, bless his heart, is ruining her life. Tommy is ungrateful. He's unrepentant. Hell, he's a criminal. Before he came along, before her sister left and stuck her with Tommy, her life was just peachy, thank you very much. Her own kids were angels. Well, they were manageable. She made it to bingo night. She made it to knitting class. She ran church committees. Now, she's getting calls from the school principal all the time: "Tommy did this," "Tommy didn't do that," "Get here right now." She's become intimately acquainted with the local police station. The church committees are excluding her. Maybe not explicitly, but her email address isn't that damn hard to remember, so why didn't anyone tell her about last week's meeting?

Because everyone in town knows: Tommy is a delinquent. Her friends in town are abandoning her. Her colleagues and neighbors are barely even polite anymore. Why shouldn't she share with her Facebook friends? Maybe the boy who sat next to her in eighth-grade civics cares, or if he doesn't care, maybe he doesn't hate her because Tommy threw eggs at his car. She needs connections, community, caring, and she doesn't have time or ability to find it closer to home. Isn't it better for her to find the support she needs to soldier on? And if she's able to enjoy free access to the digital media curation supplied by her friends in her Facebook newsfeed along the way, isn't that a nice fringe benefit?

The drive for human contact—to see and be seen, to hear and be heard, to understand and be understood—is strong and positive. That more of these social connections are now digital—in "networked space," as leading privacy theorist Julie E. Cohen calls it—does not alter this drive.[2] We aim to nurture our children with sustained, genuine connections, both with us and with others. The adult urge to connect with one another—especially to seek advice, reassurance, and commiseration around the inevitable hassles of raising children—is positive. It shows maturity. It shows emotional and psychological resilience. It shows willingness to learn from new ideas. It is positive in and of itself. It's the how, why, when, and with whom we connect that is often problematic for our children. We are connecting, but we are not reflecting. We are connecting but not necessarily sustaining ourselves or addressing those needs that are driving us to describe our most intimate challenges with our children as "status updates" or in 140 characters or to record them in the format of Nest Cam footage.[3]

What can we do to "only connect" more mindfully? We can think before we click.[4] We can reflect more on what we are hoping to accomplish when we share our children's digital data. When we share, are we really looking for something more complex and elusive than a certain number of likes? By identifying and querying our reasons for sharing certain information in a certain context, we may make more mindful choices. By being in better touch with our own needs, desires, and fears, we may direct our energies in an ever more constructive and productive fashion.[5]

We can also think about our kids before we click. You'd tell your teenager not to post a selfie from the bathtub. You should think about telling yourself not to post a shot of your toddler in the tub.[6] You'd tell your teenager to use social media to create a positive portrayal of herself so future employers will be impressed by her savvy dissection of current events rather than how many tequila shots she had at Tommy's #houseparty last weekend, so you should think about telling yourself to post only a tasteful update about your ten-year-old's success at baseball rather than the fight he got into with his younger sister after the game ended. You can think of this "digital dossier"[7] creation strategy as the "holiday card" rule of thumb: if you wouldn't put it in hard copy and mail it to a few hundred people in your life for display on their refrigerators, don't put it on the internet for thousands of people in, near, or outside of your life to repurpose and display indiscriminately.

We can think about kids, but actual youth input in and control of data-sharing decisions is largely a matter of personal and institutional connections. The law provides a limited to nonexistent framework for youth agency around whether, when, and why adults share their data. Even when kids under age thirteen go online and share their data in a commercial context, federal law doesn't require the digital service provider to get the kids' consent. Under the Children's Online Privacy Protection Act (COPPA), the provider must get consent from a parent.[8] Our legal system is deeply committed to parents as gatekeepers for their children's privacy and activities, so the primacy of parental consent isn't going to change.

The individual choices of parents, teachers, and other adults are another story. All of us can look for more and better ways to connect with the kids in our care to learn from and with them. For instance, parents can actively involve children in creating not just family media plans, as recommended by the American Academy of Pediatrics,[9] but also a family data privacy plan.

That plan can be a quick three parts: (1) familial concerns about and commitments to privacy, (2) research into the terms of use and other policies about existing or potential digital services that best align with the set of expressed preferences, and (3) some family habits that promote regular and responsible use of these or similar services. Some stock habits that might work well include the "holiday card" rule of thumb and "what would a thirteen-year-old say?"[10] "What would smart Elmo say?" is also a possibility, but it's unclear whether Muppet artificial intelligence is more or less intelligent than an average adolescent.

Teens and kids are increasingly learning about how to use their real intelligence to make decisions about their digital privacy and other parts of their digital lives. Sometimes, those decisions include blocking parents from seeing certain social media content.[11] Schools, other learning spaces, tech companies, and other institutions are offering more lessons about data privacy or "digital citizenship" more broadly.

These learning experiences are likely to become more common. Notably, in 2016, Washington state passed a law that appears to be the first of its type in the country that requires digital citizenship instruction in schools.[12] There is a movement underway to persuade other states to follow suit.

How "digital citizenship" will be defined and taught is still evolving, but under any conceivable definition, it should be a level of instruction that was not available to today's parents when they were kids back in Tom Sawyer's time. Youth today are likely to possess a level of sophistication with their digital self-creation skills that transcends their parents'. Parents presumably will continue to possess superior skills in navigating the brick-and-mortar world and its institutions and in engaging in the type of risk-assessment "executive-functioning" skills that neuroscience tells us are more the province of the "olds" than of the youngins.

The likelihood that Tommy or any other of today's Tom Sawyers will want to sit down for a family summit and action planning is slim. They're too busy white-washing the fence all by themselves, without even being asked. But even in the absence of some sort of defined plan, a parental habit of checking in with children and teens as digital data decisions are made has the potential for significant positive impact on parental practices. Teachers, educational administrators, school boards, legislative committees, vendors, and other decision makers outside the home also would do well do solicit youth input into data-handling decisions and options. Twenty-first-century Toms are lighting up digital territories. We can glean some insights from the paths they blaze.

Respect: Valuing Children's Digital Capital

You're online, flipping between your work email, your former girlfriend's Instagram pics, and your local news channel. You get a pop-up ad: "Tom & Huck Bro Co.: we give the olds a raft to ride through digital waters." Sick of meeting requests, #blessed photos, and parking structure drama, you click. You laugh. Tom & Huck is a company of teenagers offering to serve as "personal guides to help adults have fun and be cool online." They charge $50 for each consulting session and less if you do a package. You laugh some more. Then you click on their YouTube channel. You're stunned into silence. Their last "how to" video had 2 million views. Since when did kids stop painting fences and start running the internet?[13]

Most kids aren't tiny tech tycoons.[14] Most kids are players in the tech marketplace, though, through their own interactions with digital services and those of the adults in their lives. As we make decisions about whether and when to exchange our children's private data for free or low-cost digital services, we need to "follow the money." We don't need to go full Money-ball and come up with a dollar figure. We don't even need to think that we're engaging our kids in digital day labor by our handling of their data. But we do need to recognize our kids' data as a form of currency in the twenty-first-century economy. It's also a future-cy because the choices we make about our children's private data today will likely affect their life prospects for years to come.[15] And depending on the type of content we're sharenting, we may also be taking creative content from our children that could have value to them as intellectual property—a scenario that the Council of Europe addresses when it advises member states who create play-based resources online using youth contributions to have "measures in place to protect the child [creator]'s intellectual property rights."[16]

The economics behind sharenting are typically opaque to users.[17] The website for a social media platform tells you it's free. It doesn't ask for your credit card, so you don't ask what price you're paying or how you're paying it. The app for your favorite store pushes a discount code to your phone while you're shopping. You use the code to save money, and the store uses data about your purchase for its own purposes.[18] In these and many similar transactions, your children's data is part of the transaction. Your social media posts are about your kids, and your purchases are for them. You're paying for these digital and related services in part with your kids' capital.

Ask yourself: is the service you are getting worth parting with this information about your children?[19] In some cases, the answer is yes. Let's say that you need to buy diapers and you don't have a lot of money. Diapers cost a lot of money. It's worth letting your preferred retailer figure out that your four-year-old isn't toilet-trained yet to save money on those diapers. In many other instances, though, the price seems too high. You post a You-Tube video of your child's remarkable invention at summer robot camp. It gets a lot of likes, but it also spawns a lot of copycat creators who crowd the field and undermine any potential for your child to be the leading developer of her tech vision. You contact Tom & Huck for advice. Their diagnosis: epic parent fail, yo.

Parents, teachers, and other trusted adults should not be the only stakeholders tasked with bringing more transparency to the economic realities of digital tech. Other individuals and institutions across different spheres should assess their own responsibilities for bringing the transactional aspect out of the shadows and into the sun.[20]

Building on the credit report scenario, one approach might be to work on a standardized way for industry and other big data users, like governments, to show users how much they are "paying" for a given service through their data. A related regulatory initiative could be developing standardized disclosure language that so-called free services would be required to display to users that makes clear that the service isn't free. You pay by data card or social credit rather than by debit or credit card.

A more intense intervention would be to take certain types of data off the table. You can't buy a new car by selling your baby. Such a contract would be void as a matter of public policy. Should you be able to buy social media broadcasting capacity from Facebook Live by streaming videos of that baby? What if that baby is puking everywhere? Too many videos like that and the baby, when he's a teenager, might wish you had traded him in. Before that happens, let's collectively unpack and assess the financial trade-offs we're making between our digital conveniences and our children's privacy and life opportunities.

One question we might ask ourselves is whether we are getting enough in return for what we are giving up. Digital tech brings us efficiencies. It brings us opportunities for creation, education, and countless other variations on these and related themes. Should we demand even more?

Here's a question we might ask ourselves as we think about the many directions in which we might pursue respect. We're sharing a lot about our kids, and all sectors, including schools and the government, are starting to learn a lot about our kids because of this sharing. What additional opportunities could we seek for our kids as a result of this sharing rather than accepting that the sharing may put them at risk?

For example, when data-driven industries make assumptions or predictions about our kids that identify a strong likelihood of difficult and life-altering outcomes, do they have an ethical obligation to tell us as parents?[21] Should we demand that they do or take our business elsewhere? Let's go back to the oft-cited Target targeting.[22] The retail giant started mailing pregnancy-related promotions to a teenage girl, thereby outing her pregnancy to her parents. Was Target the girl's BFF? No, she hadn't confided in customer service. Target knew about her condition because it had analyzed her consumption patterns and accurately identified that she was expecting. She wasn't expecting Target to tattle.

Target apologized. Should it have? Don't we think that the parents of a pregnant minor should know about and be involved with their daughter's situation? The laws of a majority of states strongly suggest we do.[23] These laws require pregnant minors who seek to terminate their pregnancies either to tell their parents or to receive their parents' consent before getting an abortion. If parental involvement is impossible due to abuse or other familial breakdown, these minors must go before a judge and receive the judge's consent. If parental involvement is impossible due to a medical emergency that makes time of the essence, then no parental or judicial consent is required before a doctor can act. But why should we require that parents or courts be involved at all?

The answer is twofold. First, broadly speaking, the law makes parents the primary decision makers for their children's medical needs. Courts serve as a backstop. For instance, if parents' religious or other beliefs interfere with their children's receipt of vital medical care, courts will step in to protect children's health. This legal structure means that parents or courts, as a last resort, are typically involved when their children go to the doctor's office. Second, looking at abortion specifically, the law understands this medical decision as implicating the most fundamental questions of existence,[24] regardless of the age of the decision maker. The law further understands these and related questions as particularly challenging for minors. Thus, it sees a heightened urgency for parental or judicial oversight of the abortion decision.

Target, however, is not the target of parental notification or consent laws. Medical providers are. These laws have no direct bearing on the collection, storage, and use of kids' and teens' private data by private companies or other data-driven decision makers outside the doctor's office. But maybe the principles of parental involvement they contain should have some indirect bearing. Why make parents wait until their daughter belatedly announces that she's eighteen weeks pregnant and wants an abortion, at which point it may be difficult or impossible to obtain one? Teens tend to keep their secrets. If we want parents or courts involved in a pregnant minor's decision to continue or terminate her pregnancy, why not involve them as soon as practicable? If Target knows with reasonable certainty that a minor is pregnant, along with sending coupons, why doesn't it send a notice about the pregnancy to the minor's parents?

The same essential question applies to similar types of difficult circumstances that are all but guaranteed to have life-altering consequences. What if a smart baby bootie could identify with near perfect accuracy those babies who are at higher risk of SIDS? What if an ed tech app could determine which students are all but guaranteed to drop out of school? What if a child confides in a smart toy that she is being physically abused: does the company that collects that data have a mandatory reporting duty under state law?[25] Do the providers of these data-driven technologies have an ethical duty to alert the parents of the children they identify of the risks?

At first glance, these questions may seem easier than the Target query because of the tech providers' goals. The smart booty aims to empower parents with data to protect their babies. Ed tech apps aim to promote student success. Thus, the answer seems to be, "Of course, the providers should share this information. That's their raison d'être." It's like asking if Henry Ford should have made the Model T. That was the bloody point.

But the answer here isn't open and shut like a Model T door. Responding to a question about a company's ethical duty by citing its stated commercial purpose dodges the question about the ethical duty. A business motivation for a given action is not necessarily equivalent to an ethical one. Perhaps the implicit assumption is that companies have an ethical duty to fulfill their business purpose.

Even accepting that assumption, though, the question remains open. The provider could be in possession of data from past users that reveals new or updated risks. Should the tech provider have an ethical duty to continue to run ongoing analytics for past users? Such a duty would diverge from pure business interest because it would attach to individuals who were no longer paying customers, thus saying that a business's ethical duty extends only as far as its business goal risks leaving kids and their parents in harm's way. How about when these past users' data continues to inform the aggregated data set used for analytics or to teach the AI that is used to make discoveries or decisions? The provider is still deriving an active benefit from the data, even if the parents of the children whose data is being used are no longer paying customers.

We adults could use our market power and our power to lobby and vote to demand product options or the regulation of product options that would give us more access to what companies and others are learning about our kids. We could demand more bang for our buck: if you're going to gather and mine private information about our kids, give us more access to what you're learning. Learn all of the things that are serious and potentially life-altering and scary. Tell us about them so we can try to fix them. Maybe we will decide it's just not worth it to us anymore to let you learn about our kids so you can dress them, Magic Wardrobe. But if you and your friend Crystal Ball could warn us before our kids start cutting school and taking drugs that make them think talking lions are a real thing, we will gladly let you monitor their every move. We will pay for safety. We will pay for it with more private data. The world is scary. We will pay any price for security.

This is a tempting scenario. Ultimately, however, it's a trap. Adding more surveillance will only deepen the potential for dangerous or unethical third parties to misuse our children's data because more data will be available to them for such uses. And it will only deepen the difficulties that we adults are causing kids and teens as they seek to learn about themselves on their own terms.[26]

Where Did True North Go? Directions to the Dark Side

We keep our kids inside more than we used to, yet we let the outside world into our most intimate spaces via digital technologies. We let our kids' data, whether generated by us or by them with our facilitation, roam free.

As we consider how to reorient our approach to our children's digital privacy, it will be easy to spin our compass wheel aimlessly. It will be easy to lose our bearings and go right back into false trade-offs, such as the privacy versus security show-down illustrated above. It will be easy to devolve into looking for a one-stop shopping solution. It will be easy to go in wrong directions, even as we think we've found our way at last.

There are an infinite number of ways we could lose our way. Many of them fall into the category of a fear-based, "command and control" response. This solution space is tempting. It appeals to our reptilian brain. The same wiring that craves the endorphin rush of a thousand likes will, if and when our brain is convinced we need to make some changes, look for the quick fix.

Let's play out one of them. There is a longstanding legal doctrine called "attractive nuisance" that could be used as a type of deep foundation or inspiration for a more heavy-handed, "safety above all" approach to the challenges of the digital landscape. When landowners have a serious hazard on their property that is likely to appeal to children, the law requires them to take action to mitigate the risk of children coming onto their land and getting hurt.

Think about that requirement. The law recognizes that kids and teens are going to go looking for trouble and that they will follow the siren song of an abandoned well to their peril. The law places a significant burden on the well's owners to succeed where Nana failed in her duty to keep the Darling children inside, guarded against their own impulses. Why shouldn't the same animating insights and principles apply to digital terrain?[27]

These days, little Timmy can get trapped in the depths of cyberbullying, fake news, and other digital perils without leaving his couch. Data about Timmy can get attacked, misused, or repurposed beyond recognition without Timmy even pushing a button. To keep himself and his data safe, Timmy doesn't need an actual fence; he needs a virtual one: make that virtual *fences* plural.

Extrapolating from the underlying framework of attractive nuisance, we look to all the adult gate-keepers to do their part to build these boundaries around their own handling of youth digital data and the digital experiences they make available to kids and teens. The olds can't outsource this particular building task to Tommy. By and large, adults are responsible for creating digital devices and services. They are building these opportunities to be irresistible, not just attractive.[28] Are they building them to be a nuisance? Kind of. It seems unlikely that a design team sits around saying, "Let's build something that will annoy the @#$# out of everyone." But it seems very likely that a design team sits around saying, "Let's build something that everyone wants to do all the time."

When everyone stares at a screen all the time, it is a nuisance in both the colloquial and legal senses. The first sense falls into the *res ipsa loquitur* category, which is a nonobvious way lawyers say that something is obvious: "the thing speaks for itself." It's a nuisance when people walk into telephone poles because they won't look up from their screens. And this nuisance becomes a menace when a car is driven into a telephone pole for that same reason. The second sense is concerned more with that "nuisance as menace" situation. The law terms the creation of a serious potential hazard to self and others a "nuisance." In the legal sense, then, we can call it a "nuisance" when the car is driven into a telephone pole or when you apply for your first credit card and learn that your identity was stolen when you were eight days old after your proud parents posted a picture of your Social Security card online.

Under an attractive nuisance 2.0, we would say to the designers, vendors, parents, teachers, and all other adult gate-keepers of these technologies, "Put up fences. Don't let kids roam free, and don't let adults roam free with kids' data." If you don't put up the right gates—the right firewalls, the surveillance technologies, the childhood right to be forgotten as a term of use contracting, and so on—and something terrible happens, you could be legally liable for your role.

There are other legal doctrines that we could draw on to deepen a "command and control" approach. States and localities enjoy a general power to legislate to promote social welfare and protect public safety. In many places, this power is used to establish curfews for minors.[29] A curfew might say that youth under age eighteen must be home each night by 11 p.m., unless certain exceptions apply, such as going to or from a job. Sometimes, these ordinances are overly broad and struck down as violating constitutional or other rights.[30] In general, however, there is wide latitude for these types of restrictions. When a situation is known to present a heightened risk that youth will get into trouble, such as Halloween night, that line gets redrawn to permit increased regulation of youths' activities.

Social welfare and public safety legislation and regulation are also concerned with the supervision of youth even when they are back inside their homes.[31] This governmental interest commonly manifests itself in laws that require adult in-home supervision of children under a certain age, such as ten. More broadly, parents are required to supervise their children, attend to their welfare, and support them financially.[32] Typically, we don't think much about the legal foundation for these obligations placed on parents. This "parenting" subset of "adulting" gets carried out as a matter of personal responsibility and unconditional love.

But when a family is facing serious strain or dissolution, the legal system intervenes to ensure that legally acceptable parenting is in place. In divorce proceedings, the court will issue a "parenting plan" to ensure that parental responsibilities are fully and fairly allocated between the parents to ensure the "best interest of the child" is satisfied. In abuse and neglect proceedings, the court will terminate parental rights if there is no way that parents can provide baseline safety and security for their own child. These and similar legal vehicles are part and parcel of the personal freedom the law affords parents to parent as they believe to be best. Where great power goes, great responsibility should follow.

To an extent, the legal system will share this responsibility with parents. Significantly, parents who believe their child to be "in need of supervision" can ask the court to step in and essentially serve as a "super parent."[33] If a child fails to comply with lawful parental and other adult directives or otherwise engages in risky behavior, a court will issue a plan for rehabilitation. This plan can be all-encompassing in terms of the child's behavior. And it can be almost as directive when it comes to parental behavior as well. Want your unruly teen to stay away from certain peers at school or on social media? If you can get her under the court's control, you may well be able to get a "no contact" order from the court. Be careful, though, because you could wind up in court-ordered therapy yourself to explore why your teen is acting out by hanging out with the bad kids. You could also wind up for the bill for the therapy and any other services the court orders, including out-of-home placement of your child.[34] With great power and great responsibility comes massive debt.

It's plausible that also coming our way soon could be attempts by state legislatures and city councils to put together social welfare and public health requirements that tackle head on the challenges parents face as they try to raise youth in a digital age. What might a curfew on digital access look like? How different is a citywide ordinance that says "no screen time after 10 p.m. on a school night" for minors from one that says "no outside time after 10 p.m. on a school night"? You could make certain exceptions to digital curfew, as we already have with the brick-and-mortar one. Do you need to be on your laptop at 11 p.m. for your job creating fake news for a Russian troll farm? That's fine, but you can't send any late-night texts to your BFF Vladimir simply to talk about whose hands are bigger.

Most likely, your strong initial reaction here is to dismiss the digital curfew as crazy talk. Second star at the right, straight on to crazy town.[35] But it's not blowing fairy dust. Curfews are designed to ensure youth safety and public safety. These limits are intended to give parents or guardians reasonable boundaries to use to structure their kids' activities. What's the risk to youth of being outside after dark? It's that they will encounter a dangerous landscape that is too risky for them to navigate maturely. How different does that sound from many parts of the digital landscape? Would it be unreasonable for a locality or state to say, "As a matter of youth and public safety, the movement of minors across the digital landscape will be subject to reasonable safeguards, set by law or regulation, which parents will be on the front lines of imposing"? Such safeguards would be in addition to the ones already existing in law: minors can't order alcohol online, can't look at pornography, can't share personal information on most commercial websites without parental consent (if the minors are under age thirteen), and can't take many other actions.

These new "digital curfews" could be as simple as tweaking an existing curfew law: youth can't be outside their homes or on digital devices that take them virtually outside their homes after 10 p.m. What about the First Amendment, you might be thinking. Well, regular curfews also have First Amendment implications. They may limit freedom of association and the ability to engage in protected First Amendment activities, like attending a protest march that takes place after hours. They also limit the freedom to travel under the Fifth and Fourteenth Amendments. What about the Commerce Clause, the law nerds among you might be shrieking. The digital add-on to the curfew would limit interstate commerce. You are foiled, city council made of pirates. But existing curfews limit interstate commerce. If you're a seventeen-year-old living in state A and you desperately want to cross the border to state B at 10:01 p.m. to buy your favorite brand of apple pie, you're not permitted to travel that far from your home tree. So the new curfew says to parents. "Take away those digital devices after 10 p.m."

The biggest constitutional challenge will be to parental liberty and familial privacy. After all, this would be the heavy hand of the state reaching in to shake the home apple tree. In some ways, that is a bigger challenge to overcome than it would be if asserted against the brick-and-mortar version of the curfew because it involves activities taking place within the home. The brick-and-mortar curfew does too, though, albeit in a less obvious way. The brick-and-mortar one says, "You must have your kids in your home after 10 p.m." But what if you don't want your kids in your home? What if you really believe, as a parent, that the best way to raise your free-range child is for her to wander the streets, foraging for apples, all night long? Tough, the law says. You must open your home to her after 10 p.m. The add-on says. "And when she's back in your home, she can't escape outside of your home or let the outside into your home through a connected device."

What if she is prone to escaping before the sun rises? Your ten-year-old daughter has a showdown on the school bus, and bystanders share it on social media. Your daughter responds by committing suicide in her bedroom.[36] There is deep darkness there. But the darkness or sunshine of the world itself appears to have been irrelevant. Lights out on you, digital curfew!

But an actual curfew isn't the only point in the constellation of protective measures that existing and longstanding legal schemas require parents and guardians to impose. Parents and guardians are required to control their children, provide for their basic well-being, and ensure their basic safety. These broad responsibilities result in specific prohibitions like not leaving children alone in cars, not leaving them home alone under a certain age, and other safety measures. They also result in certain affirmative requirements, like wearing seatbelts, taking children to get vaccines, and taking them to school.

So let's take our digital curfew proposal, currently sulking in the shadows, and cast some new light on it. What if we think about a children's digital welfare scheme that requires parents to have knowledge of their children's digital engagement, protect their children using other reasonable safeguards, and keep children off digital devices after 10 p.m.? This legally mandated set of parental responsibilities could be enforced essentially the same way as other legal duties of parenting are: by referrals to government agencies and the justice system for alleged breaches. If a child repeatedly wanders around town in the middle of the night, the child and the parents may be hauled into court to answer for the activities. Under the new digital welfare schema, if a child repeatedly makes inappropriate or late-night social media postings, the same consequences could apply: court proceedings and, if the violations indeed happened, the imposition of conditions to ensure they don't happen again. Do you have a child who is wandering into dangerous digital environs? A court order could require the use of surveillance software that an officer can monitor. Existing children's welfare and juvenile justice laws are already written broadly enough to permit courts to micromanage almost every detail of family life for a child found to be in need of services, abused, neglected, or delinquent. Digital tools are already used to support some of this work. In some ways, there's not a lot of sunlight between what is already in place and what a new comprehensive digital welfare schema would do.

In other ways, it would be a bolt of lightning. The government wants to tell us when to make our children put away their iPhones? Yes. *Thumbs up, winky face, ambiguous ice cream turd.* And the government may have even more to say under this type of digital welfare scheme. *Frowny face, frowny crying face, lewd gif.* Remember, it's not just kids who can get themselves into trouble online.

Parents are very capable of getting their kids into trouble, too. Under a new digital welfare scheme, parents' digital choices about their kids' data would seem to be fair game. Post your child's full date, time, and place of birth? Post a booty-hanging-out photo of your toddler? Write a public blog post about your child's toilet-training challenges? You may as well be inviting identity thieves, pedophiles, and all manner of other creeps to invade your child's privacy and ruin their lives. Why don't you just drop their birth certificate off in a back alley somewhere, leave the blinds up when they bathe, and get a megaphone to talk about their "peepee in the potty" in the heart of town? Whether it is the digital version of exposure or the brick-and-mortar version, you're still failing to safeguard your children fully. Depending on the circumstances, you may even be endangering them.

Why shouldn't the government have something to say about digital neglect and abuse or even the less extreme digital failure to supervise and safeguard? Rights to free speech and liberty to raise your children have long folded in the face of important or compelling state interests in protecting children's well-being. If there is sufficient legislative fact-finding of the harms that can befall children from poor parental digital decisions and a constitutionally adequate link between regulating these decisions and preventing these harms, then state and local lawmakers and regulators legitimately could act.

But absent this foundation, they still can act, even though the results of their work would be vulnerable to constitutional challenge in the courts. Some state legislatures have already reacted in heavy-handed ways to actual or perceived threats to children's privacy. For example, in Louisiana, a relatively new law to safeguard student digital privacy carries criminal liability for violations.[37] Almost inevitably, digital welfare shades into digital surveillance shades into digital punishment.

This paradigm of digital welfare legislation is already creeping around the edges of many responses to the digital world. Significantly, in addition to actual legislators, many parents themselves are laying the foundation for an enhanced digital welfare legislative and regulatory response by using home surveillance products on their children. Sometimes, parents use them on one another or other adults, like nannies. How are we going to know whether parents themselves are properly protecting their children's digital welfare? Why, by having the government monitor us.

An old poem tells us, "Children learn what they live."[38] It's meant to remind us that, as we do to each other, we are doing to our children. And as we do to our children, they will do to themselves and to others. If we listen carefully, the poem also tells us: as we do to our children, we also do to ourselves and our world.[39] What do we want to do now?

Conclusion

How can we learn to live the kind of lives that we want our children and ourselves to have? The conversations in this book and similar ones can be uncomfortable. The digital world creates anxiety for many of us. We're insecure about our own skills and knowledge, which can cause us to swing to extremes. We may thoughtlessly over-sharent about our kids and teens or irrationally limit their and our digital engagement. Anxiety takes us wherever the rapids of the world around us or the bumpiness of our own unconscious leads. Anxiety makes us nauseated passengers, not captains, on that Tom and Huck–style raft.

Just as we need to have our kids and teens grow up through play, we need to free up ourselves to be more exploratory. We need to place greater trust in our own abilities as parents, educators, and caregivers. Now that we're through the episode of "Law & Ordinary" that is this book, you can be both judge and jury. What do you think? Do you now understand privacy the same as or differently than you did when you began? How about childhood? Are you convinced that sharenting is a problem to be solved? Or do you come away thinking that sharenting actually is a solution to living in the digital world—a way that parents, teachers, and other adults use to connect to one another and create their children's digital dossiers, which in turn creates their current and future life opportunities?

If you think sharenting is a problem, what should we do about it (other than wait around for the robots to get smart enough to fix it)? The compass spins: play, forget, connect, respect. How could these principles reorient us? And what steps would this reorientation have us take? Do we change our laws and regulations so that companies, public institutions, and other entities are prohibited from using digital data about children for certain sensitive purposes? Do we attempt to use the law to prohibit parents, teachers, and other adults from sharenting in the first place? Do we spend public money to build the equivalent of playgrounds and parks for the digital era so that we strengthen play-centered childhood and adolescent experiences rather than focus on the protection of youth data?

Or do we think nonlaw reform tools might be better? Instead of or in addition to legal change, we could look to create new tech offerings for safe sharenting. We could change our own habits in our homes, schools, and beyond. (Practicing safe sharenting seems preferable to just saying no to sharenting.) We could do all the things that have nothing to do with anything on this list.[1] What do you think you're going to do?

Whatever else we do, we should ask the children in our lives what they think we should do. We should ask because we will learn something—and because we are raising them to participate in a democracy.[2] We need our children to grow into adults who have the autonomy and agency to speak their minds and to learn to make their own decisions without a data determinism that can look suspiciously like a caste system. We need our kids and teens to be comfortable in iterative spaces and, within those spaces, to be comfortable raising tough questions and offering new solutions.[3]

The sharing we most need to do is with our children, not about them. We can share in a play-based ethos that empowers them as individuals, protects childhood and adolescence as unique life stages, and fosters democratic participation. Play is about creation and about imposing order on the world in a meaningful way. Going all the way back to your own childhood, ask yourself: does learning to participate in a democracy depend on the freedom to push each other around on the playground a bit, without the victor of a particular game of tag being added to a database? Yes, in some small way. On the playground, you're experiencing liberty, fostering the creation of order, dealing with the consequences, then trying again tomorrow. You are not being tracked, categorized, and restricted. The sky's the limit. Second star to the right, and straight on until maturity. Perhaps to infinity. You're always young enough to let the stars lead the way. What do you want to be when you grow up?

Notes

Introduction

1. You can read Mark Twain's canonical novel *The Adventures of Tom Sawyer*, which was published in 1876 but set in the 1840s, at http://www.gutenberg.org/files/74/74-h/74-h.htm.

2. See James Tomberlin, "'Don't Elect Me': Sheriffs and the Need for Reform in County Law Enforcement," *Virginia Law Review* 104 (2018): 113–156. According to Tomberlin, "The sheriff remained the most important western law enforcement officer throughout the nineteenth century" (ibid., 122).

3. For the leading account of what today's Tom Sawyer might have to say and why, check out John Palfrey and Urs Gasser, *Born Digital: How Children Grow Up in a Digital Age*, rev. ed. (New York: Basic Books, 2016). *Born Digital* focuses on the roles that youth play and ways to empower youth in their digitally connected lives. In this exploration, the authors insightfully identify that "parents are unwittingly creating problems for their children who were born digital. They sometimes make decisions for their children that are difficult, if not impossible, to undo" (ibid., 65).

4. Stacey B. Steinberg's law review article "Sharenting: Children's Privacy in the Age of Social Media," *Emory Law Journal* 66 (2017): 839–884, appears to be the first scholarly legal analysis of the "intersection of a parent's right to share and a child's interest in privacy and healthy development" (ibid., 844). Steinberg defines "sharenting" as "The ways many parents share details about their children's lives online" (ibid., 842).

5. Guardians, such as Aunt Polly, are understood to be in the "caregiver" category here, although their legal responsibilities, daily activities, and emotional ties tend to be closer to those of parents.

6. Jonathan Zittrain, *The Future of the Internet—and How to Stop It* (Harrisonburg, VA: Caravan, 2008), 233. Julie Cohen theorizes privacy along similar lines: "Privacy shelters dynamic emergent subjectivity from the efforts of commercial and government actors to render individuals and communities fixed, transparent, and predictable. It

protects the situated practices of boundary management through which the capacity for self-determination develops." Julie Cohen, "What Privacy Is For," *Harvard Law Review* 126 (2013): 1905. For a general discussion of legal concepts of privacy, see Daniel J. Solove and Paul M. Schwartz, *Privacy, Information, and Technology*, 2nd ed. (New York: Aspen, 2006), 35: "Defining privacy has proven to be quite complicated, and many commentators have expressed great difficulty in defining precisely what privacy is."

7. This definition is the author's own; however, it is broadly in keeping with an approach to privacy theory that embraces that "The way forward for privacy theory . . . [is] engaging with other scholarly traditions [such as cognitive science] that acknowledge the emergent and relational character of subjectivity . . . [in order to] explore the processes of gradual self-differentiation that individuals undergo beginning in early childhood." Cohen, "What Privacy Is For," 1908.

8. See Anne C. Dailey and Laura A. Rosenbury, "The New Law of the Child," *Yale Law Journal* 127 (2018): 1506. Dailey and Rosenbury explain how "emphasis on children's dependency and eventual capacity underlies the entire field of children and law, in large part because adult authority over children derives its primary legal justification from children's dependent status. . . . This legal conception of childhood is so widely accepted by U.S. courts, policymakers, and scholars that it has no name; it is simply the way things are," and they put an appropriate name to the "way things are": the "authorities" framework (ibid., 1456).

9. In independent scholar Edith Cobb's groundbreaking study on childhood, she argues that "childhood can be generalized as a highly creative, perhaps the most creative, phase in every human life history." Edith Cobb, *The Ecology of Imagination in Childhood* (Dallas: Spring Publications, 1993), 29. Whether we experienced (or wish we had) such a childhood ourselves, we likely feel some pull toward this vision. In their vision for a legal paradigm shift for childhood, Dailey and Rosenbury argue that the law should recognize five interests held by children, including "children's interest to exposure to new ideas." They define this "new ideas" interest as being broader than play, while recognizing that "Children's abilities [to respond to new ideas] are most clearly illustrated in the context of their pretend play." Dailey and Rosenbury, "The New Law," 1495. Other legal scholars embrace a broader definition. Notably, Julie E. Cohen sees play as "both the keystone of individual moral and intellectual development and a mode of world making." Julie E. Cohen, *Configuring the Networked Self: Law, Code, and the Play of Everyday Practice* (New Haven: Yale University Press, 2012), 54. This book uses the word *play* as a broad term for an approach to the world by people of all ages that is grounded in exploration and iteration—rather than being goal-driven—and includes a tolerance or even embrace of making and learning from mistakes.

10. This refers to the infamous Facebook–Cambridge Analytica scandal from the 2016 US presidential election. For a general overview, see Bloomberg, "Facebook

Cambridge Analytica Scandal: Ten Questions Answered," *Fortune*, April 10, 2018, http://fortune.com/2018/04/10/facebook-cambridge-analytica-what-happened.

11. As two leading family law scholars recently wrote: "Parental dissemination of private information about children's bodies—or children's lives more generally . . . largely goes unchallenged. In fact, it has become common practice for parents to detail children's lives on social media . . . often to further parents' own interests instead of those of their children." Dailey and Rosenbury, "The New Law," 1502. And scholars in disciplines outside of law also have observed the overall lack of academic challenge to or even analysis of how children are "datafied" by others through this and other types of information dissemination by adults, observing that while a "host of scholarly publications since the advent of personal computing in the 1980s has directed attention to the ways in which children use digital technologies . . . little research thus far has sought to examine how children are the objects of a proliferating range of digitized surveillance practices that record details of their lives." Deborah Lupton and Ben Williamson, "The Datafied Child: The Dataveillance of Children and Implications for Their Rights," *New Media & Society* 19 (2017): 780.

12. Dailey and Rosenbury, "The New Law," 1503.

13. For insightful, interdisciplinary, and wide-ranging coverage of parenting and technology (including topics such as promoting media literacy for kids and preventing cyberbullying between kids), visit the *Parenting for a Digital Future* blog run by Professor Sonia Livingstone at the London School of Economics and Political Science, http://blogs.lse.ac.uk/parenting4digitalfuture.

14. This query rests at the intersection of two types of privacy that are "often contrasted" within the legal scholarship: (1) information privacy, which "concerns the collection, use, and disclosure of personal information," and (2) decisional privacy, which "concerns the freedom to make decisions about one's body and family." Zittrain, *The Future of the Internet*, 1.

15. For an examination of the case method, see Russell L. Weaver, "Langdell's Legacy: Living with the Case Method," *Villanova Law Review* 36 (1991): 517–596.

16. This bedrock principle of the American legal system—a government of laws, not of men—is articulated in many sources, such as the Constitution of the Commonwealth of Massachusetts. Mass. Const. pt. 1, art. 30.

17. Martha S. Jones, *Birthright Citizens: A History of Race and Rights in Antebellum America* (Cambridge: Cambridge University Press, 2018), ix.

18. Such valuable works include Lynn Schofield Clark, *The Parent App: Understanding Families in the Digital Age* (New York: Oxford University Press, 2013), which uses sociological and communications research to examine how families use digital media and how those patterns construct broader society.

19. Spencer Kornhaber, "How 'Brangelina' Gave a Couple Its Mystique," *The Atlantic*, September 22, 2016, https://www.theatlantic.com/entertainment/archive/2016/09/brangelina-brad-pitt-angelina-jolie-divorce-vanessa-diaz-interview-celebrity-marriage-nicknames/501050.

20. The term *sharent trap* appears in Emine Saner, "The 'Sharent' Trap: Should You Ever Put Your Children on Social Media?," *The Guardian*, May 24, 2018, US edition, https://www.theguardian.com/lifeandstyle/2018/may/24/sharent-trap-should-parents-put-their-children-on-social-media-instagram.

21. For inspiration, see Ina J. Hughs, "A Prayer for Responsibility for Children," in Children's Defense Fund, *Children 1990: A Report Card, Briefing Book, and Action Primer* (Children's Defense Fund, 1990), 120. This book is out of print; you can access the cited material at the website for Cornell University, https://www.classe.cornell.edu/~seb/prayer-for-children.html.

Chapter 1

1. As Palfrey and Gasser explain: "The digital dossier is a 'superset' [of data]: it contains all of [a] young [person's] digital personally identifying information, whether that information is publicly accessible or not, and whether it is disclosed to third parties or not." John Palfrey and Urs Gasser, *Born Digital: How Children Grow Up in a Digital Age*, rev. ed. (New York: Basic Books, 2016), 39. Palfrey and Gasser offer the portrait of a "digital dossier of a hypothetical baby [called Andy]" that goes beyond the focus of this Tommy S. scenario to include contributions that Andy, his friends, his classmates, and others beyond his parents, teachers, and other adults will make to this superset of data. They correctly observe that "Andy's parents do not have much more control over some of the information in Andy's files than he does," an important reminder about the structural limitations of parental control over youth data privacy (ibid., 40–51).

2. But stay tuned: Jonathan Vanian, "IBM Filed a Patent for a Drone That Acts Like a Dog Sitter," *Fortune*, March 24, 2017, http://fortune.com/2017/03/24/ibm-drone-patent-pet-sitter.

3. Available at http://www.pleoworld.com.

4. Available at https://shopus.furbo.com

5. See Aarti Shahani, "Making Babies? Yep, There's an App for That," *NPR*, October 11, 2013, http://www.npr.org/templates/story/story.php?storyId=232238899.

6. Available at https://www.avawomen.com/order. To sign up for email list, you need to indicate whether you're interested in fertility tracking, cycle tracking, or pregnancy tracking. If you're interested in pregnancy tracking, then you're asked for the number of weeks pregnant you are in order to "receive tailored content." In

2017, researchers found that over "1000 apps related to pregnancy are now available on the market, many of which provide opportunities for pregnant women to monitor the growth, development, movements and even heart rate of their foetuses [sic.]." Deborah Lupton and Ben Williamson, "The Datafied Child: The Dataveillance of Children and Implications for Their Rights," *New Media & Society* 19 (2017): 783.

7. "At the heart of liberty is the right to define one's own concept of existence." Planned Parenthood v. Casey, 505 U.S. 833, 851 (1992).

8. For an example of what happens when these companies misstep, see Amy Pittman, "The Internet Thinks I'm Still Pregnant," *New York Times*, September 2, 2016, https://www.nytimes.com/2016/09/04/fashion/modern-love-pregnancy-miscarriage -app-technology.html.

9. Facebook collects and retains a great deal of information about its users. This information includes photos that are automatically tagged and training images— from which biometric data is extracted." Yana Welinder, "A Face Tells More Than a Thousand Posts: Developing Face Recognition Privacy in Social Networks," *Harvard Journal of Law and Technology* 26 (2012): 172. But Facebook says it doesn't sell the information. See Tom Regan, "Facial Recognition Is Exploding, but at What Cost to Your Privacy,?" WSB-TV 2 Atlanta, November 1, 2017, http://www.wsbtv.com/news/ local/facial-recognition-is-exploding-but-at-what-cost-to-your-privacy/629470235. This coverage says Facebook's facial recognition database is the largest in the world.

10. This detail is based on a true story. In fall 2017, two hospital employees were relieved of patient care duties because they "were seen in disturbing [digital] images mishandling a newborn, making obscene gestures, and calling babies 'mini Satans.'" Kristine Phillips, "Disturbing Images Show Navy Hospital Staffers Mishandling Infant, Calling Babies 'Mini Satans,'" *Washington Post*, September 19, 2017, https:// www.washingtonpost.com/news/checkpoint/wp/2017/09/19/disturbing-images -show-hospital-staffers-mishandling-an-infant-calling-babies-mini-satans.

11. "Bits of information about a child born digital may only be loosely linked to the rest of the dossier today. But as time goes on, it is becoming easier to put the pieces together and to associate them" with that child. Palfrey and Gasser, *Born Digital*, 45.

12. For example, Leah Plunkett, Alicia Solow-Niederman, and Urs Gasser, "Framing the Law and Policy Picture: A Snapshot of K–12 Cloud-Based Ed Tech and Student Privacy in Early 2014," Berkman Center Research Publication no. 2014-10, Berkman Klein Center for Internet & Society, Harvard University, June 2014, SSRN, https:// papers.ssrn.com/sol3/papers.cfm?abstract_id=2442432##.

13. "Facebook's Internal Manual on Non-Sexual Child Abuse Content," *The Guardian*, May 21, 2017, https://www.theguardian.com/news/gallery/2017/may/21/face books-internal-manual-on-non-sexual-child-abuse-content.

14. Some respected stakeholders in the advice-to-parents business are offering valuable resources to families, such as guidance from the American Academy of Pediatrics in developing a "family media use plan." HealthyChildren.org, "How to Make a Family Media Use Plan," American Academy of Pediatrics, updated October 21, 2016, https://www.healthychildren.org/English/family-life/Media/Pages/How-to-Make-a-Family-Media-Use-Plan.aspx.

15. See "FBI Investigates 'Cloud' Celebrity Picture Leaks," *BBC News*, September 2, 2014, http://www.bbc.com/news/technology-29011850.

16. See Nest Cam, https://nest.com/cameras.

17. See Anthony Cuthbertson, "How to Protect Baby Monitors from Hackers," *Newsweek*, January 29, 2016, http://www.newsweek.com/how-protect-baby-monitors-hackers-421104.

18. See Owlet, https://owletcare.com.

19. See Alice LaPlante, "Robot Nannies Are Here, But Won't Replace Your Babysitter—Yet," *Forbes*, March 29, 2017, https://www.forbes.com/sites/centurylink/2017/03/29/robot-nannies-are-here-but-wont-replace-your-babysitter-yet.

20. See Lauren Jimeson, "Fifteen Baby Book Apps for Documenting Baby's Milestones," *Babble* (blog), https://www.babble.com/baby/15-baby-book-apps-for-documenting-babys-milestones.

21. For an explanation of the *Sesame Street*–IBM collaboration, which may result in a smart Elmo or a similar smart toy, see Tony Wan, "To Tackle Early Childhood Education, Sesame Street Finds a Smart Friend: IBM Watson," *EdSurge*, April 27, 2016, https://www.edsurge.com/news/2016-04-27-to-tackle-early-childhood-education-sesame-street-finds-a-smart-friend-ibm-watson.

22. IBM, "Sesame Workshop and IBM Watson Team Up to Advance Early Childhood Education," news release, April 27, 2016, https://www-03.ibm.com/press/us/en/pressrelease/49585.wss.

23. These Barbie and teddy bear products have already been introduced to the marketplace—and caused privacy problems. See Emily McReynolds et al., "Toys That Listen: A Study of Parents, Children, and Internet-Connected Toys," Paper presented at the FTC's annual PrivacyCon, February 28, 2018, https://www.ftc.gov/system/files/documents/public_comments/2017/11/00038-141895.pdf, and Lorenzo Franceschi-Bicchierai, "Internet of Things Teddy Bear Leaked 2 Million Parent and Kids Message Recordings," *Motherboard*, February 28, 2018, https://motherboard.vice.com/en_us/article/pgwean/internet-of-things-teddy-bear-leaked-2-million-parent-and-kids-message-recordings. Other, even smarter toys are not far behind; indeed, "for roboticists, the home is the final frontier." This frontier will raise ethics questions for tech designers, such as "should a home robot intervene when

it witnesses the family's 10-year-old doing something mischievous?" Kirsten Weir, "The Dawn of Social Robots," *Monitor on Psychology*, January 2018, 52, 54.

24. Lynn Schofield Clark, *The Parent App: Understanding Families in the Digital Age* (New York: Oxford University Press, 2013), 128.

25. As one parent and technology scholar noted after giving her toddler access to Alexa, the "easy embrace of Alexa was slightly amusing but also alarming." Rachel Botsman, "Co-Parenting with Alexa," *New York Times*, October 7, 2017, https://www.nytimes.com/2017/10/07/opinion/sunday/children-alexa-echo-robots.html.

26. For example, see Tadpoles, http://www.tadpoles.com.

27. Close to 100 percent of districts in a representative sample of K–12 US public school districts used at least one type of digital ed tech in their classrooms or administrative offices. Joel Reidenberg et al., "Privacy and Cloud Computing in Public Schools," *Center on Law and Information Policy*, book 2 (2013): 11, 12, and 19, http://ir.lawnet.fordham.edu/clip/2. For a broad-brush picture of digital ed tech trends, see Plunkett, Solow-Niederman, and Gasser, "Framing the Law and Policy Picture," 5–7.

28. Sometimes, there is private foundation funding behind ed tech ventures, especially large-scale ones. A well-known example of an ultimately unsuccessful venture is inBloom, a "$100 million educational technology initiative primarily funded by the Bill & Melinda Gates Foundation that aimed to improve American schools by providing a centralized platform for data sharing, learning apps, and curricula." Monica Bulger, Patrick McCormick, and Mikaela Pitcan, "The Legacy of inBloom," working paper, Data & Society, February 2, 2017, 4, https://datasociety.net/pubs/ecl/InBloom_feb_2017.pdf. These interinstitutional collaborations can result in successful breakthroughs, but Silicon Valley–style foundations may clash with the ethos and governance structures of public education. For a deep dive into the types of clashes that can arise, see Megan Tompkins Stange, *Policy Patrons: Philanthropy, Education Reform, and the Politics of Influence* (Cambridge, MA: Harvard Education Press, 2016).

29. For example, Natasha Singer, "Silicon Valley Courts Brand-Name Teachers, Raising Ethics Issues," *New York Times*, September 2, 2017, https://www.nytimes.com/2017/09/02/technology/silicon-valley-teachers-tech.html.

30. For further discussion, see Plunkett, Solow-Niederman, and Gasser, "Framing the Law and Policy Picture," 9–12.

31. Starting with early education, "children come to be represented through their 'data doubles' or 'data doppelgangers' through a process of making education 'machine readable.'" Alice Bradbury and Guy Roberts-Holmes, *The Datafication of Primary and Early Years Education: Playing with Numbers* (New York: Routledge, 2018), 32.

32. This is a federal Family Educational Rights and Privacy Act (FERPA) release request. FERPA is discussed in chapter 5.

33. For example, see the list of reading apps compiled by the nonprofit group Common Sense Media at https://www.commonsensemedia.org/lists/reading-apps -games-and-websites.

34. The iPotty is made by CTA Digital, https://www.ctadigital.com.

35. For example, see My School Bucks, https://www.myschoolbucks.com.

36. On websites used by public schools for a variety of purposes, digital "trackers are as common . . . as microbes on a restroom door." Teachers, privacy watchdogs, and other stakeholders may be more concerned than most parents. As the president of one parent-teacher association observed, parents "'want that instant information [from the school]. . . . They don't think twice about who's tracking them.'" E. K. Moore, "The Information on School Websites Is Not as Safe as You Think," *New York Times*, August 2, 2018, https://www.nytimes.com/2018/08/02/education/learning/ school-websites-information-tracking.html.

37. For a resource for school administrators and teachers to use to learn more about privacy challenges for digital fitness trackers and related products, see Leah A. Plunkett, Dalia Topelson Ritvo, and Paulina Haduong, "Privacy and Student Data: Companion Learning Tools," Berkman Center Research Publication, Berkman Klein Center for Internet & Society, Harvard University, March 2017, 2, 7–12, http://blogs .harvard.edu/youthandmediaalpha/files/2017/03/PrivacyStudentData_Companion _Learning_Tools.pdf.

38. Sometimes, school-issued laptops "can be distributed pre-loaded with spyware enabling administrators to access extremely sensitive student information." Kade Crockford and Jessie J. Rossman, "Back to the Drawing Board: Student Privacy in Massachusetts K–12 Schools," *ACLU of Massachusetts*, October 2015, 5, https://www. aclum.org/sites/default/files/wp-content/uploads/2015/10/back_to_the_drawing _board_report_large_file_size.pdf.

39. An "industry agenda" report from the World Economic Forum, prepared in collaboration with the Boston Consulting Group, identifies social-emotional learn-ing as an area for digital tech innovation. The term *privacy* does not appear in this report. "New Vision for Education: Fostering Social and Emotional Learning through Technology," *World Economic Forum* (March 2016), http://www3.weforum.org/docs/ WEF_New_Vision_for_Education.pdf.

40. See Reidenberg et al., "Privacy and Cloud Computing."

41. "Mavis Beacon Teaches Typing" is an old-school computer program for teach-ing typing that is still available at http://www.mavisbeaconfree.com.

42. Here, the term *cloud-based ed tech* refers to products and services that "'enable the transition of computing resources—including information processing, collection, storage, and analysis—away from localized systems (i.e., on servers located at a data center away from the end user accessible through a network)' in the course of educational and/or academic administrative work." Plunkett, Solow-Niederman, and Gasser, "Framing the Law and Policy Picture," 3.

43. There is no universal way to categorize today's educational tech. See Plunkett, Solow-Niederman, and Gasser, "Framing the Law and Policy Picture," 4.

44. For more on how one teacher in Harlem has used an attendance tracker effectively, see Natasha Singer, "An App Helps Teachers Track Student Attendance," *New York Times*, January 23, 2016, https://www.nytimes.com/2016/01/24/technology/an-app-helps-teachers-track-student-attendance.html.

45. The National Association of School Nurses has taken a strong position in support of electronic health record use in schools. National Association of School Nurses, "Position Statement: School Nurse Role in Electronic School Health Records," January 2014, https://www.nasn.org/advocacy/professional-practice-documents/position-statements/ps-electronic-health-records.

46. For a discussion of the pros and cons of online gradebooks, see Laura McKenna, "Why Online Gradebooks Are Changing Education," *The Atlantic*, March 10, 2016, https://www.theatlantic.com/education/archive/2016/03/how-online-gradebooks-are-changing-education/473175.

47. For a teachable fact pattern on digitally sharing student art, see Plunkett, Ritvo, and Haduong, "Privacy & Student Data: Companion Learning Tools."

48. A capstone project from fellows at the Strategic Data Project at the Center for Education Policy Research at Harvard University offers a deep dive into this type of use of predictive analytics. Jason Becker et al., "Student Success and College Readiness: Translating Predictive Analytics into Action," Strategic Data Project, Center for Education Policy Research, Harvard University, undated, http://sdp.cepr.harvard.edu/files/cepr-sdp/files/sdp-fellowship-capstone-student-success-college-readiness.pdf.

49. For more on school surveillance and privacy concerns, see Crockford and Rossman, "Back to the Drawing Board: Student Privacy in Massachusetts K–12 Schools."

50. See Kevin Lapp, "Databasing Delinquency," *Hastings Law Journal* 67 (2015): 212–216.

51. Pedro Oliveira Jr., "Businesses Make $4M off NYC Students by Holding Their Cellphones during School," *New York Post*, June 18, 2012, https://nypost.com/2012/06/18/businesses-make-4m-off-nyc-students-by-holding-their-cellphones-during-school.

52. Leah Plunkett, "Punishing Students for Gadget Use Will Make Their Tech Etiquette Worse," *Wired*, March 19, 2014, https://www.wired.com/2014/03/zero -tolerance.

53. US Department of Education, "U.S. Department of Education and Justice Release School Discipline Guidance Package to Enhance School Climate and Improve School Discipline Policies/Practices," news release, January 8, 2014, https:// www.ed.gov/news/press-releases/us-departments-education-and-justice-release -school-discipline-guidance-package-.

54. "Congress has incentivized . . . schools nationwide to develop data-collection systems." Lapp, "Databasing Delinquency," 214.

55. For guidance for parents sending kids off to summer camp, see Leah A. Plunkett, "Summer in Cyberspace: Protecting Your Kids' Digital Privacy at Camp," *FERPA SHERPA*, July 12, 2017, https://ferpasherpa.org/plunkett1.

56. See Elana Zeide, "The Limits of Education Purpose Limitations," *University of Miami School of Law Review* 71 (2017): 504–507.

57. Zeide, "The Limits of Education Purpose Limitations," 508–509.

58. "An entire data broker industry has sprung up around profiting from our data, and our personal information is being bought and sold without our knowledge and consent." Bruce Schneier, *Data and Goliath: The Hidden Battles to Collect Your Data and Control Your World* (New York: Norton, 2015), 6.

59. According to the Future of Privacy Forum (FPF), "experts disagree about the extent to which new technologies and techniques can 'back map' de-identified data to reveal a student's identity." FPF advises that "a serious statistical analysis that ensures all direct and indirect identifiers have been removed [before a school shares data with a third party or a third party reshares that data] can be performed to ensure any re-identification risk is remote." Reg Leichty and Brenda Leong, *De-Identification and Student Data: Understanding De-Identification of Education Records and Related Requirements of FERPA* (Washington, DC: Future of Privacy Forum, August 2015), 5, https://fpf.org/wp-content/uploads/FPF-DeID-FINAL-7242015jp.pdf.

60. See Stacey B. Steinberg, "Sharenting: Children's Privacy in the Age of Social Media," *Emory Law Journal* 66 (2017): 846–854. For a summary of Steinberg's article, see Adrienne Lafrance, "The Perils of 'Sharenting,'" *The Atlantic*, October 6, 2016, https://www.theatlantic.com/technology/archive/2016/10/babies-everywhere/ 502757.

61. For example, law enforcement in Ohio chose to post a picture of a woman and a man passed out from overdosing in the front seat of a car, with the woman's four-year-old grandson sitting in the backseat. Chief John Lane, interview by Kelly McEvers and Audie Cornish, *All Things Considered*, NPR, September 12, 2016, http://

www.npr.org/2016/09/12/493654929/ohio-police-release-photos-of-couple-who
-overdosed-in-car-with-child. Note that, in the police department's original Facebook post, the four-year-old child's face was not blocked.

62. See Steinberg, "Sharenting," 852.

63. For a description of internet of things devices, see Scott R. Peppet, "Regulating the Internet of Things: First Steps toward Managing Discrimination, Privacy,
Security, and Consent," *Texas Law Review* 93 (2014): 108–112. The Federal Trade
Commission understands the "Internet of Things" as "the ability of everyday
objects to connect to the Internet and to send and receive data." Federal Trade
Commission (FTC), *Internet of Things: Privacy and Security in a Connected World*,
staff report, January 2015, https://www.ftc.gov/system/files/documents/reports/
federal-trade-commission-staff-report-november-2013-workshop-entitled-internet
-things-privacy/150127iotrpt.pdf.

64. Mia Little and Amelia Vance, "Law Enforcement Access to Student Records:
What Is the Law?," Future of Privacy Forum, September 25, 2017, https://fpf.org/
2017/09/25/law-enforcement-access-to-student-records.

65. See Lapp, "Databasing Delinquency," 208.

66. See Steinberg, "Sharenting," 846–854.

67. See Steinberg, "Sharenting," 852. For an example of how a parent's blog post
on a child's mental health crisis can bring support to the family, see "How Talking
Openly against Stigma Helped a Mother and Son Cope with Bipolar Disorder,"
Weekend Edition Sunday, NPR, April 24, 2016, https://www.npr.org/sections/health-
shots/2016/04/24/475461959/how-talking-openly-against-stigma-helped-a-mother
-and-son-cope-with-bipolar-diso.

68. See Chief John Lane, interview by Kelly McEvers and Audie Cornish.

69. As Clark asks, "at what point does it [using digital tech surveillance] become
counterproductive to the overall goal of helping young people learn from their
mistakes, because it allows them to focus on the putative mistakes of their parents
[invading their privacy] rather than their own?" Clark, *The Parent App*, 44–45.

70. See N. Cameron Russell et al., "Transparency and the Marketplace for Student
Data," *Virginia Journal of Law and Technology* 1 (forthcoming): 34, https://www
.fordham.edu/info/23830/research/10517/transparency_and_the_marketplace_for
_student_data/1.

Chapter 2

1. See Sharon K. Sandeen, "Relative Privacy: What Privacy Advocates Can Learn
from Trade Secret Law," *Michigan State Law Review* 2006 (2006): 704–705.

2. See Helen Nissenbaum, "Privacy as Contextual Integrity," *Washington Law Review* 79 (2004): 119–157.

3. See Jonathan Zittrain, *The Future of the Internet—and How to Stop It* (Harrisonburg, VA: Caravan, 2008), 233. For further discussion about the range of understandings of privacy, see Daniel J. Solove and Paul M. Schwartz, *Privacy, Information, and Technology*, 2nd ed. (New York: Aspen, 2006).

4. For instance, you could follow Steinberg's public health–based strategies for successful social media engagement as a parent, including "consider[ing] the effect sharing can have on [your] child's current and future sense of self and well-being." Stacey B. Steinberg, "Sharenting: Children's Privacy in the Age of Social Media," *Emory Law Journal* 66 (2017): 882.

5. Such "personalized learning" was the goal behind inBloom, a major ed tech initiative that came to an abrupt end in 2013. For further discussion, see Monica Bulger, Patrick McCormick, and Mikaela Pitcan, "The Legacy of inBloom," working paper, Data & Society, February 2, 2017, https://datasociety.net/pubs/ecl/InBloom _feb_2017.pdf.

6. See Jason M. Gordon, "A Shield of Disadvantage: Legal Entity Status within Guardian-Adolescent Entrepreneurial Ventures," *Entrepreneurial Business Law Journal* 9 (2014): 4–5.

7. See Bettina Elias Siegel, "Shaming Children So Parents Will Pay the School Lunch Bill," *New York Times*, April 30, 2017, https://www.nytimes.com/2017/04/30/well/ family/lunch-shaming-children-parents-school-bills.html.

8. On algorithmic potential, see Ben Williamson, *Big Data in Education: The Digital Future of Learning, Policy and Practice* (London: Sage, 2017), 63: "The result of algorithmic data mining is not simply the production of individual and social profiles, but new ways of seeing and understanding social groups that then flow back into the ways in which those groups and individuals might actually relate to themselves." For further discussion, see Alice Bradbury and Guy Roberts-Holmes, *The Datafication of Primary and Early Years Education: Playing with Numbers* (New York: Routledge, 2018), 116: "Some argue that it is possible to see a fantasized and imagined future where complex political, ethical and social problems find solutions in an online digital world supposedly free of inequality, poverty and discrimination."

9. See Dave Talbot, "AI Advance: A Community Convening at Harvard Law School to Advance the Ethics and Governance of Artificial Intelligence Initiative," *Medium*, June 1, 2017, https://medium.com/berkman-klein-center/ai-advance-may -15-2017-2c36ee9d8dc8.

10. See Lisa Fine, "Can Wearable Fitness Trackers Help Kids Gain Steps and Lose Pounds?," *KQED*, December 11, 2015, https://www.kqed.org/futureofyou/80085/can -wearable-fitness-trackers-help-kids-gain-steps-and-lose-pounds.

11. For example, "Fitness App Strava Lights Up Staff at Military Bases," *BBC News*, January 29, 2018, http://www.bbc.com/news/technology-42853072.

12. For an explanation of how social media pictures of children can be targets for pedophiles, see Steinberg, "Sharenting," 881.

13. For example, Nicole A. Poltash, "Snapchat and Sexting: A Snapshot of Baring Your Bare Essentials," *Richmond Journal of Law and Technology* 19 (2013): 14.

14. For an example of baby monitor hacking more broadly, see "Baby Monitor Hacker Delivers Creepy Message to Child," *CBS News*, April 23, 2015, https://www.cbsnews.com/news/baby-monitor-hacker-delivers-creepy-message-to-child.

15. 18 U.S.C.A. § 2256 (West 2018).

16. For legal discussion of *Dost* factors that define "lascivious exhibition of the genitals or pubic area," see United States v. Amirault, 173 F.3d 28, 31–32 (1st Cir. 1999) [citing United States v. Dost, 636 F. Supp. 828, 832 (S.D. Cal. 1986), aff'd sub nom. United States v. Wiegand, 812 F.2d 1239, 1244 (9th Cir. 1987)].

17. See ACLU, "Minnesota Teen Faces Child Pornography Charges for Sexting," December 21, 2017, https://www.aclu.org/news/minnesota-teen-faces-child-pornography-charges-sexting.

18. United States v. Amirault, 173 F.3d 28, 35 (1st Cir. 1999) (quoting Osborne v. Ohio, 495 U.S. 103, 113–114 [1990]).

19. A study from the Carnegie Mellon CyLab found that the child identification theft rate was "fifty-one (51) times higher" than the adult ID theft rate from the "same security breach population." Richard Power, "Child Identity Theft," Carnegie Mellon Cylab, 2011, 9, https://www.cylab.cmu.edu/_files/pdfs/reports/2011/child-identity-theft.pdf.

20. For more information about Utah's Child Identity Protection program, see "Child Identity Protection," ID Theft Central: Utah's Identity Theft Solution, accessed August 20, 2017, https://cip.utah.gov/cip/SessionInit.action.

21. See Nicholas Confessore, "New York Attorney General to Investigate Firm That Sells Fake Followers," *New York Times*, January 27, 2018, https://www.nytimes.com/2018/01/27/technology/schneiderman-social-media-bots.html.

22. See Selena Larson, "Hackers Are Targeting Schools, U.S. Department of Education Warns," CNN Business, October 18, 2017, http://money.cnn.com/2017/10/18/technology/business/hackers-schools-montana/index.html.

23. See Edwin Rios, "Hackers Are Stealing Sensitive Student Data—and Schools Are Paying Thousands of Dollars to Get It Back," *Mother Jones*, October 25, 2017, https://www.motherjones.com/crime-justice/2017/10/hackers-are-stealing-sensitive-student-data-and-schools-are-paying-thousands-of-dollars-to-get-it-back.

24. One security analyst predicted that children's stolen information from this breach "'will be used in waves of financial crimes' against American children for decades." Herb Weisbaum, "Millions of Children Exposed to ID Theft through Anthem Breach," NBC News, February 18, 2015, https://www.nbcnews.com/better/money/millions-children-exposed-id-theft-through-anthem-breach-n308116?cid=sm_npd_nn_fb_bt_170820.

25. Personal experience of this author when an AllClearID alert turned up suspicious information related to her child's identity.

26. For example, "At the end of July [2016], feminist writer Jessica Valenti said she was leaving social media after receiving a rape threat against her daughter, who is 5 years old." Joel Stein, "How Trolls Are Ruining the Internet," *Time*, August 18, 2016, http://time.com/4457110/internet-trolls.

27. Lynn Schofield Clark, *The Parent App: Understanding Families in the Digital Age* (New York: Oxford University Press, 2013), 29–30.

28. Clark, *The Parent App*, 28.

29. See Molly McDonough, "Sex Traffickers Use Social Media to Research Victims to Groom," *ABA Journal*, February 6, 2016, http://www.abajournal.com/news/article/sex_traffickers_use_social_media_to_research_victims_to_groom; Mark Latonero et al., *The Rise of Mobile and the Diffusion of Technology-Facilitated Trafficking*, USC Annenberg Center on Communication Leadership & Policy, November 2012, http://technologyandtrafficking.usc.edu/report/human-trafficking-online-the-role-of-social-networking-sites-and-online-classifieds/#.WhGszFWnG00; and Herbert B. Dixon Jr., "Human Trafficking and the Internet* (*and Other Technologies, Too)," *The Judges' Journal* 52, no. 1 (2013), https://www.americanbar.org/publications/judges_journal/2013/winter/human_trafficking_and_internet_and_other_technologies_too.html.

30. Ceylan Yeginsu, "Slavery Ensnares Thousands in U.K. Here's One Teenage Girl's Story," *New York Times*, November 18, 2017, https://www.nytimes.com/2017/11/18/world/europe/uk-modern-slavery.html.

31. See E. K. Moore, "The Information on School Websites Is Not as Safe as You Think," *New York Times*, August 2, 2018, https://www.nytimes.com/2018/08/02/education/learning/school-websites-information-tracking.html.

32. Bruce Schneier, *Data and Goliath: The Hidden Battles to Collect Your Data and Control Your World* (New York: Norton, 2015), 153.

33. For data-driven outreach in college admissions, see Jillian Berman, "How Colleges Aggressively Use Big Data to Target Potential Students," *Market Watch*, September 19, 2017, https://www.marketwatch.com/story/how-colleges-aggressively-use-big-data-to-target-potential-students-2017-09-19. For the use of criminal back-

ground questions in college admissions, see Judith Scott-Clayton, "Thinking 'Beyond the Box': The Use of Criminal Records in College Admissions," *Education Next*, October 2, 2017, http://educationnext.org/thinking-beyond-box-use-criminal-records -college-admissions.

34. See Emmanuel Felton, "The New Tool Colleges Are Using in Admissions Decisions: Big Data," *PBS NewsHour*, August 21, 2015, http://www.pbs.org/newshour/ updates/new-tool-colleges-using-admissions-decisions-big-data; Scott R. Peppet, "Regulating the Internet of Things," *Texas Law Review* 93 (2014): 122–125; President's Council of Advisors on Science and Technology (PCAST), *Big Data and Privacy: A Technological Perspective*, Executive Office of the President, May 2014, https:// obamawhitehouse.archives.gov/sites/default/files/microsites/ostp/PCAST/pcast _big_data_and_privacy_-_may_2014.pdf; and Karen Turner, "Schools Are Helping Police Spy on Kids' Social Media Activity," *Washington Post*, April 22, 2016, https:// www.washingtonpost.com/news/the-switch/wp/2016/04/22/schools-are-helping -police-spy-on-kids-social-media-activity.

35. Schneier, *Data and Goliath*, 3.

36. Danielle Citron and Frank Pasquale, "The Scored Society: Due Process for Automated Predictions," *Washington Law Review* 89 (2014): 22.

37. See N. Cameron Russell et al., "Transparency and the Marketplace for Student Data," *Virginia Journal of Law and Technology* (forthcoming): 1, https://www .fordham.edu/info/23830/research/10517/transparency_and_the_marketplace_for _student_data/1.

38. Russell et al., 3.

39. Russell et al., 9.

40. Russell et al., 3–4.

41. Russell et al., 3, 24.

42. Russell et al., 25.

43. Russell et al., 15.

44. Russell et al., 24.

Chapter 3

1. Narnia is a fictional land that four siblings discover through a magic wardrobe in a home in the British countryside. C. S. Lewis, *The Lion, the Witch, and the Wardrobe* (New York: Harper Trophy, 2000; first published 1950 by Geoffrey Bles).

2. "Big data" does not have a universally agreed upon definition. See President's Council of Advisors on Science and Technology (PCAST), *Big Data and Privacy: A*

Technological Perspective, Executive Office of the President, May 2014, https://obamawhitehouse.archives.gov/sites/default/files/microsites/ostp/PCAST/pcast_big_data_and_privacy_-_may_2014.pdf. "In a privacy context, the term 'big data' typically means data about one or a group of individuals, or that might be analyzed to make inferences about individuals. It might include data or metadata collected by government, by the private sector, or by individuals. The data and metadata might be proprietary or open, they might be collected intentionally or incidentally or accidentally. They might be text, audio, video, sensor-based, or some combination" (ibid., 2). This book adopts the PCAST understanding. "Big data" analytics can also take place in more specific contexts, such as "learning analytics" in education. As scholars Deborah Lupton and Ben Williamson explain: "Learning analytics platforms are designed to mine data about learners as they go about educational tasks and activities in real time and to provide automated predictions of future progress that can then be used as the basis for intervention and pre-emption." Deborah Lupton and Ben Williamson, "The Datafied Child: The Dataveillance of Children and Implications for Their Rights," *New Media & Society* 19 (2017): 785.

3. Smart bedroom objects are in the works—although a French university wisely scrapped a recent plan for a "smart bed," as described at "French Student Backlash Scuppers 'Big Brother' Connected Bed Plans," *The Local France*, September 8, 2017, https://www.thelocal.fr/20170908/student-backlash-scuppers-big-brother-connected-bed-plans.

4. The magic wardrobe is make-believe. But real-life services and products exist that combine your digital data with both big data analytics and human experts to give you and your families clothing and fashion advice. For instance, the online subscription service Stitch Fix is now offering a children's wardrobe (see https://www.stitchfix.com/). For discussion of how Stitch Fix and similar companies are gathering customers' body measurements, see Drew Harwell, "Companies Race to Gather a Newly Prized Currency: Our Body Measurements," *Washington Post*, January 16, 2018, https://www.washingtonpost.com/business/economy/companies-race-to-gather-a-newly-prized-currency-our-body-measurements/2018/01/16/5af28d98-f6e8-11e7-beb6-c8d48830c54d_story.html. And Amazon's Echo Look is "focused on style . . . [so] that Alexa [a cloud-based voice service] helps you look your best . . . [through] a second opinion on which outfit looks best [using] Style Check, a new service that combines machine learning algorithms with advice from fashion specialists." See Echo Look, https://www.amazon.com/Amazon-Echo-Look-Camera-Style-Assistant/dp/B0186JAEWK.

5. "Corporate and government surveillance interests have converged. Both now want to know everything about everyone." Bruce Schneier, *Data and Goliath: The Hidden Battles to Collect Your Data and Control Your World* (New York: Norton, 2015), 29.

6. See Stacey B. Steinberg, "Sharenting: Children's Privacy in the Age of Social Media," *Emory Law Journal* 66 (2017): 861–864. Note that under an international legal framework called the United Nations Convention on the Rights of the Child (UNCRC), a child's right to privacy is recognized; however, the United States has not signed on to the UNCRC. There may also be some growth in the ability for children to sue their parents in tort law for violations of privacy, as "the parental immunity [from children's tort suits] doctrine has broken down, and in many jurisdictions has been fully abrogated." David Pimentel, "Criminal Child Neglect and the 'Free Range Kid': Is Overprotective Parenting the New Standard of Care?," *Utah Law Review* 2012 (2012): 954. However, there does not appear to be any trend toward this type of litigation, nor would it likely be successful given both the challenges of privacy tort cases in general and the wide latitude permitted to parents' choices specifically.

7. See Dalia Topelson Ritvo, "Privacy and Student Data: An Overview of the Federal Laws Impacting Student Information Collected through Networked Technologies," Cyberlaw Clinic, Berkman Klein Center for Internet & Society, Harvard University, June 2016, 11–17, https://dash.harvard.edu/handle/1/27410234.

8. See Ritvo, "Privacy and Student Data," 6–9.

9. "Consumers have no way to control how their data might be used downstream by third parties or later aggregated into a larger portfolio of information about them." Mary Madden et al., "Privacy, Poverty, and Big Data: A Matrix of Vulnerabilities for Poor Americans," *Washington University Law Review* 95 (2017): 115.

10. See Federal Trade Commission (FTC), *Data Brokers: A Call for Transparency and Accountability*, May 2014, https://www.ftc.gov/system/files/documents/reports/data-brokers-call-transparency-accountability-report-federal-trade-commission-may-2014/140527databrokerreport.pdf. This report calls, among other things, for data brokers "to implement better measures to refrain from collecting information from children and teens, particularly in marketing products" (ibid., ix).

11. See National Consumer Law Center, *Big Data: A Big Disappointment for Scoring Consumer Creditworthiness*, March 2014, https://www.nclc.org/issues/big-data.html.

12. See Daniel J. Solove and Paul M. Schwartz, *Privacy, Information, and Technology*, 2nd ed. (New York: Aspen, 2006). One major data broker, Acxiom, "hold[s] billions of records about marital status and families and ages of children" (ibid., 191); Abby Ohlheiser, "You've Probably Never about This Creepy Genealogy Site. But It Knows a Lot about You," *Washington Post*, January 12, 2017, https://www.washingtonpost.com/news/the-intersect/wp/2017/01/12/youve-probably-never-heard-of-this-creepy-genealogy-site-but-its-heard-all-about-you. This article highlights that the site connects kids to their parents in its listings.

13. N. Cameron Russell et al., "Transparency and the Marketplace for Student Data," *Virginia Journal of Law and Technology* (forthcoming): 1–34, https://www.fordham.edu/info/23830/research/10517/transparency_and_the_marketplace_for_student_data/1.

14. For a chart of the known types of data broker clients, see Federal Trade Commission, *Data Brokers*, 39–40.

15. See Kashmir Hill, "How Target Figured Out a Teen Girl Was Pregnant before Her Father Did," *Forbes*, February 16, 2012, https://www.forbes.com/sites/kashmirhill/2012/02/16/how-target-figured-out-a-teen-girl-was-pregnant-before-her-father-did.

16. For general background on data analytics in the retail environment, see Joseph Turow, *The Aisles Have Eyes: How Retailers Track Your Shopping, Strip Your Privacy, and Define Your Power* (New Haven: Yale University Press, 2017).

17. HelloFlo, "About Us," http://helloflo.com.

18. HelloFlo.

19. Clare O'Connor, "'Like Santa for Your Vagina': Tampon Startup Hello Flo Takes on That Time of the Month," *Forbes*, August 2, 2013, https://www.forbes.com/sites/clareoconnor/2013/08/02/like-santa-for-your-vagina-tampon-startup-hello-flo-takes-on-that-time-of-the-month.

20. HelloFlo, "Privacy Policy," http://helloflo.com/privacy.

21. Madden et al., "Privacy, Poverty, and Big Data," 98. Federal antidiscrimination laws could be implicated if these data analytics somehow meant that "minority college applicants will be disproportionately excluded from admissions" (ibid. 99).

22. Madden et al., 79.

23. Madden et al., 82.

24. Madden et al. raise a related ethical question that goes beyond what parents say about their kids and asks, "Should a student [applicant] be held liable for the way their extended family members or friends or other connections behave on social media?" Madden et al., "Privacy, Poverty, and Big Data," 96–97.

25. David Rose explores the "enchanted" dimension of the internet of things in his work, available at http://enchantedobjects.com.

26. See Alina Selyukh, "Could Your Social Media Footprint Step on Your Credit History?," National Public Radio, November 4, 2015, https://www.npr.org/sections/the two-way/2015/11/04/454237651/could-your-social-media-footprint-step-on-your -credit-history.

27. Julie Cohen, "What Privacy Is For," *Harvard Law Review* 126 (2013): 1912.

28. One high-profile example is Cambridge Analytica's role in the 2016 US presidential election. See Hannes Grassegger and Mikael Krogerus, "The Data That Turned the World Upside Down," *Motherboard*, January 28, 2017, https://motherboard.vice .com/en_us/article/mg9vvn/how-our-likes-helped-trump-win.

29. For discussion of predictive analytics, see Madden et al., "Privacy, Poverty, and Big Data," 104–106.

30. Likely not, given the domination of Facebook in the facial-recognition business.

31. See Kevin Lapp, "Databasing Delinquency," *Hastings Law Journal* 67 (2015): 195–258.

32. See Jonah Engel Bromwich, Daniel Victor, and Mike Isaac, "Police Use Surveillance Tool to Scan Social Media, A.C.L.U. Says," *New York Times*, October 11, 2016, https://www.nytimes.com/2016/10/12/technology/aclu-facebook-twitter-instagram -geofeedia.html.

33. For example, Rachel Weiner and Lynh Bui, "Korryn Gaines, Killed by Police in Standoff, Posted Parts of Encounter on Social Media," *Washington Post*, August 2, 2016, https://www.washingtonpost.com/local/public-safety/maryland-woman-shot -by-police-in-standoff-posted-part-of-encounter-on-social-media/2016/08/02/ d4650ee6-58cc-11e6-831d-0324760ca856_story.html.

34. For exploration of motives of family that engaged in abusive behavior for a YouTube audience, see Abby Ohlheiser, "The Saga of a YouTube Family Who Pulled Disturbing Pranks on Their Own Kids," *Washington Post*, April 26, 2017, https://www.washingtonpost.com/news/the-intersect/wp/2017/04/25/the-saga-of-a -youtube-family-who-pulled-disturbing-pranks-on-their-own-kids.

35. Chief John Lane, interview by Kelly McEvers and Audie Cornish, *All Things Considered*, NPR, September 12, 2016, http://www.npr.org/2016/09/12/493654929/ ohio-police-release-photos-of-couple-who-overdosed-in-car-with-child.

36. The Algorithms and Justice track within the Ethics and Governance of Artificial Intelligence Initiative at the Berkman Klein Center for Internet & Society at Harvard University and MIT Media Lab at the Massachusetts Institute of Technology is doing a deep dive into these types of digital tech interventions in the criminal justice system. For more information, visit http://cyber.harvard.edu/projects/ ai-algorithms-and-justice.

37. See Matt Day, "Amazon, Microsoft Workers Sign 'Never Again' Pledge to Oppose Trump's Call for Muslim Registry," *Seattle Times*, December 15, 2016, https:// www.seattletimes.com/business/microsoft/never-again-pledge-draws-tech-workers -who-vow-not-to-help-build-possible-registry.

38. Indeed, "Reports have [already] surfaced of schools sharing [student behavior] records with noncriminal justice government agencies, such as immigration enforcement authorities." Lapp, "Databasing Delinquency," 215.

39. Compare Steinberg, "Sharenting." "There are now public Facebook groups that make fun of pictures shared by other parents" (ibid., 855).

40. For a discussion of the addictive properties of digital tech, see Nellie Bowles, "Early Facebook and Google Employees Form Coalition to Fight What They Built," *New York Times*, February 4, 2018, https://www.nytimes.com/2018/02/04/technology/early-facebook-google-employees-fight-tech.html.

41. On the other hand, there can be privacy-eroding consequences of interpersonal connectedness too. Here's a valuable thought challenge from law professors Daniel J. Solove and Paul M. Schwartz: "To some extent, people today are freer of the influence of community norms and the gossip of small towns. Does this mean that people generally have more privacy today?" Solove and Schwartz, *Privacy, Information, and Technology*, 196.

42. "Invasions of privacy can also lead to psychological harm in adolescents . . . includ[ing] the anxiety, embarrassment, or discomfort that accompany the belief that you have lost control over information about yourself and are being, will be, or have been watched or monitored." Lapp, "Databasing Delinquency," 233.

43. Hat tip to participants in a training I ran at the Children's Law Center in Brooklyn, New York, in June 2017 for sensitizing me to the interplay of social media use and custody and similar family law disputes.

44. Pam Houston, *Cowboys Are My Weakness* (New York: Washington Square Press, 1992), 124.

45. See Jean M. Twenge, "Have Smartphones Destroyed a Generation?," *The Atlantic*, September 2017, https://www.theatlantic.com/magazine/archive/2017/09/has-the-smartphone-destroyed-a-generation/534198.

46. Yes, but far fewer. Some of them have smart lockers. See Joe Heim, "Schools and Lockers: No Longer the Right Combination," *Washington Post*, January 24, 2018, https://www.washingtonpost.com/local/education/schools-and-lockers-no-longer-the-right-combination/2018/01/24/9aa4222a-fa09-11e7-ad8c-ecbb62019393_story.html.

47. Emily Dickinson dwelled in possibility. She didn't specify which type. Emily Dickinson, "I dwell in Possibility," available from the Poetry Foundation, https://www.poetryfoundation.org/poems/52197/i-dwell-in-possibility-466.

48. See Harriet Porter, "Why Cool Cats Rule the Internet," *The Telegraph*, July 1, 2016, https://www.telegraph.co.uk/pets/essentials/why-cool-cats-rule-the-internet.

49. J.R.R. Tolkien, *The Hobbit* (Boston: Houghton Mifflin, 1997), 236.

50. Esther Perel's book on adultery explores how the digital era is facilitating extra-marital affairs with past acquaintances. Esther Perel, *The State of Affairs: Rethinking Infidelity* (New York: HarperCollins, 2017).

51. Walt Whitman, "Song of Myself," *Modern American Poetry*, http://www.english .illinois.edu/maps/poets/s_z/whitman/song.htm.

52. See Ashcroft v. Free Speech Coalition, 535 U.S. 234 (2002).

53. So-called revenge porn statutes, invasion of privacy torts, and other criminal and civil avenues may provide relief for such nonconsensual adult sharing. For more on revenge porn statutes and the newest response tool, see Danielle Keats Citron and Mary Anne Franks, "Criminalizing Revenge Porn," *Wake Forest Law Review* 49 (2014): 345–391.

54. US Food and Drug Administration, "FDA Approves New Pill with Sensor That Digitally Tracks If Patients Have Ingested Their Medication," news release, November 13, 2017, https://www.fda.gov/NewsEvents/Newsroom/PressAnnouncements/ ucm584933.htm.

55. William Shakespeare, *The Tragedy of Hamlet, Prince of Denmark*, act 1, scene 3, available at http://shakespeare.mit.edu/hamlet/hamlet.1.3.html.

56. See Caroline Knorr, "Sneaky Ways Advertisers Target Kids," *Common Sense Media*, February 7, 2014, https://www.commonsensemedia.org/blog/sneaky-ways -advertisers-target-kids.

57. For instance, "Kids give advertisers lots of information just by downloading an app or clicking on a sweepstakes." Knorr, "Sneaky Ways Advertisers Target Kids."

58. As Lupton and Williamson caution: "Rendering children's behaviours, qualities and bodies into digital data, and relying principally on these data when making important assessments, judgements or inferences about them, may delimit what can be known about them and how they might be treated as a result. What is considered knowable or calculable about children and their lives becomes the outcome of the digital device and its software." Lupton and Williamson, "The Datafied Child," 787.

59. See Donna Freitas, *The Happiness Effect: How Social Media Is Driving a Generation to Appear Perfect at Any Cost* (New York: Oxford University Press, 2017).

60. More broadly, adults need what legal scholar Neil M. Richards has termed "intellectual privacy"—the "protection from surveillance or interference when we are engaged in the processes of generating ideas." Neil M. Richards, *Intellectual Privacy: Rethinking Civil Liberties in the Digital Age* (Oxford: Oxford University Press, 2015), https://ssrn.com/abstract=2554196.

61. Joni Mitchell, "Both Sides, Now," track 10 on Joni Mitchell, *Clouds*, compact disc, Siquomb Publishing Corp., 1969.

62. See Leah Plunkett and Urs Gasser, "Student Privacy and Ed Tech (K–12) Research Briefing," Berkman Center Research Publication no. 2016-15, Berkman Klein Center for Internet & Society, Harvard University, September 26, 2016, 3, https://cyber .harvard.edu/publications/2016/StudentPrivacyBriefing.

63. See Christine Emba, "Amazon Key Is Silicon Valley at Its Most Out-of-Touch," *Washington Post*, October 25, 2017, https://www.washingtonpost.com/blogs/post -partisan/wp/2017/10/25/amazon-key-is-silicon-valley-at-its-most-out-of-touch.

64. Mitchell, "Both Sides, Now."

65. See Emily Chang, *Brotopia: Breaking Up the Boys' Club of Silicon Valley* (New York: Portfolio, 2018).

66. See Pokémon Go, available at https://www.pokemongo.com/en-us.

67. See Rachel Botsman, "Co-parenting with Alexa," *New York Times*, October 7, 2017, https://www.nytimes.com/2017/10/07/opinion/sunday/children-alexa-echo -robots.html.

68. J. K. Rowling, "House-Elves," Writing by J. K. Rowling, Pottermore, accessed August 26, 2018, https://www.pottermore.com/explore-the-story/house-elves.

69. Sloan Eddleston, "Why the Future Could Mean Delivery Straight into Your Fridge," *Walmart Today* (blog), September 22, 2017, https://blog.walmart.com/innova tion/20170922/why-the-future-could-mean-delivery-straight-into-your-fridge.

70. Eddleston, "Why the Future Could Mean Delivery Straight into Your Fridge."

71. Harwell, "Companies Race to Gather a Newly Prized Currency."

72. Joni Mitchell, "The Circle Game," track 12 on Joni Mitchell, *Ladies of the Canyon*, compact disc, Siquomb Publishing Corp., 1970.

73. These divides manifest themselves in many ways, including with respect to digital tech. "Social class makes a difference in how families and individuals approach and incorporate digital, mobile, and entertainment media into their lives." Lynn Schofield Clark, *The Parent App: Understanding Families in the Digital Age* (New York: Oxford University Press, 2013), 209.

74. Shaila Dewan and Richard A. Oppel Jr., "In Tamir Rice Case, Many Errors by Cleveland Police, Then a Fatal One," *New York Times*, January 22, 2015, https:// www.nytimes.com/2015/01/23/us/in-tamir-rice-shooting-in-cleveland-many-errors -by-police-then-a-fatal-one.html.

75. For an example, see Andrea Castillo, "L.A. Father Detained by ICE after Dropping Daughter at School May Be Deported," *Los Angeles Times*, July 31, 2017, http://

www.latimes.com/local/lanow/la-me-romulo-avelica-deportation-20170731-story
.html.

76. Plyler v. Doe, 457 U.S. 202 (1982).

77. Scholars have identified a "new maternalism" in today's world, in which "social and legal reform efforts are again mobilizing white middle class mothers as a force for change. . . . [This] political mobilization [is] using the cultural forms of new maternalism to revalidate motherhood as a source of pride and moral authority for women." Naomi Mezey and Cornelia T. L. Pillard, "Against the New Maternalism," *Michigan Journal of Gender & Law* 18, (2012): 233.

Chapter 4

1. *My So-Called Life* was a TV teen drama series that aired from August 1994 to January 1995 and explored the perspectives of adolescents on the social issues of the day.

2. For examples of revenue-generating arrangements, see Ashley May, "These YouTube Moms Are Making Money Showing Real Parenting Moments," *USA Today*, May 11, 2017, https://www.usatoday.com/story/news/nation-now/2017/05/11/youtube
-moms-make-money-parenting-videos/315989001; and Mackenzie Dawson, "My Mommy Blog Ruined My Life," *New York Post*, May 29, 2016, https://nypost.com/
2016/05/29/my-mommy-blog-ruined-my-life. Dawson identifies "companies that act as the middleman between brands and bloggers and they post sponsorship opportunities—aka shopportunities" (ibid.).

3. For example, some teachers act as "brand ambassadors" for ed tech products. See Natasha Singer, "Silicon Valley Courts Brand-Name Teachers, Raising Ethics Issues," *New York Times*, September 2, 2017, https://www.nytimes.com/2017/09/02/tech
nology/silicon-valley-teachers-tech.html.

4. Alice E. Marwick, *Status Update: Celebrity, Publicity, and Branding in the Social Media Age* (New Haven: Yale University Press, 2013), 114.

5. For a report of seven-figure incomes for superstar mommy bloggers, see Bianca Bosker, "Instamom," *The Atlantic*, March 2017, https://www.theatlantic.com/
magazine/archive/2017/03/instamom/513827.

6. Compare Kathleen Kuehn, "Why Are So Many Journalists Willing to Write for Free?," *Canadian Journalism Project*, February 3, 2014, defining hope labor as "un- or under-compensated work, often performed in exchange for experience and exposure in the hopes that future work will follow."

7. Laura Ingalls Wilder, *Little House on the Prairie* (New York: Harper Trophy, 1971).

8. See Melissa Weiss, "My First Period!," *The Weiss Life*, YouTube, April 27, 2017, https://www.youtube.com/watch?v=aFLznBtKSOk. This mother-daughter YouTube

video is sponsored by a company that offers a period readiness package for preteens. In the video, the mother talks to the daughter about what to expect from her first period.

9. For an explanation of how YouTube suggestions push viewers toward more extreme content, see Zeynep Tufekci, "YouTube, the Great Radicalizer," *New York Times*, March 10, 2018, https://www.nytimes.com/2018/03/10/opinion/sunday/you tube-politics-radical.html.

10. For example, Barcroft TV, "Living with Tigers: Family Share[s] Home with Pet Tigers," YouTube video, September 25, 2013, https://youtu.be/xwidefc2wpc. This video has been viewed over 56 million times.

11. Briefly on evolution over time, one commentator suggests that the "mommy internet" has become increasingly sanitized, "miles away from what mother-hood looks like for many of us—and miles from what the mommy Internet looked like a decade ago." Sarah Pulliam Bailey, "How the Mom Internet Became a Spotless, Sponsored Void," *Washington Post*, January 26, 2018, https://www .washingtonpost.com/outlook/how-the-mom-internet-became-a-spotless-sponsored -void/2018/01/26/072b46ac-01d6-11e8-bb03-722769454f82_story.html.

12. If you're looking for a place to start your research, I recommend "FUNNY Ani-mals Trolling Babies and Kid #5." It has cute animals, cute kids, and also crying kids. Funny Babies and Pets, "FUNNY Animals Trolling Babies and Kid #5," YouTube video, December 1, 2017, https://youtu.be/BZT4eoHWVwI.

13. It can be difficult to draw the line between when commercial content is shar-enting and when it's kid-driven. For this discussion, the focus is on digital content where the parental role is fairly obvious. Even for older kids and teens, where it might seem that parents are backstage, it's unclear how much that can be the case, given all the choices kids and teens are unable to make for themselves.

14. For successful toddler digital superstars, see Katherine Rosman, "Why Isn't Your Toddler Paying the Mortgage?," *New York Times*, September 27, 2017, https://www .nytimes.com/2017/09/27/style/viral-toddler-videos.html.

15. The BlogHer 2017 conference had a session on "Intimate Writing: How to Bal-ance Your Private and Public Personas." The session description explained: "People who are transparent tend to have the most loyal audiences. But how do you share the most intimate parts of your life without sharing everything and losing yourself?" BlogHer, "#BlogHer17 Agenda," http://www.blogher.com/node/2458157/schedule.

16. One example, which includes the seemingly popular trick of disappearing ink, is available here: "Disappearing Ink Prank on Girl—Eating Bad Fish—Kids Makeup Mishap," YouTube video, February 20, 2016, https://www.youtube.com/ watch?v=SqMNdT0rF-w.

17. For example, Dawson, "My Mommy Blog Ruined My Life." Dawson claims that the term is generally disfavored by those who use it.

18. For example, Janice Brett Elspas, ed., "2018–19 Master Blog Conference Calendar for Mom, Dad and Lifestyle Influencers and Bloggers," *Mommy Blog Expert* (blog), https://www.mommyblogexpert.com/p/women-mom-blogger-conferences.html. Elspas curates information about how to effectively mommy blog, including digital content creation educational opportunities for mommy bloggers.

19. "Women have long managed both the 'second shift,' or the work of managing the household, as well as the 'third shift,' which . . . refer[s] to the emotion work of helping children to feel secure and cared for in the midst of juggling parental responsibilities of work and home." Lynn Schofield Clark, *The Parent App: Understanding Families in the Digital Age* (New York: Oxford University Press, 2013), 215.

20. Use of the term *life stage* to include conception, gestation, and labor and delivery is done in a colloquial, not legal, sense. As used here, the term is designed to reflect the felt experience of many parents that their family unit begins when they begin trying to create it or, for unplanned pregnancy, when they find out that they are on the road toward becoming parents. The term is not used to take a position on whether or how the law should recognize an unfertilized egg, an embryo, or a fetus as having life the way that newborns, infants, children, adolescents, and adults do.

21. See WhatsUpMoms, "Elle-Labor & Delivery of Presley!," YouTube video, July 17, 2013, https://youtu.be/gg_y-19iH0Y. WhatsUpMoms has over 2.2 million subscribers and identifies as the "#1 parenting channel on YouTube."

22. For example, Jessica Shyba, "Theo and Beau Welcome Evangeline," *Momma's Gone City* (blog), http://www.mommasgonecity.com/2014/09/theo-and-beau-welcome -evangeline.

23. For example, The *Something Navy* blog recommends the NEST video monitor. Arielle Charnas, "FAQs: Ruby Edition," *Something Navy* (blog), http://something-navy.com/faq-ruby-edition.

24. For a great discussion of parenting advice trends, see KJ Dell'Antonia and Jessica Lahey, "The Science of Parenting: Untangling Ever-Shifting Parenting Advice," interview with Laura Knoy, *The Exchange*, New Hampshire Public Radio, January 17, 2018, http://nhpr.org/post/science-parenting-untangling-ever-shifting-parenting -advice#stream/0.

25. For example, Kumanan Wilson and Jennifer Keelan, "Social Media and the Empowering of Opponents of Medical Technologies: The Case of Anti-Vaccinationism," *Journal of Medical Internet Research* 15, no. 5 (2013): 1–4, http://www .jmir.org/2013/5/e103. This paper explores how vaccination opponents use social media to spread information and forge connections.

26. For general discussion of "truth in advertising requirements," see Federal Trade Commission, "Truth in Advertising," Media Resources, https://www.ftc.gov/news-events/media-resources/truth-advertising.

27. For more information about the FTC's position on influencers, see Federal Trade Commission, "The FTC's Endorsement Guides: What People Are Asking," Guidance, https://www.ftc.gov/tips-advice/business-center/guidance/ftcs-endorsement-guides-what-people-are-asking.

28. This example is related to an actual FTC enforcement against Moonlight Slumber, a mattress company. Federal Trade Commission, "FTC Approves Final Consent Order in Moonlight Slumber, LLC Advertising Case," news release, December 12, 2017, https://www.ftc.gov/news-events/press-releases/2017/12/ftc-approves-final-consent-order-moonlight-slumber-llc.

29. Familiar bodies of law still exist in this space. A mommy blogger cannot avoid liability from defamation, for instance, by posting on her blog lies about another person that damage that person's reputation instead of posting them on the pages of a glossy magazine. She can't avoid liability for criminal threatening if she rants about kidnapping her playground arch-nemesis. But these and similar examples show the outer boundaries of legally permissible content in the commercial sharenting space rather than reflecting the bulk of activities that occur.

30. For an example of how ostensibly expert parental advice online can have significant real world impact, see Megan Molteni, "Anti-Vaxxers Brought Their War to Minnesota—Then Came Measles," *Wired*, May 7, 2017, https://www.wired.com/2017/05/anti-vaxxers-brought-war-minnesota-came-measles.

31. Clare O'Connor, "Forbes Top Influencers: How What's Up Moms Turned Viral Videos into a Media Company," *Forbes*, September 26, 2017, https://www.forbes.com/sites/clareoconnor/2017/09/26/forbes-top-influencers-how-whats-up-moms-turned-viral-videos-into-a-media-company.

32. For example, 5-Minute Crafts, "22 Christmas Décor and Gift Ideas without Going Broke," YouTube video, December 17, 2017, https://youtu.be/7r-lAWtpkOo.

33. For example, Shot of the Yeagers, "Family Gymnastic Challenge in Our Pool!," YouTube video, July 20, 2018, https://youtu.be/2RA1pUe_RTA.

34. For example, ClutterBug, "Decorating Tips—Decorating My Girls Shared Room on a Budget," YouTube video, November 26, 2014, https://youtu.be/TfseYsT0j3M.

35. Abby Ohlheiser, "The Saga of a YouTube Family Who Pulled Disturbing Pranks on Their Own Kids," *Washington Post*, April 26, 2017, https://www.washingtonpost.com/news/the-intersect/wp/2017/04/25/the-saga-of-a-youtube-family-who-pulled-disturbing-pranks-on-their-own-kids.

36. Ohlheiser.

37. Ohlheiser. A related query: should the companies that make smart toys also have a duty to report abuse that they learn of through their products? This law review article says yes: Corinne Moini, "Protecting Privacy in the Era of Smart Toys: Does Hello Barbie Have a Duty to Report?," *Catholic University Journal of Law and Technology* 25 (2017): 313–314.

38. See Philip DeFranco, "WOW . . . We Need to Talk about This . . . ," YouTube video, April 17, 2017, https://www.youtube.com/watch?v=fvoLmsXKkYM. DeFranco, a YouTube celebrity, removes sponsorship and advertising from this episode to focus the discussion on the issue of child safety.

39. If adverse decisions—outside the context of the home or other private life—are being made based on the perception of disability, including mental health disability, Cody should receive some protection and recourse from state and federal disability statutes and regulations.

40. "YouTube Challenge—I Told My Kids I Ate All Their Halloween Candy 2017," *Jimmy Kimmel Live*, YouTube video, November 2, 2017, https://youtu.be/bmCOjcaiXQM.

41. "YouTube Challenge—I Told My Kids I Ate All Their Halloween Candy 2017."

42. Meg van Achterberg, "Jimmy Kimmel's Halloween Prank Can Scar Children. Why Are We Laughing?," *Washington Post*, October 20, 2017, https://www.washington post.com/outlook/jimmy-kimmel-wants-to-prank-kids-why-are-we-laughing/2017/10/20/9be17716-aed0-11e7-9e58-e6288544af98_story.html. Jokes are funny when they don't perpetuate power imbalances or when the person in the subservient/lower status position is at least in on the joke.

43. A broader YouTube prank community goes beyond commercial sharents and "has long been [having] a competition for who can capture its audience's attention with the latest extreme, offensive, possibly staged video, justified as 'just a prank!'" Abby Ohlheiser, "Everyone's Outraged at the 'Acid Attack' YouTube Prank Video. It's Far from the Worst," *Washington Post*, January 30, 2018, https://www.washingtonpost.com/news/the-intersect/wp/2018/01/30/what-one-youtubers-controversial-water-prank-says-about-the-strange-world-of-prank-videos.

44. Adults also inflict "cyberhate" on one another, with "recent growth" in this unfortunate practice. Danielle Citron and Helen Norton, "Intermediaries and Hate Speech: Fostering Digital Citizenship for Our Information Age," *Boston Law Review* 91 (2011): 1438.

45. For a general discussion of cyberbullying, see John Palfrey and Urs Gasser, *Born Digital: How Children Grow Up in a Digital Age*, rev. ed. (New York: Basic Books, 2016). Palfrey and Gasser define "[c]yberbullying [as] the intentional use of any digital medium, including text-messaging, email, and phone calls, to harm others" (ibid., 100).

46. N.H. Rev. Stat. Ann. § 193-F:3(I)(a)(2).

47. N.H. Rev. Stat. Ann. § 193-F:3(I)(b).

48. N.H. Rev. Stat. Ann. § 193-F:2(IV). This provision of the statute makes it clear that the law is limited to schools.

49. For a discussion of the protected individual liberty interest in parenting, see D. Kelly Weisberg and Susan Frelich Appleton, *Modern Family Law: Cases and Materials* (New York: Wolters Kluwer, 2013), 819. Weisberg and Appleton explain that the "liberty [interest] protected by the Due Process Clause [in the US Constitution] . . . encompass[es] parental autonomy, the right to rear a child as the parent sees fit" (ibid.).

50. Taking the discussion beyond missing candy and antiparental bullying laws, Anne C. Dailey and Laura A. Rosenbury argue for reconceiving of children's relationship to law away from the law's "preoccupation with assigning control over children to parents or the state" and toward a legal structure "informed by the relationships that support children's broader interests, adult responsibilities to further those interests, and affirmative rights that best protect them." Anne C. Dailey and Laura A. Rosenbury, "The New Law of the Child," *Yale Law Journal* 127 (2018): 1506.

51. For example, Char Adams, "'Cancer Mom' Gets Real about Raising Sick Daughter: 'Please Don't Call Me Strong,'" *People*, November 13, 2017, https://people.com/human-interest/christa-keehr-cancer-mom-strong.

52. For example, Christina Smallwood, "Our Story," Fifi + Mo, https://www.fifiandmo.com.

53. For example, Team2Moms, YouTube channel, https://www.youtube.com/channel/UCCzmXhARScj7wtJ0f2co64A; and Keren Swan and Khoa Nguyen (KKandbabyJ), YouTube channel, https://www.youtube.com/channel/UCU-ZXqhx1xjsxO1ftXJELdg/featured.

54. For example, GoFundMe, "Get Help with Cancer Fundraising," https://www.gofundme.com/start/cancer-fundraising. The page explains how to use GoFundMe to "get immediate help with cancer costs." Although most users are legitimate, there have been reports of illegitimate requests, such as James Hetherington, "New York Parents Accused of Running Fake Cancer GoFundMe Page for Healthy Child," *Newsweek*, May 10, 2018, https://www.newsweek.com/new-york-parents-busted-running-fake-cancer-gofundme-page-healthy-child-918656.

55. For example, N.H. Rev. Stat. Ann. § 161-B:3. This statute describes when the state must get involved to enforce the support of dependent children.

56. For a discussion of the dangers of payday loans, see Lauren K. Saunders, Leah A. Plunkett, and Carolyn Carter, *Stopping the Payday Loan Trap: Alternatives That Work,*

Ones That Don't (Boston: National Consumer Law Center, 2010), https://www.nclc
.org/issues/stopping-the-payday-loan-trap.html.

57. See "What Are My Rights under the Military Lending Act?," Consumer Financial
Protection Bureau, updated October 7, 2016, https://www.consumerfinance.gov/
ask-cfpb/what-are-my-rights-under-the-military-lending-act-en-1783. The act places
a 36 percent military annual percentage rate cap on loans to people on active duty
and their dependents. This keeps lenders from offering the payday product.

58. Camila Domonoske, "Google Announces It Will Stop Allowing Ads for Payday
Lenders," National Public Radio, May 11, 2016, https://www.npr.org/sections/
thetwo-way/2016/05/11/477633475/google-announces-it-will-stop-allowing-ads-for
-payday-lenders.

59. For example, Save the Children's "Sponsor a Child" campaign contains some
limited identifying information about particular children. See https://support.
savethechildren.org/site/SPageNavigator/sponsorship.html.

60. See Clark, *The Parent App*, 215.

61. This longstanding differential remains true, although the proportion of single-
parent households headed by men has been rising. See Gretchen Livingston, "The
Rise of Single Fathers: A Ninefold Increase since 1960," Pew Research Center, July 2,
2013, http://www.pewsocialtrends.org/2013/07/02/the-rise-of-single-fathers.

62. You can be a successful commercial sharent and have this extent be minimal.
For example, the hilarious *Honest Toddler* blog features a generic toddler figure. See
"Apologies," Home, *Honest Toddler* (blog), http://www.thehonesttoddler.com.

63. Emma Brockes, "Is it OK to Keep Posting Photos of My Kids on Facebook?," *The
Guardian*, May 31, 2017, https://www.theguardian.com/technology/2017/may/31/
facebook-photos-children-parenting. Brockes claims that large numbers of children's
photos on Facebook are posted by women.

64. "Authenticity is negotiated symbolically; information disclosure is used to
determine its presence or absence, but is an incomplete measure at best." Marwick,
Status Update, 121.

65. For an example of such content, see Wills Robinson, "And the Baby Makes
Three! Napping Toddler and Puppy Who Charmed the World Are Now Joined by
Little Sister," *Daily Mail*, January 18, 2015, http://www.dailymail.co.uk/news/article
-2915776/And-baby-makes-three-Napping-toddler-puppy-charmed-joined-adorable
-baby-sister.html.

66. For a leading theoretical framework of this and related challenges of self-
presentation, see Erving Goffman, *The Presentation of Self in Everyday Life* (New York:
Doubleday, 1959).

67. Through interviews with college students, researcher Donna Freitas concluded that "By the time our children reach college, they know that a large part of their job is to present a happy face to the world. . . . [W]e (the parents, teachers, coaches, and mentors in their lives) have helped push them to this place." Donna Freitas, *The Happiness Effect: How Social Media is Driving a Generation to Appear Perfect at Any Cost* (New York: Oxford University Press, 2017), xvii.

68. See Andrew Ross, "In Search of the Lost Paycheck," in *Digital Labor: The Internet as Playground and Factory*, ed. Trebor Scholz (New York: Routledge, 2012), 26. Ross defines the term as "gladsome work" (ibid.).

69. For further discussion, see Lauren Gelman, "Privacy, Free Speech, and 'Blurry-Edged' Social Networks," *Boston College Law Review* 50 (2009): 1315–1344.

Chapter 5

1. William Wordsworth, "My Heart Leaps Up When I Behold," *Bartleby.com*, http://www.bartleby.com/145/ww194.html.

2. In this iconic twentieth-century novel by William Golding, an island governed by children becomes increasingly dystopian.

3. That background sound was actually a trombone, suggesting that adults are speaking with jazz rather than expelling hot air. Andy Lewis, "Peanuts Producer: Where That Adult 'Mwa-Mwa-Mwa' Sound Came From," *Hollywood Reporter*, January 30, 2015, http://www.hollywoodreporter.com/news/peanuts-producer-adult-mwa-mwa-767418.

4. "U.S. Society has tended to view young people either as vulnerable and in need of protection or as a potential menace to be controlled and contained." Lynn Schofield Clark, *The Parent App: Understanding Families in the Digital Age* (New York: Oxford University Press, 2013), 49. For further discussion, see Anne C. Dailey and Laura A. Rosenbury, "The New Law of the Child," *Yale Law Journal* 127 (2018): 1448–1537. Daily and Rosenbury argue that the law's "narrow focus on children's dependency under a regime of parental and state authority has multiple shortcomings" (ibid., 1467).

5. The United States Supreme Court has long recognized a broad "liberty [that] parents and guardians [have] to direct the upbringing and education of children under their control." Pierce v. Society of the Sisters of the Holy Names of Jesus & Mary, 268 U.S. 510, 534–535 (1925). Guardians also enjoy significant protection, although not as robust as parents.

6. The home is a "quintessentially private space." Jeannie Suk, "Criminal Law Comes Home," *Yale Law Journal* 116 (October 2006): 5.

7. In what appears to be the first deep-dive analysis of "online sharing about parenting" in a law review article, Stacey B. Steinberg explains that "parents are seemingly the natural protector of their child's digital identity." Stacey B. Steinberg, "Sharenting: Children's Privacy in the Age of Social Media," *Emory Law Journal* 66 (2017): 843.

8. Today, government involvement in the home as the result of a breakdown in family cohesion and safety, such as abuse, is likely to include the use of the criminal law toolkit, which increases the scope and impact of state intervention. See Suk, "Criminal Law Comes Home," 6.

9. In certain circumstances, attempts by an outside party to force entry into a home can be met with lawful violence by the homeowner. See 40 C.J.S. *Homicide* § 221 (2017).

10. From the perspective of youth today, "there is no 'online life' and 'offline life.' There's just 'life.'" John Palfrey and Urs Gasser, *Born Digital: How Children Grow Up in a Digital Age*, rev. ed. (New York: Basic Books, 2016), 2.

11. A recent sociological study of parenting styles and technology found that the "professional middle-class parents interviewed for this study generally began with a concern about care when they explained why they eagerly use devices of connection such as baby monitors and cell phones." Margaret K. Nelson, *Parenting Out of Control: Anxious Parents in Uncertain Times* (New York: New York University Press, 2010), 165.

12. The "umbrella field known as science and technology studies (STS) . . . [has long held] that artifacts constrain ('regulate') behavior." Julie E. Cohen, *Configuring the Networked Self: Law, Code, and the Play of Everyday Practice* (New Haven: Yale University Press, 2012), 26. The impact of digital "artifacts" within the home seems to be increasing with today's current and emerging digital technologies.

13. Daniel Tiger, a cartoon continuation of the children's TV classic *Mister Rogers' Neighborhood*, is available at http://pbskids.org/daniel.

14. For an example of how data recorded over a digital home device may be used to resolve disputes far more serious than those over the tails(!) of a talking tiger, see Amy B. Wang, "Can Amazon Echo Help Solve a Murder? Police Will Soon Find Out," *Washington Post*, March 9, 2017, https://www.washingtonpost.com/news/the-switch/wp/2017/03/09/can-amazon-echo-help-solve-a-murder-police-will-soon-find-out.

15. J. M. Barrie's childhood classic *Peter Pan, or The Boy Who Wouldn't Grow Up* can be read at https://www.gutenberg.org/files/16/16-h/16-h.htm.

16. "These days, average American adults check their phones every six and a half minutes." Sherry Turkle, *Reclaiming Conversation: The Power of Talk in a Digital Age* (New York: Penguin Press, 2015), 42.

17. As leading technology and social media scholar danah boyd has found, "many teens complain about parents who look over their shoulders when they're on the computer." danah boyd, *It's Complicated: The Social Lives of Networked Teens* (New Haven: Yale University Press, 2014), 32.

18. "Children have no control over the dissemination of their personal information by their parents." Steinberg, "Sharenting," 846.

19. "Information privacy law is an interrelated web of tort law, federal and state constitutional law, federal and state statutory law, evidentiary privileges, property law, contract law, and criminal law." Daniel J. Solove and Paul M. Schwartz, *Privacy, Information, and Technology*, 2nd ed. (New York: Aspen, 2006), 2.

20. J. K. Rowling, "Potions," Writing by J. K. Rowling, Pottermore, accessed August 20, 2017, https://www.pottermore.com/writing-by-jk-rowling/potions.

21. J. K. Rowling, "Invisibility Cloak," Writing by J. K. Rowling, Pottermore, accessed August 20, 2017, https://www.pottermore.com/explore-the-story/invisibility-cloak.

22. "Notice and consent is, today, the most widely used strategy for protecting consumer privacy. . . . In some fantasy world, users actually read these notices, understand their legal implications (consulting their attorneys if necessary), negotiate with other providers of similar services to get better privacy treatment, and only then click to indicate their consent. Reality is different." President's Council of Advisors on Science and Technology (PCAST), *Big Data and Privacy: A Technological Perspective*, May 2014, 38, https://obamawhitehouse.archives.gov/sites/default/files/microsites/ostp/PCAST/pcast_big_data_and_privacy_-_may_2014.pdf.

23. "As a useful policy tool, notice and consent is defeated by exactly the positive benefits that big data enables: new, non-obvious, unexpectedly powerful uses of data. It is simply too complicated for the individual to make fine-grained choices for every new situation or app." PCAST, *Big Data and Privacy*.

24. For example, "Consumers do not typically read privacy policies and other online disclosures, even for products like Gmail that they use every day." Lior Jacob Strahilevitz and Matthew B. Kugler, "Is Privacy Policy Language Irrelevant to Consumers?," *Journal of Legal Studies* 45 (2016): S72.

25. Zooming in on the connected baby monitor example: privacy policies on internet of things devices may be particularly difficult to find because the digital object itself may not have space for any fine print. Scott R. Peppet walks through this problem in "Regulating the Internet of Things: First Steps toward Managing Discrimination, Privacy, Security, and Consent," *Texas Law Review* 93 (2014): 89–90.

26. "Even when consumers do read privacy policies, their belief about the nature of their bargains with technology companies seem to depend more on their preexisting

expectations than on the terms of the policies." Strahilevitz and Kugler, "Privacy Policy Language," S71.

27. In its 2014 report, the President's Council of Advisors on Science and Technology (PCAST) called for the exploration of new methods to detect and sanction privacy violations that don't rest with consumers because "Privacy policies . . . are only effective to the extent that they are realized and enforced." PCAST, *Big Data and Privacy*, 42–43.

28. State tort law offers people a vehicle to seek remedies, usually financial, for certain invasions of privacy. For discussion of privacy protections in tort law, see Solove and Schwartz, *Privacy, Information, and Technology*, 26.

29. In such circumstances, the FTC typically relies on "Section 5 of the FTC Act, which bars unfair and deceptive acts and practices in or affecting commerce." Federal Trade Commission, "Enforcing Privacy Promises," Protecting Consumer Privacy, Media Resources, https://www.ftc.gov/news-events/media-resources/protecting -consumer-privacy/enforcing-privacy-promises.

30. Compare Federal Trade Commission, "Recovering from Identity Theft," Identity Theft, Consumer Information, https://www.consumer.ftc.gov/features/feature-0014 -identity-theft. The FTC tries to educate the public on protective measures to discourage and mitigate fallout from privacy breaches because after the private information is out, it's essentially impossible to claw it back.

31. See US Department of Health and Human Services, "Summary of the HIPAA Privacy Rule," Health Insurance Portability and Accountability Act (HIPAA) for Professionals, https://www.hhs.gov/hipaa/for-professionals/privacy/laws-regulations/ index.html.

32. See Dalia Topelson Ritvo, *Privacy and Student Data: An Overview of the Federal Laws Impacting Student Information Collected through Networked Technologies*, Cyberlaw Clinic, Berkman Klein Center for Internet & Society, Harvard University, June 2016, 4–9, https://dash.harvard.edu/handle/1/27410234.

33. See Elana Zeide, "Student Privacy Principles in the Age of Big Data: Moving beyond FERPA and FIPPS," *Drexel Law Review* 8 (2016): 374.

34. See Ritvo, *Privacy and Student Data*, 3.

35. See Leah Plunkett, Alicia Solow-Niederman, and Urs Gasser, "Framing the Law and Policy Picture: A Snapshot of K–12 Cloud-Based Ed Tech and Student Privacy in Early 2014," Berkman Center Research Publication no. 2014-10, Berkman Klein Center for Internet & Society, Harvard University, June 4, 2014, 12–15, SSRN, https://papers.ssrn.com/sol3/papers.cfm?abstract_id=2442432##.

36. See Zeide, "Student Privacy Principles," 356.

37. See Joel Reidenberg et al., *Privacy and Cloud Computing in Public Schools*, Center on Law and Information Policy, book 2 (2013), 21, http://ir.lawnet.fordham.edu/clip/2.

38. "In practice . . . FERPA creates a structure in which [educational] institutions, not individuals, manage student privacy." See Zeide, "Student Privacy Principles," 123.

39. See Ritvo, *Privacy and Student Data*, 7.

40. See Plunkett, Solow-Niederman, and Gasser, "Framing the Law and Policy," 12–14.

41. See N. Cameron Russell et al., "Transparency and the Marketplace for Student Data," *Virginia Journal of Law and Technology* (forthcoming): 1–34, https://www.fordham.edu/info/23830/research/10517/transparency_and_the_marketplace_for_student_data/1. None of the schools responding to information requests for this study said they were "giving or selling student information to data brokers or to any other third party for marketing purposes" (ibid., 18). However, if schools are using digital services absent a negotiated and monitored contract directly with the service-provider, they may not know up-front or be in a position to monitor exactly what information they are giving or what is being done with it. A previous study by the Center on Law and Information Policy (CLIP) at Fordham looked at a nationally representative sample of school districts and found that "districts were rarely in control of the terms and conditions of data transfers" done through cloud-based digital ed tech. See Reidenberg et al., *Privacy and Cloud Computing in Public Schools*, 24.

42. 20 U.S.C.A. § 1232h (West 2018). See Lynn M. Daggett, "Student Privacy and the Protection of Pupil Rights Act as Amended by No Child Left Behind," *U.C. Davis Journal of Juvenile Law & Policy* 12 (2008): 55.

43. See Ritvo, *Privacy and Student Data*, 16.

44. See Ritvo, 18.

45. See Ritvo, 20.

46. For a deeper dive into the lessons Orwell holds, see Richard A. Epstein, "Does Literature Work as Social Science? The Case of George Orwell," *University of Colorado Law Review* 73 (2002): 987–1011.

47. For example, Frances Jensen, interview by Terry Gross, *Fresh Air*, NPR, April 15, 2016, http://www.npr.org/2016/04/15/474348291/why-teens-are-impulsive-addiction-prone-and-should-protect-their-brains: "We talk a lot about the downside of the limitations of . . . the teen brain . . . no insight, no judgment. . . . But . . . this is a wonderful time in life for teenagers . . . because of their enhanced synaptic plasticity . . . they can learn faster."

48. For example, Henry L. Roediger and Bridgid Finn, "Getting It Wrong: Surprising Tips on How to Learn," *Scientific American*, October 20, 2009, https://www.scientific american.com/article/getting-it-wrong. Roediger and Finn summarize research findings that show "learning becomes better if conditions are arranged so that students make errors."

49. For example, Julie Lythcott-Haims, *How to Raise an Adult: Break Free of the Overparenting Trap and Prepare Your Kid for Success* (New York: Henry Holt, 2015), excerpted at *MindShift* (podcast), KQED, June 9, 2015, https://ww2.kqed.org/mind shift/2015/06/09/what-overparenting-looks-like-from-a-stanford-deans-perspective. Haims offers a former Stanford University dean's take on how "humans need some degree of weathering in order to survive the larger challenges life will throw our way . . . [and wonders] why did parenting change from preparing our kids *for* life to protecting them *from* life" (ibid.).

50. In a seminal case on the rights of juvenile offenders, *In re* Gault, the United States Supreme Court reviewed the history of the juvenile justice system, observing that among the "highest motives and most enlightened impulses" of the reformers who created the system were the ideas that the "child was to be 'treated' and 'rehabilitated' and the procedures . . . were to be 'clinical' rather than punitive." 387 U.S. 1, 17 (1967).

51. For example, Laurence Steinberg and Elizabeth Cauffman, "The Elephant in the Courtroom: A Developmental Perspective on the Adjudication of Youthful Offenders," *Virginia Journal of Social Policy and the Law* 6 (1999): 393. Steinberg and Cauffman comment: "Ironically, it is these very features of adolescence as a [dynamic] developmental period that make it simultaneously interesting to developmental psychologists and perplexing to policy-makers and legal practitioners" (ibid.).

52. This quote is attributed to Fred Rogers, a towering figure in the world of child development and entertainment through his classic TV show, *Mister Rogers' Neighborhood*. For further discussion of the work of childhood, see Deborah Farmer Kris, "Creative Play: The Real Work of Childhood," Expert Tips & Advice, PBS Parents, February 22, 2016, http://www.pbs.org/parents/expert-tips-advice/2016/02/creative-play-real-work-childhood.

53. Provocatively, Dailey and Rosenbury suggest that trusted adults other than parents might promote play better than parents can due to their focus on "children's needs and incapacities." Dailey and Rosenbury, "The New Law," 1487.

54. "As the social state is reconfigured as a punishing state [in the post 9/11 era], youth become the enemy in hiding." Henry A. Grioux, *Youth in a Suspect Society: Democracy or Disposability* (New York: Palgrave Macmillan, 2009), 72. There is a "burgeoning [sociological academic] literature on the 'new surveillance' . . . which brings new populations and 'not just the official deviant' . . . under the 'watchful gaze' of others . . . [through] practices [that] have become part of our daily lives and

occur within personal and social relations." Margaret K. Nelson, "Watching Children: Describing the Use of Baby Monitors on Epinions.com," in *Who's Watching: Daily Practices of Surveillance among Contemporary Families*, ed. Margaret K. Nelson and Anita Ilta Garey (Nashville: Vanderbilt University Press, 2009), 220–221. Indeed, "Surveillance is already the business model of the internet." Bruce Schneier, "Snoops May Soon Be Able to Buy Your Browsing History. Thank the US Congress," *The Guardian*, March 30, 2017, https://www.schneier.com/essays/archives/2017/03/snoops_may_soon_be_a.html.

55. "The surveillance of children has been framed in a language of safety, protection, and care." Benjamin Shmueli and Ayelet Blecher-Prigat, "Privacy for Children," *Columbia Human Rights Law Review* 42 (2011): 760. For exploration of the "protective impulses" that underlie the juvenile justice system, see Kevin Lapp, "Databasing Delinquency," *Hastings Law Journal* 67 (2015): 207; compare Nelson, "Watching Children," 221, explaining that "surveillance does not just threaten, but that it also protects" and flagging the need for further academic research into the "balance between care and control that characterizes the use of these [surveillance] technologies [in families]," an inquiry relevant to spheres outside the home as well.

56. See Anita Ilta Garey, "'Nested Responsibility' and the Monitoring of Children and Parents in Family Court," in *Who's Watching: Daily Practices of Surveillance among Contemporary Families*, ed. Margaret K. Nelson and Anita Ilta Garey (Nashville: Vanderbilt University Press, 2009). Garey describes how government "intervenes [in family life] . . . to protect others from children—and to protect children from themselves" (ibid., 19).

57. "Monitoring has become associated with good parenting." Shmueli and Blecher-Prigat, "Privacy for Children," 760.

58. "Teachers are increasingly relying on behavior monitoring software not only to keep kids on track, but to track them, too." Adriene Hill, "A Day in the Life of a Data Mined Kid," *Marketplace*, NPR, September 15, 2014, https://www.marketplace.org/2014/09/15/education/learning-curve/day-life-data-mined-kid. For a legal analysis of the ever-broadening scope of student monitoring, see Emily F. Suski, "Beyond the Schoolhouse Gates: The Unprecedented Expansion of School Surveillance Authority under Cyberbullying Laws," *Case Western Reserve Law Review* 65 (2014): 63–119. "In a majority of states, they [cyberbullying laws] arguably provide schools with unlimited or nearly unlimited authority to conduct electronic surveillance of students' online and electronic activity whenever and wherever that activity occurs" (ibid., 67).

59. "The criminal justice system collects a remarkable amount of information about youth." Lapp, "Databasing Delinquency," 208.

60. "This specific historical moment [is] . . . one in which the *technological* possibilities for monitoring (and for the invasion of privacy) have expanded in ways never

before considered." Margaret K. Nelson and Anita Ilta Garey, "Who's Watching? An Introductory Essay," in *Who's Watching: Daily Practices of Surveillance among Contemporary Families*, ed. Margaret K. Nelson and Anita Ilta Garey (Nashville: Vanderbilt University Press, 2009), 1.

61. Surveillance instruments may hide in plain sight. For example, location data obtained by your cell phone "is so valuable that cell phone companies are now selling it to data brokers, who in turn resell it to anyone willing to pay for it." Bruce Schneier, *Data and Goliath: The Hidden Battles to Collect Your Data and Control Your World* (New York: Norton, 2015), 3.

62. And little monkeys are curious indeed, especially that iconic one named George. You can see his adventures at http://www.pbs.org/parents/curiousgeorge.

63. For example, in the sphere of schools' responses to undesirable, difficult, or dangerous behavior, digital ed tech provider ABE Systems states that 484,902 students are "managed using ABE [Alternative Behavior Educator]." ABE Systems, home page, accessed August 19, 2017, http://www.abesystems.com. One feature of ABE is that "Each student receives [digitally delivered] personalized modules that are automatically assigned based on over 50 targeted behaviors such as fighting, substance abuse, or disrespect." The first two categories are straightforward. The third is not. ABE Systems, last accessed August 19, 2017, http://www.abesystems .com/mid-high-school.php.

64. "Schools are not just sharing behavioral information with law enforcement. Reports have surfaced of schools sharing records with noncriminal justice government agencies, such as immigration enforcement authorities." Lapp, "Databasing Delinquency," 215.

65. For the definition of "delinquent act," see Office of Juvenile Justice and Delinquency Prevention, "Glossary," Statistical Briefing Book, https://www.ojjdp.gov/ ojstatbb/glossary.html.

66. According to the Bureau of Justice Statistics, "prosecution of juveniles in criminal court is generally reserved for those charged with the quite serious crimes of murder, robbery, and aggravated assault." Office of Justice Programs, "Juvenile Defendants," Bureau of Justice Statistics, https://www.bjs.gov/index.cfm?ty=tp&tid=236.

67. Lapp, "Databasing Delinquency," 212–213.

68. "While black students represent 16% of student enrollment, they represent 27% of students referred to law enforcement and 31% of students subjected to a school-related arrest. . . . Students with disabilities . . . represent a quarter of students arrested and referred to law enforcement, even though they are only 12% of the overall student population." U.S. Department of Education Office for Civil Rights, *Data Snapshot: School Discipline*, March 2014, https://ocrdata.ed.gov/downloads/ crdc-school-discipline-snapshot.pdf. "A growing body of research has also found

that the school-to-prison pipeline is affecting lesbian, gay, bisexual, and transgender (LGBT) youth." "Dropout, Push-Out, and the School-to-Prison Pipeline," GLSEN, https://www.glsen.org/article/dropout-push-out-and-school-prison-pipeline.

69. "According to the CRDC [U.S. Department of Education's Civil Rights Data Collection], during the 2011–2012 school year, schools referred approximately 260,000 students to law enforcement, and approximately 92,000 students were arrested on school property." Sarah E. Redfield and Jason P. Nance, *School-to-Prison Pipeline: Preliminary Report*, American Bar Association, February 2016, 14, https://www.american bar.org/content/dam/aba/administrative/diversity_pipeline/stp_preliminary_report _final.authcheckdam.pdf.

70. According to Lapp, "schools have criminalized normal adolescent behavior." Lapp, "Databasing Delinquency," 212–213.

71. "Once students are so disciplined [by schools,] they are significantly likely to find themselves moving further along the pipeline toward prison." Redfield and Nance, *School-to-Prison Pipeline*, 23.

72. "Results of being out of school directly disadvantage the students and the impact is likely circular and cumulative." Redfield and Nance, *School-to-Prison Pipeline*, 22.

73. Judges do have discretion to require specific types of educational experiences as part of juvenile justice sentencing. For instance, a judge in Virginia recently ordered teens who vandalized a "historic black schoolhouse . . . [to] read one book each month for the next 12 months and write a report about it. . . . [The books] must address some of history's most divisive and tragic periods." Christine Hauser, "Teenagers Who Vandalized Historic Black Schoolhouse Are Ordered to Read Books," *New York Times*, February 8, 2017, https://www.nytimes.com/2017/02/08/us/black -school-racist-sexist-graffiti.html. That this type of case disposition made national news reflects it is an exception rather than the rule.

74. Rehabilitation is at the core of juvenile justice system design. See *In re* Gault, 387 U.S. at 14.

75. The United States Supreme Court has recognized that there can be a big gap between rehabilitative intent and reality: "Juvenile Court history has . . . demonstrated that unbridled discretion [by judges], however benevolently motivated, is frequently a poor substitute for principle and procedure." *In re* Gault, 387 U.S. at 18.

76. The juvenile delinquency statutory scheme in New Hampshire, where the author previously represented juvenile clients, offers an illustrative example of the broad scope of "services, placements [,] and programs" that the court can order. See N.H. Rev. Stat. Ann. §§ 169-B:19, 169-B:21; N.H. Cit. Ct. Fam. Div. R. 3.6.

77. For instance, juvenile offenders in New Hampshire who are subject to monitoring by a Juvenile Parole and Probation Officer (JPPO) are required to "be of good

behavior and remain arrest free, obey all laws and cooperate with your parent(s) or custodian at all times." N.H. Cit. Ct. Fam. Div. R. 3.6(b). Cooperation with parents at all times is a lot to ask of any kid or teenager.

78. Guidance from the National Reentry Resource Center encourages juvenile justice system stakeholders to move way from this common problem in the juvenile justice system: "Relying on restrictive forms of supervisions that don't promote public safety or positive youth behaviors but do create bloated juvenile corrections budgets." Elizabeth Seigle, Natassia Walsh, and Josh Weber, *Core Principles for Reducing Recidivism and Improving Other Outcomes for Youth in the Juvenile Justice System* (New York: Council of State Governments Justice Center, 2014), 7, https:// csgjusticecenter.org/wp-content/uploads/2014/07/Core-Principles-for-Reducing -Recidivism-and-Improving-Other-Outcomes-for-Youth-in-the-Juvenile-Justice -System.pdf.

79. This Silicon Valley buzz-phrase is actually on point here. For example, Dominic Basulto, "The New #Fail: Fail Fast, Fail Early and Fail Often," *Washington Post*, May 30, 2012, https://www.washingtonpost.com/blogs/innovations/post/the-new-fail -fail-fast-fail-early-and-fail-often/2012/05/30/gJQAKA891U_blog.html.

80. Tragically, we seem to be doing so even for kids who are most in need of actual protection: "The county shelters in the nation's largest foster care system are supposed to serve as a refuge for vulnerable children removed from unsafe homes. Instead, they have funneled hundreds of children, some as young as 8 years old, into the criminal justice system for relatively minor incidents, a *Chronicle* study has found." Karen de Sá, Joaquin Palomino, and Cynthia Dizikes, "Dubious Arrests, Damaged Lives: How Shelters Criminalize Hundreds of Children," *San Francisco Chronicle*, May 18, 2017, http://projects.sfchronicle.com/2017/fostering-failure.

81. "Maybe you heard about the Tamir Rice case and wondered: How does a 12-year-old boy with a toy gun on a playground get shot to death on-camera by the police without anyone getting charged?" Sean Flynn, "The Tamir Rice Story: How to Make a Police Shooting Disappear," *GQ*, July 14, 2016, https://www.gq.com/story/ tamir-rice-story.

82. For a criticism of a Washington state trial court that found "a juvenile who sends a sexually explicit selfie is a victim of his own act of child pornography," see Amy Roe, "Teens Who Engage in 'Sexting' Should Not Be Prosecuted as Sex Offenders," *Speak Freely* (blog) ACLU, April 19, 2017, https://www.aclu.org/blog/privacy-technology/ teens-who-engage-sexting-should-not-be-prosecuted-sex-offenders. Zooming in on the registry piece: sex offender registries are theorized by psychological and criminological experts as having no meaningful deterrent effect on teens who engage in sexting and similar behaviors because "certain nonviolent sexual offenses that warrant registration are perceived as developmentally normative (e.g., consensual sex between similar-aged peers, sexually explicit text messaging or 'sexting')." Cynthia J.

Najdowski, Hayley Cleary, and Margaret Stevenson, "Adolescent Sex Offender Regis-tration Policy: Perspectives on General Deterrence Potential from Criminology and Developmental Psychology," *Psychology, Public Policy, and Law* 22 (2016): 115.

83. The lines between conduct that constitutes playful youthful exploration versus conduct that should be regulated by an institutional authority are far from clear. For instance, in 2015, when Yale University issued guidelines on Halloween cos-tumes to try to avoid choices that might be offensive or intimidating to members of minority or other marginalized groups, some students resented the intrusion. Others resented the response of one faculty member who "drew on her scholarship and career experience, and . . . invit[ed] the community to think about the controversy through an intellectual lens [early child development and its emphasis on play] that few if any had considered." Conor Friedersdorf, "The New Intolerance of Student Activism," *The Atlantic*, November 9, 2015, https://www.theatlantic.com/politics/archive/2015/11/the-new-intolerance-of-student-activism-at-yale/414810.

84. The full text of Twain's novel is available at http://www.gutenberg.org/ebooks/76.

85. "The phrase 'orphan train' was first used in 1854 to describe the transportation of children outside of their homes localities on the railways." Rebecca S. Trammell, "Orphan Train Myths and Legal Reality," *The Modern American* 5 (Fall 2009): 4.

86. Some of them were not actually orphans. Trammell, "Orphan Train Myths," 5.

87. "Older boys wanted to be paid for their labor." Trammell, "Orphan Train Myths," 5–6.

88. "Child labor was a fact of life" in that era, for orphan train riders and other kids, but "'Many [orphan train riders] were used as strictly slave farm labor.'" Dan Scheuerman, "Lost Children: Riders on the Orphan Train," *Humanities*, November/December 2007, https://www.neh.gov/humanities/2007/novemberdecember/feature/lost-children-riders-the-orphan-train.

89. This tendency may persist even after kids reach the age of majority. See Noam Scheiber, "When Helicopter Parents Hover Even at Work," *New York Times*, June 21, 2017, https://www.nytimes.com/2017/06/21/business/millennial-work-parent-lavar-lonzo-ball.html.

90. One powerful example: analysts at McKinsey estimate that "Increasing the use of student data in education [which impacts students, parents, schools, and other constituencies] could unlock between $900 billion and $1.2 trillion in global eco-nomic value." Michael Chui and Jimmy Sarakatsannis, "Protecting Student Data in a Digital World," McKinsey & Company, April 2015, http://www.mckinsey.com/industries/public-sector/our-insights/protecting-student-data-in-a-digital-world.

91. Many stakeholders have used some version of the "Wild West" description to advance a range of observations and arguments. For example, Eric T. Schneiderman

(then attorney general of New York), "Taming the Digital Wild West," *New York Times*, April 22, 2014, https://www.nytimes.com/2014/04/23/opinion/taming-the-digital -wild-west.html. Schneiderman asks "cybercowboys [digital companies] to realize that working with the sheriffs is both good business and the right thing to do."

92. "Adolescents face a litany of challenges in entering or contributing to the U.S. workforce . . . [and] federal and state child labor standards have developed to place limits on the ability of adolescents to work for others." Jason M. Gordon, "A Shield of Disadvantage: Legal Entity Status within Guardian-Adolescent Entrepreneurial Ventures," *Ohio State Entrepreneurial Business Law Journal* 9 (2014): 5.

93. For information about federal laws and regulations on child labor, visit US Department of Labor, "Child Labor," Wage and Hour Division, https://www.dol .gov/whd/childlabor.htm.

94. If a minor does enter into a contract, in most circumstances, that "contracting minor may repudiate the contract at any time before reaching majority or within a reasonable time afterwards." Lapp, "Databasing Delinquency," 203.

95. Irwin Reyes et al., "Won't Somebody Think of the Children? Examining COPPA Compliance at Scale," *Proceedings on Privacy Enhancing Technologies* (Barcelona: Privacy Enhancing Technologies Symposium, 2018), 63, https://petsymposium.org/ 2018/files/papers/issue3/popets-2018-0021.pdf.

96. There are some limited exceptions to this requirement. For an overview of COPPA, see Ritvo, *Privacy and Student Data*, 12–17.

97. Ritvo, 9, 13.

98. Reyes et al., "Think of the Children," 65.

99. David R. Hostetler and Seiko F. Okada, "Children's Privacy in Virtual K–12 Education: Virtual Solutions of the Amended Children's Online Privacy Protection Act (COPPA) Rule," *North Carolina Journal of Law & Technology Online Edition* 14 (2013): 176.

100. 16 C.F.R. § 312 (2013).

101. Hostetler and Okada, "Children's Privacy in Virtual K–12 Education," 168.

102. Hostetler and Okada, 168.

103. See Chris Jay Hoofnagle and Jan Whittington, "Free: Accounting for the Costs of the Internet's Most Popular Price," *UCLA Law Review* 61 (2013): 606–670. "Currently, consumers are left in a gray zone. . . . They paid nothing for the service and should expect to get what they paid for" (ibid., 611).

104. In general, there is no one-stop-shopping way to define employers: "Due to the [Fair Labor Standards Act] statute's linguistic circularity, the task of defining

these terms [employee and employer] has been left largely to courts." Kimberlianne Podlas, "Does Exploiting a Child Amount to Employing a Child? The FLSA's Child Labor Provisions and Children on Reality Television," *UCLA Entertainment Law Review* 17 (2010): 51.

105. US Department of Labor, "Employment by Parents," Youth & Labor, www.dol .gov/general/topic/youthlabor/employmentparents.

106. US Department of Labor.

107. 2 Les A. Schneider and J. Larry Stine, *Wage and Hour Law: Compliance and Practice* §14:28 (2018).

108. Podlas, "Does Exploiting a Child," 69.

109. Some state labor law frameworks, including state investigatory powers, have covered reality TV. For an example, see Associated Press, "'Jon & Kate' under Investigation," *Hollywood Reporter*, May 29, 2009, https://www.hollywoodreporter.com/news/jon-amp-kate-investigation-84713.

110. These state laws may be more about protecting grown-ups who work with child actors. Also note that the original of these types of statutes was named for a child actor, Jackie Coogan, whose parents took advantage of his earnings from movies such as *Tom Sawyer*. Ethan Bordman, "Are You Ready for Your Close-Up? You May Face Entertainment Law Issues, Regardless of Your Practice Area," *New York State Bar Journal* 84-Sep (September 2012): 41.

111. Glenda K. Harnad, Employment of Minors § 5:46, in vols. 19–21A, *Employment and Labor Relations*, of *Summary of Pennsylvania Jurisprudence* 2nd ed. (2018).

112. Harnad, § 5:46.

113. 43 Pa. Stat. Ann. § 40.5.

114. In the commercial sharenting space, intellectual property (IP) law might seem to offer another avenue for children to assert some control over the sharenting choices their parents make for them by arguing that they own their images and other creative content. This avenue seems unlikely to offer much promise, especially for children who are not celebrities in their own right and lack teams of other adult professionals to help them navigate this tricky terrain while they are still minors. Even for child celebrities, this type of argument is often foreclosed because of the central role that laws typically give parents in decision making on their children's behalf. A well-known case in this area is model-actress Brooke Shields' lawsuit to have nude images taken of her as a child (with her mother's consent) barred from use when she was an adult. The highest court in New York State denied her request because state statutory law had authorized her mother to enter into the initial contract. The right to enter into or to later abrogate the contract did not belong to Shields herself. Shields v. Gross, 58 N.Y.2d 338 (N.Y. 1983).

115. Compare President's Council of Advisors on Science and Technology (PCAST), *Big Data and Privacy*, 19: Big data "is big in the quantity and variety of data that are available to be processed . . . [and] in the scale of analysis . . . that can be applied."

116. For example, *The Digital Campus: Big Data*, Chronicle of Higher Education, April 5, 2017, at http://www.chronicle.com/specialreport/The-Digital-Campus-Big-Data/105. This special report delves into a number of issues facing higher education institutions, including data privacy vulnerabilities as "college campuses . . . are under constant attack . . . by a group of criminal hackers who have professionalized, and industrialized, their efforts in the past few years." Lee Gardner, "Keeping Up with the Growing Threat to Data Security," special report, Chronicle of Higher Education, April 9, 2017.

117. For example, Neil M. Richards and Jonathan H. King, "Big Data Ethics," *Wake Forest Law Review* 49 (2014): 398–399. Richards and King describe the ever-expanding landscape of big data, including industry and government examples.

118. See Richards and King.

119. The "notice and consent" mechanism by which users typically give digital providers access to their data "is defeated exactly by the positive benefits that big data enables: new, non-obvious, unexpectedly powerful uses of data." PCAST, *Big Data and Ethics*, 38.

120. Educators are alarmed at how "smart phones and social media" may contribute to "suicide clusters" among teens by sharing details of deaths. See Hanna Rosin, "The Silicon Valley Suicides," *The Atlantic*, December 2015, https://www.theatlantic.com/magazine/archive/2015/12/the-silicon-valley-suicides/413140.

121. "Recent estimates indicate that a year's worth of data is worth $50 to $5,000 per consumer to Google and $45 to $190 per consumer to Facebook." Strahilevitz and Kugler, "Privacy Policy Language," S79.

122. See Scott Goodson, "If You're Not Paying for It, You Become the Product," *Forbes*, March 5, 2012, https://www.forbes.com/sites/marketshare/2012/03/05/if-youre-not-paying-for-it-you-become-the-product. "The bargain you make, again and again, with various companies is surveillance in exchange for free service." Schneier, *Data and Goliath*, 5.

123. See Leah Plunkett, "Pay Your Own Way Government Has a Body Count," *Huff Post* (blog), June 16, 2014, http://www.huffingtonpost.com/leah-plunkett/pay-your-own-way-governme_b_5500172.html.

124. See Leah Plunkett, "Captive Markets," *Hastings Law Journal* 65 (2013): 61–63.

125. For a description of a state public defender reimbursement framework, see Kate Levine, "If You Cannot Afford a Lawyer: Assessing the Constitutionality of Massachusetts's Reimbursement Statute," *Harvard Civil Rights-Civil Liberties Law Review* 42 (2007): 192–193.

126. See Plunkett, "Captive Markets," 84–86.

127. See Plunkett, 101–102.

128. See Peppet, "Regulating the Internet of Things," 106–108 (car insurance example); Darrell M. West, "How Digital Technology Can Reduce Prison Incarceration Rates," *Brookings Institute*, March 31, 2015, https://www.brookings.edu/blog/techtank/2015/03/31/how-digital-technology-can-reduce-prison-incarceration-rates (justice system monitoring example).

129. To learn more about the strategy of this campaign, see Kevin Allen, "Win the Pitch: Tips from MasterCard's 'Priceless' Pitchman," *Harvard Business Review*, May 8, 2012, https://hbr.org/2012/05/mastering-the-art-of-the-pitch.

Chapter 6

1. Avi Selk, "Terrorists Are Building Drones. France Is Destroying Them with Eagles," *Washington Post*, February 21, 2017, https://www.washingtonpost.com/news/worldviews/wp/2017/02/21/terrorists-are-building-drones-france-is-destroying-them-with-eagles.

2. For many "questions that arise [about youth and digital life], common sense leads to surprisingly good answers." John Palfrey and Urs Gasser, *Born Digital: How Children Grow Up in a Digital Age*, rev. ed. (New York: Basic Books, 2016), 11.

3. "Many parents begin to construct a public digital profile for their children before they are even born, [but] research suggests that they have not yet considered the implications for their children of divulging information about them online, including privacy risks and security issues." Deborah Lupton and Ben Williamson, "The Datafied Child: The Dataveillance of Children and Implications for Their Rights," *New Media & Society* 19 (2017): 788. Researchers themselves are in a similar boat, as "Internet studies scholars have only just begun to confront the issue of children's rights in the digital age" (ibid., 789).

4. Compare "The Creativity Compass," *Joi Ito* (blog), July 30, 2013, https://joi.ito.com/weblog/2013/07/30/the-creativity.html.

5. These principles and related ones are complex and, at times, highly contested in the broad body of legal scholarship on privacy. In keeping with this book's aim of having a more general conversation, this book does not engage comprehensively with all threads of the legal academic discussion but draws on them selectively to benefit from the weight and texture they bring to the fabric of the discussion here in this book.

6. For example, China is already committed to what it calls a "'credit system that covers the whole society.'" This system aims for "every Chinese citizen to be trailed by a file compiling data from public and private sources by 2020, and for those files to

be searchable by fingerprints and other biometric characteristics." This use of "social credit is an attempt at a softer, more invisible authoritarianism." Mara Hvistendahl, "You Are a Number," *Wired*, January 2018, http://contentviewer.adobe.com/s/Wired/ 5857345fd35d4d1f9a1f00273013f68a/WI0118_10_Folio/5010_2601FF_socialcredits .html. In her analysis of this system, scholar Rachel Botsman observes: "On the one hand, a social credit system will almost certainly encourage people to act more honestly and to abide by the rules. On the other, it's a deeply disturbing version of reputation economics that will give governments unprecedented control over what they consider good and bad ways to behave." Rachel Botsman, *Who Can You Trust? How Technology Brought Us Together and Why It Might Drive Us Apart* (New York: Hachette Book Group, 2017), 170. And according to Danielle Keats Citron and Frank Pasquale: "Although predictive algorithms may not yet be ranking high school students nationwide . . . they are increasingly rating people in countless aspects of their lives." Danielle Keats Citron and Frank Pasquale, "The Scored Society: Due Process for Automated Predictions," *Washington Law Review* 89 (2014): 2.

7. See Craig Lambert, "Universal Tennis Rating Is a New System for Grading Tennis Players," *Sports Illustrated*, October 6, 2015, https://www.si.com/tennis/2015/10/06/ universal-tennis-rating-boston-open.

8. Ant Financial, one of the companies in China that has government approval to "develop their own private credit scoring platforms," already uses student data for credit scoring purposes. "In June 2015, as 9.4 million Chinese teenagers took the grueling national college entrance exam . . . Ant Financial hoped to obtain a list of students who cheated, so that the fraud could become a blight on their Zhima credit [social credit] records." Hvistendahl, "You Are a Number." And Professors Palfrey and Gasser caution: "We are only steps away from a world where detailed data about our young people, collected and analyzed by powerful companies, will influence which schools they attend, what loans they can receive, the amount they will pay for health or car insurance, and so on." Palfrey and Gasser, *Born Digital*, 61.

9. N. Cameron Russell et al., "Transparency and the Marketplace for Student Data," *Center on Law and Information Policy* 4 (2018), https://www.fordham.edu/info/23830/ research/10517/transparency_and_the_marketplace_for_student_data/1.

10. Russell et al., 21.

11. Russell et al., 22–23.

12. Software that predicts dangerousness is biased against African Americans. See Julia Angwin et al., "Machine Bias," *ProPublica*, May 23, 2016, https://www.pro publica.org/article/machine-bias-risk-assessments-in-criminal-sentencing.

13. "If we want our own children to value our time with them, we need to model that we are not spending time with them only because we don't currently have a more interesting or demanding call to take or email to answer." Lynn Schofield

Clark, *The Parent App: Understanding Families in the Digital Age* (New York: Oxford University Press, 2013), 219–220.

14. Jenny S. Radesky et al., "Patterns of Mobile Device Use by Caregivers and Children during Meals in Fast Food Restaurants," *Pediatrics* 133, no. 4 (April 2014): e844, http://pediatrics.aappublications.org/content/early/2014/03/05/peds.2013-3703.

15. See Leah Plunkett, "Punishing Students for Gadget Use Will Make Their Tech Etiquette Worse," *Wired*, March 19, 2014, https://www.wired.com/2014/03/zero-tolerance.

16. Julie Cohen theorizes privacy as inextricably bound up in play for people of all ages, explaining that "situated subjects [people existing within networks] exercise a deliberate, playful agency. Everyday practice can be enormously creative in ways that work around or push back against the institutional, cultural, and material constraints that people encounter." Julie Cohen, "What Privacy Is For," *Harvard Law Review* 126 (2013): 1910. Cohen also links a concept of "home"—which is both a legally and pragmatically significant construct in young people's lives, although Cohen isn't focused on this demographic—to the importance of play: "A viable theory of privacy for the networked information age must consider the extent to which the 'privacy of the home' has served as a sort of cultural shorthand for a broader privacy interest against exposure. . . . we might envision a zone of personal space that permits (degrees of) unconstrained physical and intellectual movement . . . furnish[ing] room for a critical, playful subjectivity to develop." Julie E. Cohen, *Configuring the Networked Self: Law, Code, and the Play of Everyday Practice* (New Haven: Yale University Press, 2012), 142–143.

17. See Melanie Thernstrem, "The Anti-Helicopter Parent's Plea: Let Kids Play!," *New York Times*, October 19, 2016, https://www.nytimes.com/2016/10/23/magazine/the-anti-helicopter-parents-plea-let-kids-play.html.

18. Jonathan Zittrain describes the internet's "generative" roots in *The Future of the Internet—and How to Stop It* (Harrisonburg, VA: Caravan, 2008), 7–8. The particular ethos of digital development has varied considerably across time and context. For example, Franklin Foer talks about "infinitely resourceful nerd cowboys. . . . In MIT's labs, during the sixties and seventies, they broke any rule that interfered with the stuff of early computing." *World without Mind: The Existential Threat of Big Tech* (New York: Penguin Press, 2017), 57.

19. See Brad Peters, "The Big Data Gold Rush," *Forbes*, June 21, 2012, https://www.forbes.com/sites/bradpeters/2012/06/21/the-big-data-gold-rush/#3442bee9b247.

20. Privacy advocacy groups have mounted successful campaigns against some of the digital products and services that most egregiously threaten children's privacy. One example is the smart doll My Friend Cayla, which was reportedly sending "recordings [of kids' voices] to a software company that sells 'biometric solutions'

to law enforcement and the military." Jeff John Roberts, "Privacy Groups Claim These Popular Dolls Spy on Kids," *Fortune*, December 8, 2016, http://fortune .com/2016/12/08/my-friend-cayla-doll. Compare Kevin Lapp, "Databasing Delinquency," *Hastings Law Journal* 67 (2015): 249, where Lapp calls for limits on information gathering in juvenile delinquency context.

21. See President's Council of Advisors on Science and Technology (PCAST), *Big Data and Privacy: A Technological Perspective*, May 2014. This report, from a multistakeholder expert council convened by the Obama administration, recommends that privacy protection focus on regulating data use.

22. Available at https://www.youtube.com/yt/kids/ and https://www.kiddle.co.

23. Compare, generally, Ethan Zuckerman, "Who Filters Your News? Why We Built Gobo.social," *MIT Media Lab*, November 16, 2017, https://medium.com/mit-media -lab/who-filters-your-news-why-we-built-gobo-social-bfa6748b5944. Zuckerman discusses why and how we might take more ownership over the social media content we see. Could this or a similar service have a role to play in blocking the social media content we see about kids?

24. See Leah Plunkett and Urs Gasser, "Student Privacy and Ed Tech (K–12) Research Briefing," Berkman Center Research Publication no. 2016-15, Berkman Klein Center for Internet & Society, Harvard University, September 26, 2016, 6–8, https://cyber .harvard.edu/publications/2016/StudentPrivacyBriefing. This article draws on Gasser's work on internet governance to identify different governance toolkits that could be used in the student privacy space.

25. In contrast, when Germany's privacy regulator determined that a doll was spying on children, it stated that it was not "planning any legal actions against the parents who bought the toy," implying that it could contemplate and undertake such action. Brandon Conradis, "German Regulator Tells Parents to Destroy 'Spy' Doll Cayla," *Deutsche Welle*, February 21, 2017, http://www.dw.com/en/ german-regulator-tells-parents-to-destroy-spy-doll-cayla/a-37601577.

26. Student Online Personal Information Protection Act, Cal. Bus. & Prof. Code § 22584 (2014).

27. Dylan Peterson, "Edtech and Student Privacy: California Law as a Model," *Berkeley Technology Law Journal* 31 (2016): 974. Many other states are also getting into the business of regulating student data privacy. Providing an analysis of these developments is beyond the scope of this work. For updates on state law developments, please visit the Data Quality Campaign at https://dataqualitycampaign.org.

28. See Elana Zeide, "Student Privacy Principles for the Age of Big Data: Moving beyond FERPA and FIPPS," *Drexel Law Review* 8 (2016): 379.

29. Council of Europe, "Recommendation CM/Rec(2018)7 of the Committee of Ministers to Member States on Guidelines to Respect, Protect and Fulfill the Rights of the Child in the Digital Environment," Committee of Ministers, adopted July 4, 2018, https://search.coe.int/cm/Pages/result_details.aspx?ObjectID=09000016808b79f7.

30. Council of Europe.

31. Council of Europe.

32. The playground reform movement in New York City "got the City's official recognition in 1897, when Mayor William L. Strong appointed the Small Parks Advisory Committee." New York City Parks, "History of Playgrounds in Parks," https://www.nycgovparks.org/about/history/playgrounds.

33. "In the Wilderness Act of 1964, Congress adopted a policy of securing wilderness areas for the benefit of present and future generations of Americans." National Park Service, "National Park System Timeline (Annotated)," History E-Library, https://www.nps.gov/parkhistory/hisnps/NPSHistory/timeline_annotated.htm.

34. See Urs Gasser, "Perspectives on the Future of Digital Privacy," *Zeitschrift für Schweizerisches Recht* 134 (2015): 341–342.

35. Tracey Lien, "Tech Workers Pledge to Never Build a Database of Muslims," *Los Angeles Times*, December 14, 2016, http://www.latimes.com/business/technology/la-fi-tn-tech-oppose-muslim-database-20161214-story.html.

36. For example, Britt Faulstick, "A Handshake in a Backpack: Drexel Freshmen among First to Try Out Programmable Packs," *Drexel News Blog* (blog), Drexel University, September 15, 2017, https://newsblog.drexel.edu/2017/09/15/a-handshake-in-a-backpack-drexel-freshmen-among-first-to-try-out-programmable-packs.

37. Mattel, "Mattel Strengthens Leadership Team to Help Drive Transformation Strategy," news release, October 3, 2017, https://news.mattel.com/news/mattel-strengthens-leadership-team-to-help-drive-transformation-strategy.

38. Toys "R" Us added one in 2016, but that goes in the "too little, too late" category, given that chain's bankruptcy status.

39. "Be Internet Awesome," Google, https://beinternetawesome.withgoogle.com/en.

40. Palfrey and Gasser, *Born Digital*, 11.

41. William Shakespeare, *Twelfth Night*, ed. Barbara A. Mowat and Paul Werstine (New York: Washington Square Press, 2004), 1.1.1.

42. This challenge isn't unique to children: "It's getting harder and harder to be ephemeral." Bruce Schneier, *Data and Goliath: The Hidden Battles to Collect Your Data and Control Your World* (New York: Norton, 2015), 150–151.

43. Other legal scholars who are also parents have noted this divide between the "analog" records of their youth and the digital ones of their children's. See, for example, Robert A. Heverly, "Growing Up Digital: Control and the Pieces of a Digital Life," in *Digital Youth, Innovation, and the Unexpected*, ed. Tara McPherson (Cambridge: MIT Press, 2008), 199–200.

44. For Roger Ebert's summary of the film, see https://www.rogerebert.com/reviews/ great-movie-say-anything-1989.

45. Lapp does see it more in that second category, calling for delinquency record destruction. Lapp, "Databasing Delinquency," 252–255.

46. Who counts as a "data subject" under GDPR is unclear. A good working understanding is that it includes EU citizens, even if they travel or move away, and those residing in the EU. See Moyn Uddin, "GDPR: The Data Subject, Citizen or Resident?," *GDPR Blogs*, Cyber Counsel, January 29, 2017, https://cybercounsel.co.uk/ data-subjects.

47. General Data Protection Regulation (GDPR), art. 17, https://gdpr-info.eu/ art-17-gdpr.

48. GDPR., art. 17, pt. 1.

49. GDPR, art. 17, pt. 1(b), Recital 65.

50. Milda Macenaite and Eleni Kosta, "Consent for Processing Children's Personal Data in the EU: Following in US Footsteps?," *Information & Communications Technology Law* 26, no. 2, (2017): 148, https://www.tandfonline.com/doi/full/10.1080/1360 0834.2017.1321096.

51. At least one state—California—does have a law on the books that allows for youth under age eighteen to remove content that they share about themselves with most online and mobile operators if they later regret it. The law does not apply to sharented information. Cal. Bus. & Prof. Code § 22,581 (2014).

52. However, even these historical protections have been eroding. See Lapp, "Databasing Delinquency," 217–219.

53. For example, in New Hampshire (where this author used to represent juvenile clients), such disclosure would be a misdemeanor. N.H. Rev. Stat. Ann. § 170-G:8-a(V).

54. Zittrain, *The Future of the Internet*, 228–229.

55. For example, Facebook, "I Don't Want My Child's Name or Profile Photo to Be Paired with Ads," Help Center, https://www.facebook.com/help/11635665511 8482?helpref=related.

56. Recall that the Constitution binds public, not private, actors. Because social media companies are private actors, to paint with a broad brush, any such constitutional claims would be that the government passed laws that limited protected speech in a quasi-public forum, not that the companies themselves violated the Constitution. As legal scholars Anupam Chander and Uyen P. Le explain: "[T]he First Amendment [has] posed a substantial hurdle to broad privacy regulations like those passed in other advanced economies. . . . Congress is reluctant to regulate privacy because such statutes might impinge on free speech." "Free Speech," *Iowa Law Review* 100 (2015): 518.

57. Pierce v. Society of the Sisters of the Holy Names of Jesus & Mary, 268 U.S. 510 (1925).

58. Prince v. Massachusetts, 321 U.S. 158, 166 (1944).

59. Reputation history is more important in the digital world than a credit history. UNICEF, *The State of the World's Children 2017: Children in a Digital World* (New York: UNICEF, 2017), 92, https://www.unicef.org/eapro/SOWC_2017_ENG _EMBARGOED.pdf.

60. The desirability of a type of credit bureau system around digital privacy has been explored by legal academics. See Palfrey and Gasser, *Born Digital*, 87–89. Such a system would require careful design, however, because adding another layer for digital assessment of status could potentially lead to more privacy problems, depending on how the layer is structured. Citron and Pasquale have developed a thorough and thoughtful credit bureau model for today's algorithmically "scored society" that would give individuals "'technological due process'—procedures ensuring that predictive algorithms live up to some standard of review and revision to ensure their fairness and accuracy." Citron and Pasquale, "The Scored Society," 19.

61. "Senator to Ex-CEO: Equifax Can't Be Trusted with Americans' Personal Data," *Morning Edition*, hosted by David Green, NPR, October 4, 2017, http://www. npr.org/2017/10/04/555651379/senator-to-ex-ceo-equifax-can-t-be-trusted-with -americans-personal-data.

62. This entertaining and informative show about car safety is available from National Public Radio at https://www.npr.org/podcasts/510208/car-talk.

63. Wallace Stegner, *Crossing to Safety* (New York: Modern Library, 2002).

64. For an explanation of what a credit report is, see National Consumer Law Center, "Credit Reports," Issues, https://www.nclc.org/issues/credit-reports.html.

65. See National Consumer Law Center, *Disputing Errors in a Credit Report*, Facts for Older Consumers (Boston: National Consumer Law Center, 2014), http://www.nclc .org/images/pdf/older_consumers/cf_disputing-errors-in-a-credit-report.pdf.

66. Senator Elizabeth Warren's office has a detailed report on this failure: Office of Elizabeth Warren, "Bad Credit: Uncovering Equifax's Failure to Protect American's Personal Information," February 2018, https://www.warren.senate.gov/files/documents/2018_2_7_%20Equifax_Report.pdf.

67. See Alicia Solow-Niederman, "Beyond the Privacy Torts: Reinvigorating a Common Law Approach for Data Breaches," *Yale Law Journal Forum* 127 (2018): 614–634; Daniel J. Solove and Danielle Keats Citron, "Risk and Anxiety: A Theory of Data Breach Harms," *Texas Law Review* 96 (2018): 737–786.

68. Office of Elizabeth Warren, "Bad Credit," 9.

69. Office of Elizabeth Warren, 9.

70. The potential for tech-based approaches to facilitate forgetting by digital technologies has long been part of the privacy solution space. Notably, almost ten years ago, Viktor Mayer-Schonberger proposed: "One way we can mimic human forgetting in the digital realm is by associating information we store in digital memory with expiration devices that users set." Viktor Mayer-Schönberger, *Delete: The Virtue of Forgetting in the Digital Age* (Princeton, NJ: Princeton University Press, 2009), 171.

Chapter 7

1. E. M. Forster, *Howards End* (London, 1910; Project Gutenberg, 2008), chap. 22, https://www.gutenberg.org/files/2946/2946-h/2946-h.htm.

2. "Flows of information through networked space alter social patterns of interaction and resource allocation in important ways. Even so, networked space remains real space inhabited by real people." Julie E. Cohen, *Configuring the Networked Self: Law, Code, and the Play of Everyday Practice* (New Haven: Yale University Press, 2012), 33.

3. "Computers offer the illusion of companionship without the demands of friendship and then, as the programs [have] got[ten] really good, the illusion of friendship without the demands of intimacy." Sherry Turkle, *Reclaiming Conversation: The Power of Talk in a Digital Age* (New York: Penguin Press, 2015), 7; Lynn Schofield Clark, *The Parent App: Understanding Families in the Digital Age* (New York: Oxford University Press, 2013), 26. Clark shares that her own "personal struggle as a parent in a digital age is . . . about resisting the temptation to engage in technologically enabled multitasking in order to make the most out of every moment simultaneously."

4. Variations of this phrase are popping up in public discourse around online security and privacy. For example, Aleksander Yampolskiy, "Cybersecurity Expert: Think before You Click," CNBC, May 15, 2017, https://www.cnbc.com/video/2017/05/15/cybersecurity-expert-think-before-you-click.html.

5. Turkle stresses the need for self-reflection in the psychoanalytic tradition. Turkle, *Reclaiming Conversation*, 80.

6. Stacey B. Steinberg makes this recommendation in "Sharenting: Children's Privacy in the Age of Social Media," *Emory Law Journal* 66 (2017): 881.

7. For a definition of "digital dossier," see John Palfrey and Urs Gasser, *Born Digital: How Children Grow Up in a Digital Age*, rev. ed. (New York: Basic Books, 2016), 39.

8. Dalia Topelson Ritvo, "Privacy and Student Data: An Overview of the Federal Laws Impacting Student Information Collected through Networked Technologies" Cyberlaw Clinic, Berkman Klein Center for Internet & Society, Harvard University, June 2016, 11–12, https://dash.harvard.edu/handle/1/27410234.

9. American Academy of Pediatrics, "Media and Children Communication Toolkit," AAP Health Initiatives, https://www.aap.org/en-us/advocacy-and-policy/aap-health -initiatives/Pages/Media-and-Children.aspx.

10. See Steinberg, "Sharenting," 881. Steinberg recommends that parents give kids "'veto power' over online disclosures."

11. For example, Donna Freitas, *The Happiness Effect: How Social Media Is Driving a Generation to Appear Perfect at Any Cost* (New York: Oxford University Press, 2017), 64–65.

12. Media Literacy Now, "Digital Citizenship and Internet Safety Law in Washington State Is National Model," April 4, 2016, https://medialiteracynow.org/digital -citizenship-and-internet-safety-education-law-in-washington-state-is-national-model.

13. For example, "Stories," Hatch, She Knows, http://www.sheknows.com/special -series/hatch.

14. But some are. See Amanda Hess, "The Teenage Life, Streamed Live and for Profit," *New York Times*, June 6, 2017, https://www.nytimes.com/2017/06/06/arts/lively -the-teenage-life-streamed.html.

15. Recognizing whether, when, and how we are giving up this digital data is difficult in today's system of "surveillance capitalism," as Shoshana Zuboff refers to today's "new form of information capitalism [that] aims to predict and modify human behavior as a means to produce revenue and market control." Shoshana Zuboff, "Big Other: Surveillance Capitalism and the Prospects of an Information Civilization," *Journal of Information Technology* 30 (2015): 75–76. In some instances, digital companies are openly buying data from people. See Stacy-Ann Elvy, "Paying for Privacy and the Personal Data Economy," *Columbia Law Review* 117 (2017): 1369–1459.

16. Council of Europe, "Recommendation CM/Rec(2018)7 of the Committee of Ministers to Member States on Guidelines to Respect, Protect and Fulfill the Rights of the

Child in the Digital Environment," Committee of Ministers, adopted July 4, 2018, https://search.coe.int/cm/Pages/result_details.aspx?ObjectID=09000016808b79f7.

17. The economics are far less opaque to the companies themselves. See Jaron Lanier, *Who Owns the Future?* (New York: Simon & Schuster, 2013). Lanier explains that "troves of dossiers on the private lives and inner beings of ordinary people, collected over digital networks, are packaged into a new private form of elite money" (ibid., 108).

18. See Joseph Turow, *The Aisles Have Eyes: How Retailers Track Your Shopping, Strip Your Privacy, and Define Your Power* (New Haven: Yale University Press, 2017), 3–5.

19. We should also ask whether the tech we're using—that we're "paying" for at least in part with our children's information—has negative implications for the economy and public welfare more broadly. Clark writes: "If we truly want to counter the commercialization of childhood, we need to recognize that there are links between an unregulated marketplace that places profit above public welfare and sells to children and an unregulated marketplace that outsources jobs, keeps wages artificially low, and makes it difficult for families to meet their basic needs." Clark, *The Parent App*, 226.

20. Notably, Jaron Lanier has proposed defending privacy and preserving autonomy by moving toward a more transparent economic bargain around digital data, such that "any cloud computer operator, whether it is a social network, an eclectic Wall Street scheme, or even a government agency, is required to pay you for useful data that is derived from you." Lanier, *Who Owns the Future?*, 317.

21. Compare a new New York bill that would make algorithms public when used by government actors for decisions, including school placement. The response is that the algorithm already is public: Benjamin Herold, "'Open Algorithms' Bill Would Jolt New York City Schools, Public Agencies," *Education Week*, November 8, 2017, http://blogs.edweek.org/edweek/DigitalEducation/2017/11/open_algorithms_bil l_schools.html.

22. See Kashmir Hill, "How Target Figured Out a Teen Girl Was Pregnant before Her Father Did," *Forbes*, February 16, 2012, https://www.forbes.com/sites/kashmirhill/ 2012/02/16/how-target-figured-out-a-teen-girl-was-pregnant-before-her-father-did.

23. Henry J. Kaiser Family Foundation, "Parental Consent/Notification Requirements for Minors Seeking Abortions," State Health Facts, updated April 1, 2017, https:// www.kff.org/womens-health-policy/state-indicator/parental-consentnotification.

24. See Planned Parenthood v. Casey, 505 U.S. 833 (1992).

25. Corinne Moini unpacks this question and proposes an amendment to COPPA that would clearly require such a duty. "Protecting Privacy in the Era of Smart Toys:

Does Hello Barbie Have a Duty to Report?," *Catholic University Journal of Law and Technology* 25 (2017): 281–318.

26. Jane Barnbauer argues that "freedom from thought [receiving unwanted self-knowledge] may be a promising form of privacy and dignity rights." Jane Barnbauer, "Freedom from Thought," *Emory Law Journal* 65 (2015): 221.

27. Thanks to Mike McCann for this suggestion, which is underdeveloped in the legal literature. An exception to this underdevelopment is Kevin A. Cranman, "Privacy and Technology: Counseling Institutions of Higher Education," *Journal of College and University Law* 25 (1998): 69–103.

28. Former big tech employees are now mobilizing against social media because of its impact on youth. See Alex Langone, "Ex Google and Facebook Employees Are Banding Together to Protect Kids from Social Media Addiction," *Time*, February 5, 2018, http://time.com/5133185/ex-facebook-google-fight-tech-addiction.

29. For example, Luke Broadwater, "Baltimore Summer Youth Curfew Begins Friday; Police Will Take Kids Home Instead of to City-Run Centers," *Baltimore Sun*, May 25, 2018, http://www.baltimoresun.com/news/maryland/baltimore-city/bs-md-curfew-20180525-story.html.

30. For example, City of Sumner v. Walsh, 148 Wash. 2d 490 (2003).

31. Surveillance is especially acute for low-income families: "Our new digital tools [for poverty management] spring from punitive, moralistic views of poverty and create a system of high-tech containment and investigation." Virginia Eubanks, *Automating Inequality: How High-Tech Tools Profile, Police, and Punish the Poor* (New York: St. Martin's Press, 2017), 16.

32. "During the nineteenth century, through judicial and legislative action, parents' moral duty to support their children evolved into an obligation legally enforceable in the private realm. The law linked this legal obligation to parents' right to control their children, and defined parents' duty to support their children in ways that maximized parental authority." Leslie J. Harris, Dennis Waldrop, and Lori Rathbun Waldrop, "Making and Breaking Connections between Parents' Duty to Support and Right to Control Their Children," *Oregon Law Review* 69 (1990): 692.

33. For example, N.H. Rev. Stat. Ann. § 169-D.

34. See Leah Plunkett, "Captive Markets," *Hastings Law Journal* 65 (2013): 105–106.

35. Or to the Google City that's being built. See "A Google-Related Plan Brings Futuristic Vision, Privacy Concerns to Toronto," *All Things Considered*, hosted by Ari Shapiro, NPR, November 20, 2017, https://www.npr.org/sections/alltechconsidered/2017/11/20/565352403/a-google-related-plan-brings-futuristic-vision-privacy-concerns-to-toronto.

36. Lisa Marie Segarra, "'Bullycide': Ten-Year-Old Girl's Suicide Was Result of Bullying Video, Parents Say," *Time*, updated December 1, 2017, http://time.com/5044974/
ashawnty-davis-10-year-old-suicide-bullying.

37. In a new student privacy law effective in 2016, Louisiana created criminal
penalties for adults who violate the student privacy requirements. La. Rev. Stat. §
17:3914(G), http://legis.la.gov/legis/Law.aspx?d=920124.

38. Dorothy Law Nolte, "Children Learn What They Live," http://www.cdatribe
-nsn.gov/eclctribal/eclc/poem3.pdf.

39. For a thoughtful analysis of the "moral obligation to protect one's own privacy"
in the age of Big Data, including how "individuals can act collectively to constrain
and improve Big Data practices" despite the overwhelming nature of big data, see
Anita L. Allen, "Protecting One's Own Privacy in a Big Data Economy," *Harvard Law
Review Forum* 130 (2016): 76.

Conclusion

1. For instance, we could turn to the wisdom of ancient philosophers for guidance
on contemporary parenting, as Rebecca Goldstein does so delightfully in her book,
Plato at the Googleplex: Why Philosophy Won't Go Away (New York: Pantheon Books,
2014).

2. "For cyberspace to remain a positive domain, for the Internet to continue to be
a driver of economic prosperity but also simply universal human freedoms . . . we
need to tackle the burgeoning pollution of this environment." Alexander Klimburg,
The Darkening Web: The War for Cyberspace (New York: Penguin Press, 2017), 318.

3. A danger of surveillance is that "people around us will be less likely to proclaim
new political or social ideas, or act out of the ordinary." Bruce Schneier, *Data and
Goliath: The Hidden Battles to Collect Your Data and Control Your World* (New York:
Norton, 2015), 116.

Index